The Rise and Decline of the Nation State

Edited by

Michael Mann

Basil Blackwell

First published 1990

Basil Blackwell Ltd
108 Cowley Road, Oxford, OX4 1JF, UK

Basil Blackwell, Inc.
3 Cambridge Center
Cambridge, Massachusettes 02142, USA

British Library Cataloguing in Publication Data

A CIP catalogue record for this book is available from the British Library.

Library of Congress Cataloging in Publication Data

The Rise and Decline of the Nation State/edited by Michael Mann.
 p   cm.
   "The essays contained here (apart from my introduction) were originally presented at a conference held in Emmanuel College, Cambridge, in September 1988. This was the first of a series of four annual conferences under the general title of 'Structural change in the West'"—Pref.
Includes bibliographical references.
ISBN 0-631-17125-8
1. Imperialism—History—Congresses.
2. Capitalism—History—Congresses.
3. Geopolitics—History—Congresses. I. Mann, Michael, 1942-
JC359.R53 1990
325'.32'09-dc20

Typeset in Ehrhardt on 10/11.5 pt
by Setrite Typesetters Ltd
Printed in Great Britain by
T.J. Press Ltd, Padstow, Cornwall.

Contents

Contents

Preface

The essays contained here (apart from my introduction) were originally presented at a conference held at Emmanuel College, Cambridge in September 1988. This was the first of a series of four annual conferences under the general title of 'Structural Change in the West'. The series, continuing through until 1991, is devoted to discussing issues arising from one of the major social transformations of the twentieth century – the changing relations between individual national economies and societies on the one hand, and the international order on the other. The subject requires an inter-disciplinary and international approach, and our participants are anthropologists, economists, geographers, historians, international relations specialists, political scientists and sociologists from various countries – mostly represented by our essayists here. As it is hoped to publish the major papers of each conference, this book may be the first in a series of four.

The conference series has been most generously financed by the Council of the United Kingdom Economic and Social Research Council to whom sincere thanks are due. I also express thanks to my co-organizers of the conferences, Fred Halliday and John Hobson, to Blackwell's efficient, helpful and sympathetic editor, Sean Magee, and to all the participants at our 1988 conference.

Michael Mann
University of California at Los Angeles

Abbreviations

AmEcR	*American Economic Review*
BHR	*Business History Review*
CJE	*Cambridge Journal of Economics*
EcHR	*Economic History Review*
EcJ	*Economic Journal*
EcPW	*Economic and Political Weekly*
EHR	*English Historical Review*
ERP	*Economic Report of the President* (Washington, DC: US Government Printing Office).
ExEcH	*Explorations in Economic History*
HJ	*Historical Journal*
ISQ	*International Studies Quarterly*
JEcH	*Journal of Economic History*
JEurEcH	*Journal of European Economic History*
JICH	*Journal of Imperial and Commonwealth History*
JPE	*Journal of Political Economy*
JRSS	*Journal of the Royal Statistical Society*
OBES	*Oxford Bulletin of Economics and Statistics*
OEP	*Oxford Economic Papers*
QJE	*Quarterly Journal of Economics*

1

Introduction: Empires with Ends

Michael Mann

Virgil declared that Romulus had been granted 'the gift of Empire without end'. This was, of course, false. Rome did decline, and so did all the other great empires and powers of history. So recently did Great Britain, and so will the United States. Given that all empires have ends, 'rise and decline' is not in itself a terribly interesting issue. Rather more interesting are the issues of whether there are common patterns of rise and decline, how we recognize their onset, how far decline need go and how much of it is reversible. These are the major issues raised in this volume. Given recent history and contemporary reality (as well as the nationalities of most contributors), it is natural to focus discussion on the British and American cases and on their comparison. Yet to avoid Anglo-Saxon ethnocentrism we have also extended our vision to other countries and to examine the nature of the broader world inhabited by the nation state.

To discuss rise and decline we need to make two preliminary conceptual distinctions. First, we may be talking about different types of rise and decline – economic, military, political, cultural, moral etc. Here we focus on two of these, economic and military–geopolitical. National economies rise and de-cline, so do great powers. The two processes are usually entwined but they are not identical. Prussia rose to be a great power while its economy was still second-rate; Japan today is the reverse, its economy almost rivalling that of the US, its military and geopolitical posture still controlled largely by the US. Decline may be on both dimensions of power simultaneously, it may be on one which then induces decline on the other, or it may occur only on one. All these, for example, are possibilities for the US today. My main points in this introduction concern the separability yet contingent conjunction of these two economic and geopolitical processes. This precludes easy analogies between different historical cases of rise and decline of the kind which have been recently fashionable. It leads toward a rather different view of the problem of American decline.

Second, we must distinguish between inevitable and avoidable levels of decline. When we consider the case of Britain or the US, we must remember that quite unusual circumstances led to an extraordinary degree of world dominance, and this simply had to diminish. Britain was first with the industrial revolution. After the destruction of Napoleonic France Britain was also left with control of the seas and of international trade and currency, while the other great powers were concerning themselves principally with the affairs of continental Europe. The US, along with the more economically backward Soviet Union, was also left in the driving seat by the fortunes of war — by the military and economic exhaustion of the European powers, their empires and Japan. In both cases it was inevitable that other countries would rebuild, emulate and eventually rival the leader, sometimes aided by the benefits of lateness (discussed by Pollard in this volume). In the case of Britain relative decline might eventually go some distance, since Britain is only a moderately sized and resourced country. The inevitable part of American decline is probably rather less, since the US is a large continent with far more resources. Yet most observers would probably agree that British decline has gone somewhat further down than this natural slippage. This is a quite common feature of once-dominant powers — some, like Rome, are destroyed altogether; others, like Spain, sink into near-obscurity. Is there something in the institutional structures of great powers that prevents them from adapting to their changed, more modest circumstances and that induces what we might call 'supra-natural decline'?

Both distinctions are necessary when examining the British case. Though no two scholars agree exactly on the causes of British 'supranatural' decline, there is now emerging some overall consensus among historians and sociologists as to its general contours. Our contributors start from this and take it further. It is helpful, first, to look at the nature of Britain's dominance, distinguishing economics from geopolitics. Britain's geopolitical dominance after 1815 rested, in Patrick O'Brien's words, upon 'An effective fiscal system, an outstanding navy and an expanding industrial economy (in that order) . .'. Britain's mid-nineteenth-century dominance over the world economy resided in the same three factors, but probably in something like reverse order. By then the industrial revolution was maintaining the decisive lead, though Britain's commercial, fiscal and naval institutions were important too. Our two main contributors on British decline, Pollard and O'Brien, argue in different ways that the 'supra-natural' level of British decline is at least partly explained by the sacrifice of economic priorities to geopolitical ones.

Patrick O'Brien, the radical — liberal heir of Cobden and Hobson, is explicit: imperialism, or as it is often expressed, 'imperial overstretch' helped ruin Britain. Going through the evidence, and relying principally on Davis and Huttenback's (1986) data on the costs of empire,[1] he argues that the empire

1   L. E. Davis and R. A. Huttenback, *Mammon and the Pursuit of Empire* (Cambridge: Cambridge University Press, 1986).

was not more profitable for British investors than alternative fields of investment and did not pay for the cost of its own defence. The empire was but a 'splendid and showy equipage' that ultimately over-stretched Britain and impoverished the working class (as Hobson had originally argued). It was not only economically unprofitable and socially undesirable; it eventually became geopolitically unnecessary. Faced with the rising threat of Germany, Britain was forced just before World War I to pull back the navy to home waters. The empire proved largely irrelevant to Britain's needs.

While accepting much of O'Brien's case, I would situate it in a broader comparative and geopolitical perspective. I would be inclined to interpret the fiscal side of the argument in a different way. Though it is true that, as Davis and Huttenback argue, British people paid more per capita for defence than the subjects of any other major state of the time, they were also the second richest (after Americans). If we calculate defence costs as a proportion of GNP among the great powers in 1910, then the ordering is France (4.1 per cent), Germany (about 2.9 per cent − it was 3.1 per cent of national income), Britain (2.8 per cent), Austria-Hungary (2.7 per cent), with the US trailing (1.2 per cent) (all these figures should be raised slightly to take account of the small but usually uncalculable part of debt repayments that went on the military.[2] France seems distinctly over-stretched and the US under-stretched, and the other three are very close together in the middle. However, contemporaries and historians have generally argued that Austria (spending almost the same proportionately as Britain) was not spending enough on its military to maintain great power status! Moreover, even without empire Britain would have high per capita defence costs because its island position required a predominantly naval defence strategy, and navies cost more in peacetime than armies did (though they needed less manpower). So O'Brien's argument may be less applicable to Britain than he believes.

Could the logic of his argument have been pressed at the time? Of course, a more detailed cost−benefit analysis might have revealed a more nuanced conclusion. Perhaps India paid its way indirectly, its looted wealth allowing Britain the gold reserves to become the world's financial centre. Perhaps Argentina's trade was worth a substantial Royal Navy presence. Perhaps a handful of colonies and client states could have been profitably maintained while jettisoning the rest of empire. The same reasoning could be applied in other powers. A cost−benefit analysis might have indicated, for example, that Austria-Hungary should have held on to industrializing Czechoslovakia while abandoning impoverished Ruthenia and costly Balkan adventures.

But this is all with the benefit of hindsight. At the time of acquisition of imperial powers and responsibilities over a territory it was usually impossible to judge its future profitability. This was particularly so in a period of rapid economic advance involving new products, often requiring new, perhaps as yet

2 M. Mann, *The Sources of Social Power*, vol. 2, *A History of Power, 1760−1914* (Oxford: Basil Blackwell, forthcoming).

undiscovered, raw materials. Imperialism, in Europe or the globe, claimed a way of bypassing the impossibilities of nuanced cost–benefit rationality. It argued that holding territory and dominating client states would ultimately protect the power from the uncertainties of competitive market processes. In the end control of territory would *guarantee* market dominance. This meant, of course, that the pursuit of power and empire became a very broad mind-set, resilient to the carping costings and liberal rhetoric of a Hobson, reluctant to retreat from territorial control anywhere.

Perhaps imperialism could have guaranteed market dominance in the long run. If the British Empire survived today in its territories and its dominance over client states, Britain might be rather wealthy. So might Austria-Hungary. But the principal weakness of imperialism was that it prompted counter-imperialisms which reinforced the original imperialism and led closer to catastrophic war. If Austria rationally backed out of the Balkans, Russia would move in, which would be very threatening — so Austrians plausibly argued. If Britain withdrew from Africa, France and Germany would surely move in, and the consequent growth in their navies would be threatening to the British Isles themselves. Contemporary governments felt they could not divorce economic rationality from geopolitics. Yet their geopolitical rivalries ended in great wars which exhausted them all.

As John Hall points out in his paper, the main British 'imperial overstretch' occurred during the two world wars that Britain nominally won but which really liquidated its wealth and power. The first war totally destroyed Austria-Hungary, and the two wars ended the German and French Empires. They left Europe in decline, and its two Russian and American flanks in the ascendant. Austria-Hungary, France, perhaps Britain (as O'Brien argues) might have boosted their economies by converting guns into butter. But their main problem was that those who live by the sword die by it — before the sword can fulfil its promise of delivering eternal butter!

Sidney Pollard's essay has two main parts. The first carefully assembles the economic evidence, sector by sector, decade by decade, as to whether Britain's decline began before the First World War. He is ultimately unsure, because the evidence does not point decisively in either direction. But this gives him confidence enough to declare that, even if it had already begun, it had not yet gone far and was still reversible. He also notes a distinctive late Victorian and Edwardian trend: a shift from manufacturing industry to trade and finance. By 1914 British industrial capitalism was subordinated to finance and commercial capitalism. Others have also noted this subordination — though some believe it had always characterized British political economy.[3]

But Pollard carries his analysis further than others have done, onto the comparative level. He suggests that the same switch had also characterized the

---

3   G. K. Ingham, *Capitalism Divided? The City and Industry in British Social Development* (London: Macmillan, 1984); M. Mann, 'The Decline of Great Britain', in his *States, War and Capitalism* (Oxford: Basil Blackwell, 1988).

beginnings of decline for two previous economic leaders, Holland in the seventeenth century and the Italian city states in the fifteenth. The switch from industry to trade and finance begins to look like that traditional depiction of the decline of empires – in Rome, for example, from those energetic, abstemious republicans who created empire, to those effete luxury-loving rentiers who used it up. As some US observers are claiming to detect the same switch occurring today, watch out America!

Andrew Gamble provides a broad overview of the British experience, relating the principal historical phases of decline to the main schools of theory that have emerged to explain it. He agrees that 'imperial over-stretch' and the dominance of internationally oriented finance capital were causes of decline. The latter is discussed as an obstacle to the development of what was powering other early twentieth-century economies, corporate 'Fordism', involving state and/or banking assistance to domestic industry. After 1945 Britain did develop a belated, social democratic version of Fordism which stuttered on into the crisis of the 1970s, and thence to Thatcherism, a return to Britain's internationalist, *laissez-faire* past. Gamble finds the Thatcherite reactionary revolution to be more ideology than substance, but he is more impressed by the changing nature of the global economy. Fordism may have had its day. The traditional internationalism of the British economy may be more appropriate to the late than the early twentieth century. The sun did not rise again on Holland or the Italian city states. Is Britain to be uniquely favoured, not with Empire, but with comfortable prosperity without end? Gamble might be offering some much-needed cheer to the current depressed generation of British academics.

Mancur Olson operates with a more general theory. In keeping with his previous work,[4] he argues that decline is attributable directly to 'distributional coalitions', special interest groups that have managed to institutionalize their private interests into the power structure of the society at large. Britain is unusually well-supplied with these and so is an obvious candidate for decline. Though he does not give these as his examples, his model might work well with the two principal 'distributional coalitions' identified by our other contributors – the financial and commercial interests of the City–Bank of England–Treasury nexus and the military–imperial connection. These are, after all, still at the heart of the British Establishment.

However, Olson asks whether this might be offset by the unusual strength and sophistication of British economic theory. Drawing from another of his theoretical concepts, the rational ignorance of the voter, he argues that not economic theories but simple rival ideologies, asserting that the role of government in the economy is either good or harmful, have actually dominated in Britain. Reviewing the evidence he concludes that there is no evidence either

4 M. Olson, *The Rise and Fall of Nations* (New Haven, Connecticut: Yale University Press, 1982).

way that the size or activism of government has significant economic effects in Western economies. From this rather gloomy tale of vested interests and ignorance he manages a ray of optimism: that more creative, sophisticated ideas may attain some influence when contrary distributional coalitions cancel each other out.

The main linkage between Britain's past and America's present is provided by John Hall in the context of a critique of 'hegemonic stability theory'. This theory asserts first that the international economy benefits from having a single hegemonic power – Britain in the nineteenth century, the United States since 1945 – to provide military stability and international financial instruments in the global system. But secondly, this order cannot last: the hegemon is drained by imperial over-stretch, its rivals can emulate and free-ride, and a more fragile multi-polar order ensues. The Victorians agreed with this theory. They called it 'The White Man's Burden'. Modern America prefers labels that are non-racist and social scientistic. But their similarity underlies Hall's title: 'Will the United States decline as did Britain?'

His answer is clearly 'No'. He regards both arguments as self-serving. He is sceptical of the military burdens of either case and more sensitive to another aspect of the hegemonic role, geopolitical mistakes. If America is suffering imperial over-stretch, that is because of particular mistakes, in Vietnam and in its unwillingness to enter into partnership with Third World nationalist regimes. This recalls O'Brien's charge that the British had also foolishly over-committed themselves to overseas empire. Hall continues that American economic power is still great; its military hegemony unchallenged. There is no rival commensurate with the challenge Germany posed to Britain. World wars destroyed British power. It is up to the intelligence of American leaders to avoid a comparable fate.

I would go further in rejecting what Charles Maier has called the 'seductive analogies' of writers like Immanuel Wallerstein and Paul Kennedy,[5] who have compared the American faltering with other cases of imperial decline in European history. The problem with comparing recent American hegemony with British nineteenth-century power, or Dutch seventeenth-century power, is that neither Britain nor Holland was indeed hegemonic. Holland was the leader in commercial capitalism and naval power, but she was not the greatest power of the age (an honour which would go to the Habsburgs of Spain and Austria, followed by France). Britain succeeded Holland as the commercial capitalist leader and the greatest naval power, and strengthened this by pioneering the industrial revolution. But Britain never dominated the European continent, had the smallest army of the great powers and after 1815 never sought to station troops in Europe. The nineteenth-century peace was kept by a balance of power, not British hegemony. Two pivotal powers, Britain and

5 I. Wallerstein, *The Politics of the World Economy* (Cambridge: Cambridge University Press, 1984); P. Kennedy, *The Rise and Fall of the Great Powers* (London: Unwin, 1988).

Russia, aided by Austria and Prussia, first kept down France and then admitted her to their number. The system collapsed when a rising power, Germany, directly challenged Russia and France, rather than Britain, though this inevitably brought Britain into the conflagration too.

The leading capitalist country is not necessarily the greatest power. The history of capitalism is not history *tout court*. Nonetheless, as the power of the capitalist economy has developed, so its leading national exponent has come closer to achieving great power hegemony. Holland was nowhere near this hegemony, Britain was rather closer, and the United States clearly achieved it in 1945 — at least over the capitalist world. The United States has been the greatest capitalist country, but she has also had the greatest army, navy and air force, plus a monopoly over the use of nuclear weapons (whatever British and French Governments might say). This combination of economic and military power was not present in prior European history. American power is qualitatively greater than anything known in this area of civilization since the Romans.

Thus Americans might have been excused sharing Virgil's delusion of having received the gift of 'Empire without End'. But there are two differences between then and now. First, unlike the Romans, many Americans are not sure they want it. Second, unlike the barbarians, the empire's rivals want it even less. These points are taken up by our other contributors.

David Calleo's essay analyses the US defence burden. Lucidly examining America's fiscal history since Eisenhower, he finds some support for imperial over-stretch. US defence costs have been higher than those of other major states. When they rise, as they cyclically have done, they have ushered in budget deficits, an unstable dollar and a steadily worsening trade deficit. These may be contributing to American economic decline — and currency instability may be bad for the global economy, too.

Yet Calleo refuses to simply blame defence spending. As he pertinently notes, state budgets actually contain three principal items: defence spending, civilian spending, and receipts (principally taxes). Why blame one of these? Why not blame the two others: governmental refusal to cut civilian spending or raise taxes? As both refusals are politically popular, why not blame the American electorate for failing to make sacrifices for empire by shouldering the real defence burden? American defence spending is actually rather low in historical terms for a great power.

Calleo notes that blame may not be appropriate, for the American government and electorate may have found an apparently rational policy alternative. American control of the world monetary system has allowed US policy makers to manipulate the dollar such that foreigners have funded the deficit and so paid for the increasing costs of American defence. The reader should digest this argument rather carefully since it involves some technical economic analysis. The other side of this equation is that Europeans and Japanese are unwilling to finance their own defence forces, but willing to rent American mercenaries! American hegemony turns out to be quite consensual.

Such 'imperial taxation' might be thought only right and proper since

American forces are defending the whole free world. Patrick O'Brien shows us that the British were never able to make the empire pay for its own defence. The Americans have devised a cleverer system — though Calleo warns us that it may encourage a 'casino capitalism' which may be harmful in the long term. There are two responses which a non-American like me might well make to this. First, whatever its justice regarding the Japanese and Europeans (most of whom do want American defence), its burdens fall equally upon the Third World which is least able to afford them. Moreover, the Third World needs very little of the nuclear and hi-tech aspects of the American military, and only some of its regimes and political interest groups (generally the more repressive ones) actually want any American defence at all.

Second, even America's allies are paying for a level and type of American defence for which they have not voted. True, they sometimes exercise political pressure on American defence policy (on the deployment of cruise missiles, for example). But their dismay at the 'star wars' defence system has been universal and unheeded. If 'the free world' is paying for American defence, should it not be allowed an American principle of freedom: no taxation without representation? This is especially appropriate since we may doubt whether many of the defence increases catalogued by Calleo were in fact necessary for the defence of America or the free world. Rhetoric about 'windows of vulnerability' and 'evil empires' may have little basis in geopolitical reality. It may have more resonance in the United States than elsewhere partly because of the peculiar virulence of American anti-communism. But it may be aided by the fact that Americans do not have to pay for the cost of such rhetoric in higher taxation. The burdens and the political vices of imperial taxation have come full circle since the Boston Tea Party.

So, how far is America declining, and how far will it sink? Our contributors are agreed that relative economic decline is occurring though not yet down to its 'natural' level of perhaps 16–18 per cent of world wealth.[6] But there is no real sign of military–geopolitical decline. As the Warsaw Pact dissolves, the USSR, not the United States, is revealed as imperially overstretched. The CIA Director has stated that not even resurgent Soviet conservatives would want the Cold War back. Nor do America's free world rivals show military ambition. Perhaps Germany and Japan have finally found the peaceful route to a global power which their earlier militarism denied them. Indeed, if they or the Soviet Union did mount a serious military challenge to American domination, it would threaten far worse than American decline. It might signal the end of the world. This seems well understood by the powers themselves, as do the lessons of twentieth-century history. Unlike the rivals of 1914 they recognize that military and economic power are indeed separable, that the economic well-being of the major nations need not depend on a commensurate

6 As given by its population and resource base, estimated by Kennedy in *The Rise and Fall*, p. 53.

geopolitical power. For the near future the American empire seems unchallenged, and imperial taxation reduces its own fiscal burdens to manageable levels.

In the medium and long term, however, economic problems may well loom. America may be gradually declining to somewhere around its 'natural' level, just as the European economy may be in the last phase of expansion to its own natural level. Japan, on the other hand, is in the contemporary period expanding somewhat beyond the level conferred by its population and resources, having found distinctive corporate structures that may produce more effectively than those of the West at this particular juncture in the development of capitalism – though there is no reason for thinking that Japan has been conferred the gift of 'Efficiency without End'. In the Third World only relatively small economies are showing remarkable growth rates – though as these are also mostly in East Asia, the possibility arises of a shift in economic power to that region, away from the West altogether.

The question is, whether these rivals plus American institutional rigidities may lead to the kind of 'supra-natural' economic decline as occurred to earlier great powers. This would probably stem less from the military burdens than from the possible historical scenario laid out by Pollard: the imperial power shifts from industry to finance and commerce, and from productive enterprise to luxury consumption. In this respect imperial taxation may be an immediate fiscal solution but a long-term economic disaster.

The rise of two East Asian rivals, Japan and China, concerns Gilbert Rozman. He focuses on the emergence of a distinctive form of state, neither severely limited as in the Western capitalist tradition, nor strongly interventionist as in the Russian 'northern', latterly socialist, tradition, but offering an intermediate level of non-coercive 'guidance' to society. He chronicles its origins in Confucian states, its Japanese revival from the Meiji restoration up to today, and the dilemmas of Chinese Communist leaders in trying to recreate a contemporary version of it in reaction to their over-interventionist beginnings. In Japan and in modern conditions its general virtues are the cultural solidarities it provides, and its high valuation of education and indicative planning. More particularly what he seems to be describing is an unusually self-conscious and influential administrative elite, constantly discussing Japan's place in the world, the experience of the other major nation states, and future strategies. All this is distinctively useful in the economic rise of Japan in the multi-state system of advanced capitalism.

But lest we get too obsessed with picking winning and losing nations, two contributors remind us that the nation itself is not natural, but a particular and developing historical construct. Meghnad Desai takes pains to remind us that the rise of the Dutch, the British and the Americans was only one part of a broader hegemony: that of the Europeans and their white colonists over the world. Preoccupation with the nation obscures the transnational aspects of this hegemony, its capitalist, Christian, sometimes international liberal but usually racist character. This helps explain why Europe shares too many cultural and capitalist solidarities with the United States to become its serious geopolitical rival in a nuclear age. But it also creates a new research problem: why do particular nations arise at all amid these broader solidarities?

Desai takes two cases, one in central Europe, the other in the Indian subcontinent. How did Germany and India emerge as modern nation states? In both cases other emergent states were possible over these areas (which he calls Germania and Indica). Had Germania as a whole been a single state, as it was briefly under Hitler, it would have comprised the whole German Confederation of the nineteenth century and its two great powers, Prussia and Austria. Instead the smaller, *Kleindeutsch*, Prussian-dominated state we know as Germany emerged. Desai argues that there were at least three other possible German states, all involving a more significant Austrian presence than actually occurred. There was no inevitability about the outcome; instead complex inter-relations between economic, cultural, military and geopolitical causes narrowly produced that Germany we too often regard as a 'natural' nation state. Indian developments were in two respects very different. A dominant imperial power, Britain, was significantly involved, and the formal division of Indica into two states, India and Pakistan, did not last as the latter was itself broken into two. But Desai finds the same complex web of economic, cultural, military and geopolitical events and causes narrowly determining one outcome rather than another. Contingencies mattered as we see again in the unexpected emergence of a *fifth* Germany, uniting the two 'rump' states of 1945 − *Kleiner deutsch* than Desai's four nineteenth-century alternatives. It is no more 'natural' a Germany but it may endure.

Wolfgang Mommsen tackles another aspect of the contingency of the nation. He charts the changing character of nationalism and the nation state. Though states existed at the beginning of the nineteenth century, and though some of these were in a sense 'national', the nation state, reinforced by strong nationalist ideologies, was basically a creation of that century. Moreover, as it developed, nationalism changed from being liberal and emancipatory to being aggressive and militarist abroad and sometimes repressive at home. Similarly imperialism, at first largely confined to the periphery of Europe, was then generalized into its heartland as Europe slid towards the world wars. Though this is a grim tale, it poses what might be an optimistic moral: that the really dangerous part of great power rivalry, the conjunction of elite geopolitical strategies with mass, xenophobic nationalism, is not natural but conjunctural. Perhaps it is even anachronistic in the modern world − 'evil empires' notwithstanding. Germany was crucial to the nineteenth-century shift from liberal to repressive nationalism. Germany is again crucial to a reverse shift.

Taking these points to heart, we can see that there are actually two main tensions in the contemporary world affecting the 'rise and fall' issue. One centres on the rivalry of the great nation states, the other on how dominant and aggressive that rivalry is to become *vis-à-vis* the more internationalist tendencies of the global system. I return to one of the two distinctions with which I started. It is evident in the world today that economic and military-geopolitical rivalry have become largely separated. The supreme military-geopolitical rivalry concerns the United States and the Soviet Union. Hopefully, even this appears to be easing at the present time — though political events in either country could reverse this. But the Soviet Union is not a significant economic rival to the United States. True, the two superpowers are also engaged in a mixed economic—ideological—geopolitical rivalry over the Third World. Here I endorse John Hall's argument. The United States would do much better — with greatly improved consequences for the Third World itself — if it allowed its economic advantages to flower by coming to terms with Third World nationalism and indigenous socialism, so detaching those forces from Soviet-style socialism.

But the economic rivals to the US are its geopolitical friends. The growing intensity of their economic competition shows no signs of reducing this friendship. This might not endure for ever. If the Soviet Union no longer appeared as a threat to any of the major capitalist powers, and if their economic power were to overtake that of the US, then they might seek more military autonomy and grandeur. But it is worth observing how historically unusual the behaviour of West Germany and Japan has already become. Major economic powers who do not bother to defend themselves are rather rare. It is now 45 years since the end of World War II. German and Japanese reluctance to re-arm now seem less like war-guilt, more like a rational, openly-discussed response to a changed reality, the operation of two distinctively late twentieth-century forces. First, the global capitalist economy has produced more genuine internationalism, weakening nation-state divisions, than at any period in the historical development of nation states. Second, the advent of nuclear (to say nothing of chemical and biological) weapons has cast considerable doubt on the historical norm that militarism and war were useful instruments of economic aggrandizement and national greatness. Germany and Japan may eventually raise their defence commitments rather closer to the level of their economic powers. But the level of capitalist interdependence and rational nuclear strategy is more likely to replace America with a fairly stable consortium of capitalist powers than with cut-throat imperialist rivalry or a successor hegemon.

Thus the major shortcoming of drawing contemporary lessons from historical analogies of rise and decline is provided by a new stage in the contingent conjunctions of economic and military power: the rising economic powers may not now be as interested in securing military domination. And in turn this might have the effect of slowing down the rate of decline of the hegemon itself. It is probable that the United States will not experience the really severe level of imperial over-stretch which has come historically only during major wars. Or if it does, it — and the world as a whole — will experience a far worse fate. Unless this terrible fate ensues, these essays carry a more optimistic message both for the United States and for the other major powers than would a mere emphasis on historical analogies of rise and fall.

2

The Imperial Component in the Decline of the British Economy before 1914

Patrick K. O'Brien

The Imperial Question Redefined

In 1914 the Government of a small kingdom located on the edge of continental Europe (sustaining some 45 million subjects on a land mass of just 87,500 square miles) exercised sovereignty over India (a sub-continent of 2 million square miles and a population of 322 million people). It also ruled directly over 60 dependent colonies extending over 3.2 million square miles and populated by 5.2 million 'natives'. In addition British jurisdiction and political influence intruded into the affairs of five dominions containing 24 million (mainly white) citizens and including an area of 7.6 million square miles. Whether this complex institutional edifice of supra-national power (representing the largest occidental empire since Rome) brought tangible gains to anything like a majority of British people is a large question, which has in recent years attracted growing attention in modern economic history.

Clearly a historical problem of this kind must be reformulated and constrained in time, scope and scale. Thus this essay will not be concerned with the costs and benefits of acquiring the enormous empire that remained under British rule after the Treaty of Vienna. That grand theme, encompassing the origins and consequences of some three centuries of mercantilist warfare for control of the seas and of territories beyond Western Europe, is the disputed academic province of historians of global development and world systems.[1] In an earlier paper I argued that both these 'Marxistante schools' exaggerated the economic gains that Western Europe in general, and Britain in particular, derived from

This article is an amended version of the author's 'The Costs and Benefits of British Imperialism 1846–1914', which first appeared in *Past and Present: A Journal of Historical Studies*, no. 120 (August 1988), pp. 163–200. (World Copyright: The Past and Present Society, 175 Banbury Road, Oxford, England)

war, conquest and international trade before 1815. The assumption that European and British industrialization rested in large part upon the spoils of successful mercantilism and proceeded at the expense of Asian, African and Latin American economies is inherently implausible.[2] For purposes of this survey the historical origins of Britain's political and industrial pre-eminence in the mid-nineteenth century can be set on one side because I will be concerned with the *material* costs and benefits for British society as a whole, imputable to political decisions to retain and extend the empire from the onset of free trade through to the First World War, 1846 to 1914.

In selecting the question of gains from imperialism for discussion modern economic historians have rejoined and revitalized a debate which originated with Adam Smith's famous synthesis of 1776, and which continued throughout the long nineteenth century between supporters and denigrators of the British Empire. Among opponents of the 'imperial idea' are to be found a line of classical economists and several famous economic historians. Most of their arguments against empire (which range from positive enmity in the cases of Cairnes, Goldwin Smith, Fawcett, Thorold-Rogers and Hobson, to the ambivalent position of John Stuart Mill and the sceptical antipathies of neo-classical economists such as Jevons and Marshall) can be traced back to the *Wealth of Nations*.[3] It was Smith who first argued that colonies imposed heavy and unfair burdens on British taxpayers, distorted the allocation of investible funds, and increased threats of war and the probability of political corruption at home.[4] Mill, Fawcett and Cairnes agreed with his fundamental point that Britain required an empire neither for trade nor for defence. When Cairnes wrote in 1864 'We do not any longer ask — we certainly do not receive — from our colonies any commercial advantages which are not equally open to the whole world, which we should not equally command though the political connection were 'severed tomorrow', he simply reiterated very old arguments.[5]

With proponents of imperialism, nineteenth century radicals debated four topics of central concern for this enquiry: the emigration of British labour overseas; the profitability of investing money to support capital formation in the empire; the potential gains from sustaining and using the political ties binding Britain to the dominions and its colonies for purposes of trade and

1 I. Wallerstein, *The Modern World System* (New York, 1974); A. G. Frank, *World Accumulation* (London, 1978); S. Amin, *Accumulation on a World Scale*, 2 vols (New York, 1974).

2 P. K. O'Brien, 'Economic Development: The Contribution of the Periphery', *EcHR*, 2nd ser., xxxv (1982), pp. 1–18.

3 This literature is surveyed by J. C. Wood, *British Economists and the Empire* (London, 1983).

4 A. Smith, *Wealth of Nations* (Cannan edn, New York, 1937), pp. 560–84 and 607–26. On the complexities of Smith's position see B. Semmel, *The Rise of Free Trade Imperialism* (Cambridge, 1970), pp. 24–30.

5 J. E. Cairnes, *Essays in Political Economy* (London, 1873), pp. 311–12.

commerce; and the kingdom's security. Again and again radicals expressed
strong scepticism towards views ably expounded by more conservative economists, such as Wakefield, Giffen, Ashley, Cunningham and Hewins, who argued
that the empire provided the British economy with profitable outlets for its
'surplus' population, capital and commodities.[6] In a classic study of 1902
Hobson launched an eloquent attack on imperialism, which he saw as a costly
and ineffective alternative to social reform and as an obstacle to the structural
changes required for the future vitality of the British economy.[7]

Modern economic historians have reopened this venerable discussion by
resorting to their favourite heuristic device, a counterfactual question. Predict-
ably they now ask what might have happened to British exports (visible and
invisible), to its imports and to flows of capital and labour (the entire nexus of
economic connections between Britain and her empire) as well as to the
defence budget and taxation if the dominions and colonies had become
independent polities from the middle of the nineteenth century onwards.
After all, commercial relations with France, Spain, the United States, even
with Brazil, were not predicated upon similar degrees of political intrusion by
the British government. Might not British businessmen, with or without the
Raj, have been engaged in similar kinds and levels of commerce with India?
With or without the Colonial Office might not trade with Jamaica have been
much the same as it was over the period 1850–1914? Taking the existence,
persistence and extension of empire as given, economic historians have now
attempted to specify (and where possible to measure) the *incremental* costs and
extra benefits to British society as a whole, imputable to the political arrangements and institutions of 'formal' imperial rule. In pursuing this line of *ex post*
evaluation, questions have been reformulated and new evidence uncovered
dealing with trade; with flows and rates of return on capital invested in the
empire and with taxes, national security and transfers of income effected
through imperial budgets. And some kind of preliminary balance sheet for the
costs and benefits of sustaining and expanding the British Empire can now be
drawn up, at least from the perspective of 1914.

Commodity Trade

The British economy became increasingly dependent upon international commerce over the nineteenth century.[8] That involvement is best measured by the

6 Semmel, *Rise of Free Trade Imperialism*, pp. 82–90 and 100–24 and 126; Wood,
   British Economists, pp. 181–223.
7 J. A. Hobson, *Imperialism* (Ann Arbor Paperback edition Michigan, 1967), pp.
   81–93 and 140–4; Wood, *British Economists*, pp. 245–56. For a subtle analysis
   of the complexities of Hobson's thought see P. J. Cain, 'J. A. Hobson, Cobdenism
   and the Radical Theory of Economic Imperialism', *EcHR*, 2nd ser., xxxi (1978),
   pp. 565–84.
8 P. Mathias, *The First Industrial Nation* (London, 1969), p. 244; D. McCloskey,
   Enterprise and Trade in Victorian Britain (London, 1981), pp. 145–7.

ratio of retained imports to national income, which rose from around 12 per cent in the 1830s, up to 30 per cent in the 1870s but fell back slightly to 27 per cent from 1900–13.[9] Almost all accounts of the Victorian and Edwardian economies analyse the connections between foreign trade and economic growth over the long run and also over particular cycles of economic activity from 1815 to 1914.[10] Britain's dependence upon overseas markets for the sale of manufactured exports and upon foreign and imperial sources of supply for foodstuffs and raw materials was unique among European nations, with the possible exceptions of very small countries such as Holland, Belgium and Switzerland.[11] Population growth, rising standards of living and marked specialization on industry and urban services within the British economy was sustained by ever increasing supplies of imported food and industrial raw materials. By 1913 agriculture produced only about half of non-tropical foodstuffs consumed within the United Kingdom. Apart from coal, 90 per cent of the raw materials processed by domestic industry came from abroad.[12]

Of course the empire had contributed to the emergence of the first industrial nation and from the mid-nineteenth century onwards it continued to exchange primary produce for the manufactured exports of the metropolis. But the significance of Britain's colonies and dominions as sources of supply for foodstuffs and raw materials and as markets for goods and services should not be exaggerated. In 1860 only a fifth of imports emanated from the Empire and that proportion rose to a quarter before the Great War.[13] Imperial wheat, tea, cheese, tin, jute, oil seeds and rubber seem to have been statistically important. Between 1860 and 1913 the Empire provided more food (particularly non-tropical foodstuffs) than raw materials, and the self governing dominions increased their share of primary produce sold to Britain relative to India and

9 F. Crouzet, 'Towards an Export Economy: British Exports during the Industrial Revolution', *ExEcH*, xvii (1980), pp. 77–84; C. Lee, *The British Economy Since 1700* (Cambridge, 1986), pp. 109, 219.

10 R. C. O. Mathews, C. H. Feinstein and J. Odling-Smee, *British Economic Growth, 1856–73* (Oxford, 1982), pp. 454, 525; Lee, *British Economy*, pp. 107–24, 218–23; D. H. Aldcroft and P. Fearon (eds), *British Economic Fluctuations 1700–1939* (London, 1972), pp. 97–160.

11 P. Bairoch, *Commerce extérieur et développement économique de l'Europe au XIXe Siècle* (Paris, 1974), pp. 78–80. This peculiar feature of British economic development has recently been analysed by N. F. R. Crafts, 'Patterns of Development in Nineteenth Century Europe', *OEP* xxxvi (1984), pp. 448–53.

12 P. Mathias, *First Industrial Nation*, pp. 232–3; F. Crouzet, *The Victorian Economy* (London, 1982), p. 343. The strategic significance of this dependence on imports is discussed by D. French, *British Economic and Strategic Planning* (London, 1982), pp. 11–13.

13 F. Crouzet, 'Trade and Empire: The British Experience from the Establishment of Free Trade until the First World War' in B. M. Radcliffe (ed.), *Great Britain and her World, 1750–1914* (Manchester, 1975), p. 215.

other dependent countries.[14] No commodities delivered from the Empire were, however, unobtainable elsewhere in the world economy and British consumers paid competitive prices for imported primary produce regardless of its origins.

The share of exports despatched to the Empire fluctuated between a quarter and one third (with a peak of 39 per cent in 1902). Taking this period as a whole it is possible to observe shifts from exported textiles to metallurgical products and to capital goods and some tendency for the dominions to overtake India and the colonies as markets for British manufactured exports.[15] It seems impossible to estimate the proportions of services (shipping, banking, insurance and distribution) sold to the Empire, although the ratio is unlikely to have differed from the percentages cited above for commodity exports. Clearly the significance of the Empire for British commerce should not be minimized, but it was far from overwhelming. And its significance had not increased in proportion to the massive acquisition of territory, resources and people that occurred during the high tide of imperialism from 1880 to 1900.[16] But what might have happened to Britain's imports and exports if the imperial connections had been severed at mid century?

Given that the self-governing dominions displayed no inhibitions in exercising their legal rights to impose tariffs on imports from the mother country, the transfer of sovereignty to India and other colonies would almost inevitably have led to augmented levels of protection on markets formerly open and free to imports from any part of the world.[17]

Edelstein attempted to quantify the potential effects of a counterfactual situation where governments, released from the constraints of imperial rule, imposed tariffs at the *ad valorem* rates favoured by the United States for 1870 and for 1913. His analysis proceeds on the basis of two assumptions (both biased heavily in favour of the economic significance of Empire): firstly that the resources embodied in the production of British exports sold to colonies and the dominions possessed *no* potential for employment elsewhere in the

14 S. B. Saul, *Studies in British Overseas Trade* (Liverpool, 1960), pp. 222–9; Crouzet, 'Trade and Empire', pp. 214–20.

15 M. Barratt Brown, *The Economics of Imperialism* (London, 1974), pp. 104–5; Crouzet, 'Trade and Empire', pp. 220–4; E. A. Benians (ed.), *Cambridge History of the British Empire*, iii (1959) pp. 206–8.

16 Crouzet observed 'imperial trade tended to move in unison with fluctuations in world trade', in 'Trade and Empire', p. 223. The point was strongly emphasized by Hobson, *Imperialism*, pp. 28–40 in 1902. This does not, however, invalidate the argument that a quest for markets may have been a motive for the annexation of territory from 1880 to 1900 – see D. K. Fieldhouse, *Economics and Empire*, (London, 1973), pp. 10–13.

17 Benians, *Cambridge History of the British Empire*, iii, pp. 185–6; W. T. Easter-brook and H. G. J. Aitken, *Canadian Economic History* (Toronto, 1979), pp. 392–3; P. J. Cain, 'Colonies and Capital: Some aspects of Anglo-colonial Financial Relations after 1850' (unpublished paper, Birmingham, 1986), pp. 8–9.

domestic economy and secondly that the infant industries located behind tariff walls in territories granted independence would not have boosted demand for British capital goods and industrial inputs.[18] On the assumptions specified, Edelstein guessed that upper bound estimates for the magnitude of losses on account of commodity trade from dismantling the Empire could have amounted to 1.1 per cent of Britain's gross national product for 1870 and 3.3 per cent for 1913.[19] Of course more complex models are required to work through the entire range of effects which might in theory follow from the premature end of Empire.[20] For example, if Britain's former colonies became, for whatever reasons, less integrated into the world economy, international trade and specialization might have declined more radically than Edelstein's 'partial equilibrium' analysis assumes.[21] Furthermore, India's large deficit on account of its commercial and political relations with the United Kingdom provided the metropolis with the means required to settle its trade deficits with North America and industrial Europe.[22] Several historians assert that the Anglo-Indian relationship played an essential role in the pattern of multilateral settlements and down to 1914 sustained the development of both British and international trade.[23]

But is there any need to accept suggestions that this particular imperial connection was indispensable for the continuation of international commerce or the viability of multilateral settlements from 1846 to the Great War? Why should an independent India have withdrawn from trade with the United

18 M. Edelstein, 'Foreign Investment and Empire 1860–1914', in R. C. Floud and D. N. McCloskey (eds), *The Economic History of Britain Since 1700*, ii (Cambridge, 1981), pp. 90–2.

19 Edelstein, 'Foreign Investment and Empire', pp. 92–3.

20 Examples of the kind of models and statistical testing required to work through the full range of potential effects flowing from changes in tariffs are to be found in J. James, 'The Welfare Effects of the Antebellum Tariff: A General Equilibrium Analysis', *ExEcH* xv (1978), pp. 231–56; and J. James, 'The Optimal Tariff in the Antebellum United States', *AmEcR* lxxi (1981), pp. 726–34.

21 Edelstein, 'Foreign Investment and Empire', p. 93 also works with stronger assumptions prescribing more drastic losses of gains from imperial trade. His revised estimates fall within the range of 3.6 per cent and 5.4 per cent of British national income.

22 The original data and analysis dealing with the pattern of multilateral settlements is Saul, *Studies in British Overseas Trade*, pp. 43–64. The argument is repeated in Crouzet, *Victorian Economy*, p. 358; by E. J. Hobsbawm, *Industry and Empire* (New York, 1968), p. 123; and by A. J. H. Latham, *The International Economy and the Underdeveloped World, 1865–1914* (London, 1978), pp. 68–92. India's balance of payments statistics have been assembled and analysed by A. K. Banerji, *Aspects of Indo-British Relations* (Oxford, 1982), pp. 157, 206, 244–6.

23 The whole issue remains under debate, see A. G. Frank, 'Multilateral Merchandise Trade Imbalances and Uneven Economic Development', *JEurEcH* v (1976), pp. 407–29; and Frank's controversy with Pollard in *JEurEcH*, vi (1977), pp. 745–53 and with Latham's in vii (1978), pp. 33–51.

Kingdom? Without India Britain could have settled her payments deficits with the United States and Europe by negotiating mutually agreed tariff reductions which, free traders argue, would have pushed the industrializing countries of Europe and North America towards greater specialization and even higher levels of production and specialization. And, to return to Edelstein's interesting arithmetic, it is implausible to assume (as he does simply for heuristic purposes) that a mature and sophisticated economy such as Britain's (with its rich resource base and diversified structure of output) was incapable of adjusting to whatever changes occurred as a direct consequence of relinquishing its Empire. Even if (to take a worst-case scenario) former imperial possessions had refused to trade with Britain, substitute sources of imports were certainly available elsewhere in the world economy or, in the case of temperate food-stuffs, by expanding domestic agriculture.[24] Given that exports to the Empire represented only small proportions of national output the reallocation of re-sources (capital and labour) engaged in production for imperial customers to production for sale on foreign and domestic markets could almost certainly have been achieved without any pronounced losses in efficiency or drastic and permanent falls in output and employment.[25]

Finally, those who agree with Hobsbawm's view that for some three or four decades before the First World War, sheltered and accessible imperial markets unfortunately allowed British industry to postpone necessary adjustments to growing German and American competition might also surmise that an earlier delinking of the economy from commerce with the Empire may have promoted faster productivity growth and the structural changes required by the British economy to meet the challenges of the twentieth century.[26]

The Migration of Capital and Labour

Access to official and more or less accurate figures for exports and imports means that the trade account can be sorted out and rough orders of magnitude assigned to the potential consequences of Britain's hypothetical withdrawal from Empire at mid-century. Unfortunately, the data available for the capital

24 The decline and slow growth of factor productivity in British agriculture was not inevitable – see C. O. Grada, 'Agricultural Decline 1860–1914' in Floud and McCloskey, *Economic History*, ii, pp. 175–97; and see W. W. Wade, *Institutional Determinants of Technical Change and Agricultural Productivity Growth: Denmark, France and Great Britain 1870–1965* (New York, 1981).
25 McCloskey, *Enterprise and Trade*, pp. 142–51. For an exaggeration of the role of trade see B. Porter, *Britain, Europe and the World, Delusions of Grandeur 1850–1982* (London, 1983), pp. 16–20, 66–7.
26 Hobsbawm, *Industry and Empire*, pp. 116–26; Bairoch, *Commerce extérieur*, pp. 202–17. This view has recently been reinforced by N. F. R. Crafts and M. Thomas, 'Comparative Advantage in U.K. Manufacturing Trade 1910–35', *EcJ* xcvi (1986), pp. 642–5.

account are scarce and far more difficult to analyse. Ideally we require a run of statistics which might reveal how the savings of British citizens were allocated in order to support the formation of capital at home, in foreign territories overseas, or within the Empire. Did British capitalists and the institutions that garnered and invested their savings, find the Empire a particularly attractive outlet for their surplus funds?

Unfortunately the data set available (and used by a long line of economists from Hobson to Dunning) is far from comprehensive.[27] It consists of statistics, copied from *Stock Exchange Yearbooks*, the *Investors Monthly Manual* and other parts of the financial press which refer to capital 'called up' for shares, debentures and bonds sold on behalf of governments and private incorporated firms on the London capital market. These figures obviously exclude: investments undertaken by unincorporated enterprises (including proprietorships, partnerships and private companies) as well as the funds raised by incorporated firms through provincial stock exchanges.[28] Furthermore, they do not bring into view the flows of British funds directly invested by all forms of business (merchants, commercial and financial agencies, small and large firms) which originated from retained profits or emanated from financial intermediaries, personal incomes and interpersonal loans.[29]

In other words the accessible data only records part of the total flow of British savings channelled through London *en route* for investment in the Empire, elsewhere in the world or within the frontiers of the United Kingdom. And there is now hard evidence which suggests that a rather high proportion of funds which supported the formation of capital outside the home economy travelled directly to foreign and imperial locations and by routes that bypassed the metropolis.[30] Obviously, those flows cannot be detected or classified from

27 C. K. Hobson, *The Export of Capital* (London, 1914), ch. vii; J. H. Dunning, *Studies in International Investment* (London, 1970), pp. 16−18, 44−5, 143−95; Thomas, 'The Historical Record of International Capital Movements to 1913', in J. H. Dunning (ed.), *International Investment* (London, 1972), pp. 27−55.

28 The data and its limitations are well reviewed in: H. Segal and M. Simon, 'British Foreign Capital Issues 1865−94', *JEcH* xxi (1961), pp. 567−81; M. Simon, 'The Pattern of New British Portfolio Foreign Investment 1865−1914', in A. R. Hall (ed.), *The Export of Capital from Britain 1870−1914* (London, 1968), pp. 16−23; P. L. Cottrell, *British Overseas Investment in the 19th Century* (London, 1975), pp. 27−64.

29 D. C. M. Platt, 'British Portfolio Investment before 1870: Some Doubts', *EcHR* 2nd ser. xxxiii (1980), pp. 1−16 and D. C. M. Platt, *Britain's Investment Overseas on the Eve of the First World War* (Basingstoke, 1986); S. J. Nicholas, 'British Multinational Investment Before 1939', *JEurEcH*, xi (1982), pp. 605−30.

30 The distinction between 'direct' and 'portfolio' investment is taxonomic and important for questions of control and business organization. It is not the immediate concern of this paper. But see P. Sverdberg, 'The Portfolio − Direct Composition of Private Foreign Investment in 1914 Revisited', *EcJ* lxxxviii (1978), pp. 763−77; I. Stone, 'British Direct and Portfolio Investment in Latin America Before 1914', *JEcH* xxxvii (1977), pp. 693−722.

records dealing solely with paper assets sold on the London stock exchange. Indeed by 1914 'direct' investment may have constituted up to 35 per cent of the value of the stock of assets owned by British capitalists which was located beyond the frontiers of their own country.[31] Finally, not all the paper assets traded on the London or even on the provincial stock exchanges found their way into the portfolios of the local capitalists. Some proportion (probably a minor percentage) attracted the savings of foreigners who simply invested their money through British financial intermediaries.[32]

Although business history has made us aware that the statistics available for manipulation and analysis are less than comprehensive, its attention to the details of where particular enterprises obtained funds for investment or how certain investors constructed their portfolios will never lead to a set of macro accounts which might reveal just how attractive and profitable British capitalists found the Empire before 1914.[33] The only way to approach that problem (which remains central for any overall economic assessment of imperialism) is to use the available familiar and defective set of figures in order to ascertain where (and for what kinds of return) those capitalists who opted to channel their savings through London, placed their money. There is no reason to assume that information available to and perceptions of that particular group differed radically from British investors as a whole.[34] Furthermore, although only a proportion of the total flow of British savings passed through the metropolis, that share was far from insignificant. It almost certainly increased over time. It also became more 'representative' of the entire annual flows of savings, because from the 1860s onwards national and international markets for capital became steadily more integrated into and with London money markets.[35]

31 P. Hertner and G. Jones (eds), *Multinationals Theory and History* (Brookfield, 1986), p. 6; Sverdberg, 'The Portfolio Direct Composition', p. 769; S. Nicholas, 'Agency Contracts, Institutional Modes and the Transition to Foreign Direct Investment by British Manufacturing Before 1939', *JEcH* xliii (1983), pp. 675−7.

32 Platt, 'British Portfolio Investment', pp. 6, 15 and 16; L. E. Davis and R. Huttenback, *Mammon and the Pursuit of Empire* (Cambridge, 1986), pp. 36, 209; R. Mitchie, 'The London and New York Stock Exchanges 1850−1914', *JEcH* xlvi (1986), pp. 177−87.

33 S. D. Chapman, 'British Based Investment Groups before 1914', *EcHR* 2nd ser., xxxviii (1985), pp. 229−47; R. C. Turrell and J. J. Van-Helten, 'The Investment Group: the Missing Link in British Overseas Economic Expansion before 1914', *EcHR* 2nd ser., xl (1987), pp. 267−73.

34 Davis and Huttenback, *Mammon and the Pursuit of Empire*, pp. 198−217.

35 R. C. Mitchie, 'The London Stock Exchange and the British Securities Market', *EcHR* 2nd ser., xxxviii (1985), pp. 61−82; L. Neal, 'Integration of Capital Markets: Quantitative Evidence from the Eighteenth to Twentieth Centuries', *JEcH* xlv (1985), pp. 219−26.

Direct investment or investment through conduits and methods which bypassed London was more likely to have formed a higher proportion of funds used to finance capital formation *within* the United Kingdom; higher that is compared to the savings that flowed to fund governments and private enterprises located beyond its borders.[36] Although direct investment overseas was far from negligible before 1914, the annual totals were certainly well below the shares *directly* invested in the home economy.[37] Thus when historians such as Davis and Huttenback use information which records only the flow of corporate finance passing through the London capital market, they are aware that this particular set of statistics does not encompass the aggregate flow of British savings but they should make it clear that the share of funds raised in the City for investment outside the United Kingdom represents an *upper bound estimate* of the *proportion* of national savings that were allocated to support capital formation and government expenditures located on both foreign and imperial soil. Their recent research which provides revised geographical breakdowns showing the destinations of funds raised largely (but not exclusively) on the London capital market from 1865 to 1914 is summarized in tables 1 and 2.

Tables 1 and 2 indicate that, at the outside, only a quarter of British investible funds flowed into the Empire. On private account that share was less than a fifth. Foreign assets emerge as considerably more attractive to British capitalists than securities and shares sold on behalf of imperial governments and imperial enterprises.[38] Table 2 demonstrates that the shares, bonds

Table 1 The geographical distribution of called-up capital, 1865–1914

	UK (£m)	(%)	Foreign[a] (£m)	(%)	Imperial (£m)	(%)
Private	1089	37	1282	44	561	19
Government	398	23	656	38	664	39
Total	1487	33	1939	42	1226	25

[a] Outside the UK and its Empire.

Source: L. E. Davis and R. Huttenback, *Mammon and the Pursuit of Empire* (Cambridge, 1986), pp. 40–1.

36 P. L. Cottrell, *Industrial Finance* (London, 1980), pp. 249–70; Mitchie, 'London Stock Exchange', pp. 71–82.
37 The macro data are set out in M. Edelstein, *Overseas Investment in the Age of High Imperialism* (London, 1982), p. 178; 'Direct' investment flows have not been accurately estimated but they were probably not more than 40 per cent of capital exports: see Nicholas, 'Agency Contracts', pp. 675–7; Hertner and Jones (eds), *Multinationals*, p. 6.
38 Earlier breakdowns of a similar kind were published by Simon, 'The Pattern of New British Portfolio Foreign Investment', pp. 23–44 and H. Feis, *Europe the World's Banker* (London, 1930), p. 33.

Table 2   The geographical distribution of called-up capital issued for imperial
governments and enterprises 1865–1914

	Dominions (£m)	(%)	Colonies (£m)	(%)	India (£m)	(%)
Private	369	65	84	16	108	19
Government	503	66	31	14	131	20
Total	872	71	115	10	239	19

Source: L. E. Davis and R. Huttenback, *Mammon and the Pursuit of Empire* (Cambridge, 1986), pp. 40–1.

and debentures of governments and firms located in 'white dominions', with a considerable degree of political autonomy, appealed far more to British investors than the securities sold on behalf of enterprises located in India or other colonial possessions. But the latter represent locations where it might be supposed that the political power of the metropolitan government could have been used to safeguard and boost returns on British capital invested within the Empire.[39]

If, as many polemicists both for and against imperialism alleged, the Empire was maintained and expanded in order to support safe and unusually profitable outlets for British capital these data (which have been around for some time now) challenge them to explain why colonies within that supranational institution failed to attract anything more than a tiny proportion of British funds available year after year from 1865 to 1914.[40] When they placed their surpluses beyond national frontiers British investors preferred foreign to imperial regions by a large margin. If the Empire represented an effective set of political arrangements which guaranteed exploitative profits for British capitalists, why was so little capital exported there from 1860 to 1914?

Official emigration statistics tell approximately the same story. From 1853 to 1910 around two-thirds of people leaving the United Kingdom travelled to destinations outside the Empire – the vast majority to the United States.[41] Not until 1911–13 did the Empire receive more than half of all emigrants leaving the British Isles, and even then most families settled in the autonomous dominions.[42] Neither outflows of labour nor capital from the United Kingdom to other parts of the world seemed to depend in any significant degree on the

39 A point that seems to escape P. J. McGowan and B. Kordan, 'Imperialism in World System Perspective: Britain 1870–1914', *ISQ* xxv (1981), p. 64.
40 An argument developed by Fieldhouse, *Economics and Empire*, pp. 38–62, and in his collection D. K. Fieldhouse, *The Theory of Capitalist Imperialism* (London, 1967), pp. xiii–xix. See also R. Winks (ed.), *British Imperialism* (New York, 1963).
41 D. E. Baines, *Migration in Mature Economy: Emigration and Internal Migration in England and Wales 1861 – 1900* (Cambridge, 1985), pp. 62–5.
42 Wood, *British Economists and the Empire*, p. 22.

institutional framework, political guarantees and security provided by imperial rule.

Relative Returns on Investment in the Empire

From mid-century onwards, in no sense was the visible presence of British power a precondition for emigration or for investment overseas, but did the apparatus of imperial defence and rule help to generate rates of return that turned out *post hoc* to be higher within the Empire than returns on British-owned capital located at home or placed in independent parts of the world economy? Our problem seems best posed in this way because historians, following Mill or deriving their views from Marxist–Leninist theory, depict the Empire as providing havens and outlets for Britain's surplus capital which staved off diminishing returns to investments within the home economy.[43] Two sources seem potentially helpful for purposes of comparing rates of return on domestic, foreign and imperial investments for the years down to 1914. Firstly there are quotations of prices and yields of paper securities traded on the London Stock Exchange, and secondly the reports and records of companies operating in one or other of these three locations.

Early quantitative research by Lehfeldt and Cairncross compared yields on the bonds of foreign, colonial and UK governments and they indicated that interest obtainable in the Empire was above British but below foreign interest rates, but the gap had narrowed to insignificance by 1914.[44]

By far the most sophisticated analysis of home and overseas returns from paper assets traded on the Stock Exchange has been conducted by Edelstein, who worked with a sample of 566 securities (equities, preference shares and debentures) quoted in the *Investors Monthly Manual*.[45] His study hardly constitutes a representative sample and varies in size and composition over the period studied, from 1870 to 1913. But it makes the point that on average and over these 43 years, British capitalists secured higher rates of return by investing outside the United Kingdom by a margin (adjusted for risk) of around 1.58 per cent a year — not a huge gap but significant enough. British investors (this test reveals) behaved rationally. No blame attaches to them or

43 The classical argument that capital exports represented a response to diminishing returns in the home economy is traced by Fieldhouse, *Economics and Empire*, *passim* and in its Marxist form by A. Brewer, *Marxist Theories of Imperialism* (London, 1980), pp. 44–60, 79–127, 274–93.
44 A. K. Cairncross, *Home and Foreign Investment 1870–1913* (Cambridge, 1953), pp. 222–35. R. A. Lehfeldt, 'Rate of Interest on British and Foreign Investments', *JRSS* lxxvii and lxxviii, (1914 and 1915), pp. 432–5 and 452–3.
45 First published as M. Edelstein, 'Realized Rates of Return on U.K. Home and Overseas Portfolio Investment in the Age of High Imperialism', *ExEcH* xiii (1976), pp. 283–329.

to financial intermediaries who garnered their savings for neglecting potentially more profitable investments at home because the prices of first and second class securities quoted in London provided signals that placing money overseas would probably yield higher returns (in the form of capital gains, interest and dividends) than investing in companies located in Britain − at least compared with domestic companies whose shares also happened to be traded on the Stock Exchange.[46]

Average yields, which ostensibly sum up the experience of 43 years, are tricky to construct and difficult to interpret. Edelstein weights his overall averages by the 1913 values of securities contained within the portfolio of paper assets he selected for study − a selection which appears to be dominated by the stocks and shares of railways and other forms of social overhead capital.[47] Furthermore, when he tracks variations in domestic and foreign yields through time and along the business cycle, the tabulation reveals that foreign equities enjoyed extraordinary differentials over UK equities in two sub-periods − 1897 to 1909 (when home yields slumped to below 1 per cent per annum) and from 1877−86 (when the return on foreign equities rose to almost double the level of returns available in the UK). Outside these particular and unexplained phases of the cycle no incremental gains accrued to those who exported their capital overseas.[48] Finally, this particular set of financial data reveals no tendency for trends in profitability between home and overseas investments to widen. It lends no clear support to the Marxist hypothesis that capital exports offset a predicted tendency to diminishing returns to capital formation within the United Kingdom.[49]

It is difficult to disentangle returns to the specifically imperial component of the overall flow of British funds overseas. That can only be accomplished for a small subset of the securities studied by Edelstein and which refers again to railways, banks and social overhead capital. Again, if those years of abnormally depressed yields on UK securities (1896−1909) are omitted from the calculations, then returns from investments in private incorporated enterprises located in the Empire were below foreign and on a par with domestic rates for most years from 1870 to 1914.[50]

---

46 Edelstein, *Overseas Investment*, p. 138. The best short summary of his research is in Edelstein, 'Foreign Investment and Empire', pp. 70−87; S. Pollard, 'Capital Exports, 1870−1914', *EcHR* 2nd ser., xxxviii (1985), p. 498 disputes the methods utilized by Edelstein to adjust for risk. The average unadjusted differential is only 1.12 per cent (Edelstein, 'Foreign Investment', p. 79 and Edelstein, *Overseas Investment*, p. 126).

47 Edelstein, *Overseas Investment*, pp. 115−20.

48 Edelstein, 'Foreign Investment and Empire', p. 79 and *Overseas Investment*, p. 148. The difficulties with variations along the cycle are discussed by Pollard, 'Capital Exports', pp. 496−8.

49 Edelstein, *Overseas Investment*, pp. 141−59. Cycles seem to dominate trends and as usual disaggregation obfuscates the picture.

There is little in Edelstein's sophisticated research (which is focused anyway on the rationality of exporting capital overseas) that undermines the radical argument that the Empire would turn out to be a waste of investors' money. Furthermore, the kind of financial information he uses cannot really settle the question of whether estimated *ex post* realized rates of return on British investment placed in the Empire were more or less profitable than potential returns available in the UK or elsewhere in the world economy. Prices of the securities of companies, quoted on the London Stock Exchange, reflect past capital gains, recent distribution of dividends and the current expectations of capitalists about future returns. Over the long run, in a perfectly competitive market and with full information about the realized returns, capital gains and dividends (emanating from paper claims sold on the Stock Exchange) and the real flows of profits accruing to companies selling such paper assets should, in theory, converge.[51] But before 1914 shares traded on all major and inter-connected stock exchanges represented the assets of only a minority of firms engaged in economic activity around the globe.[52] Information available to investors was far from perfect. The perceptions of those buying and selling paper securities were often so badly formed as to render the prices of equities and bonds tenuous indicators of the actual returns obtained from capital under the control of British, foreign or imperial firms.[53] Too many economists have exposed the 'higgledy piggledy' or 'random' connections in modern times between stock market quotations on the one hand and the long-term profitability of companies on the other for historians to accept the prices of securities printed in the *Investors Monthly Manual* as anything more than a proxy for the costs firms would have to pay if they attempted to raise funds on the London capital market at particular times between 1870 and 1914.[54] For purposes of

---

50 Davis and Huttenback, *Mammon and the Pursuit of Empire*, p. 81, citing an unpublished mimeographed paper by Edelstein.

51 These analytical issues concerned with the demand and supply prices for investible funds are discussed in J. H. Lorie and M. Hamilton, *The Stock Market: Theories and Evidence* (Homewood, 1973).

52 Research on the degree of integration achieved by international markets for long term capital is only beginning to emerge: see Neal, 'Integration of Capital Markets', pp. 219–26; Edelstein, *Overseas Investment*, pp. 81–110; Mitchie, 'The London and New York Stock Exchanges', pp. 61–82; K. E. Born, *International Banking in the 19th and 20th Centuries* (Leamington, 1977), pp. 115–60.

53 The subject is a long way from the level of sophistication attained by studies of the integration of national capital markets – see J. James, *Money and Capital Markets in Postbellum America* (Princeton, 1978); Mitchie, 'The London Stock Exchange', pp. 61–82; Cottrell, *Industrial Finance*, chapters 4–8.

54 The most accessible are B. G. Malkie, *A Random Walk Down Wall Street* (New York, 1975) and I. M. D. Little, *Higgledy Piggledy Growth Again: An Investigation of the Predictability of Company Earnings and Dividends in the UK* (London, 1971).

assessing gains to British capitalists from investment in the Empire, calculations which simply expose the *ex ante* expectations of those buying securities on the London Stock Exchange seem useful but inconclusive.

Historians require accounts which reveal the *ex post* and realized rates of return on British investments in the Empire. Davis and Huttenback are, therefore, to be highly commended for analysing surviving records of some 482 firms of varying types and sizes located at home, abroad, and within the Empire. But, their set of company records is also neither random nor representative.[55] As they frankly admit 'the firms included in the sample vary greatly in size — there are companies with total assets of less than £100 and others with assets in millions'.[56] The authors have, however, reconstructed surviving accounts in order to provide consistent and inclusive definitions of profit which are then related to the current values of assets under the command of an impressively large number of firms.[57] Their painfully mined and carefully presented statistics will be subjected to critical scrutiny from historians who will point to a data set dominated by incorporated enterprises, exhibiting rates of return on capital possibly above or possibly below those attained by proprietorships, partnerships, private companies and mercantile and interlocking business groups.[58] Many business historians will remark on the daunting complexities of transforming the accounts of a bygone age into acceptable and consistent measures of profitability.[59] (Most of them don't even try!) Sample size by industry and by location (particularly for the decades before the 1880s) may be small enough to represent nothing more than the accidental survival of business records. Finally there are some inexplicable movements in rates of profit from period to period, even after smoothing by means of five-year averages.[60]

Nevertheless, unless and until business histories of British firms accumulate to include a large enough number of cases to qualify and supercede it, the Davis — Huttenback set of company accounts, summarized in table 3, constitutes

55 First published in L. Davis and R. Huttenback, 'The Political Economy of British Imperialism: Measures of Benefits and Support', *JEcH* xlii (1982), pp. 122–6.
56 Davis and Huttenback, *Mammon and the Pursuit of Empire*, p. 84.
57 Davis and Huttenback, *Mammon and the Pursuit of Empire*, pp. 81–5 and the list of companies cited in appdx. 3.1 and pp. 326–37.
58 See M. Edelstein, 'Discussion', *JEcH* xlii (1982), pp. 131–2. For a list of firms not included in the Davis–Huttenback sample see: Chapman, 'British Based Investment Groups', pp. 243–5; Turrell and Van Helten, 'The Investment Group', pp. 267–73; Chapman, 'Investment groups in India and South Africa', pp. 275–80; C. Newberry, 'Technology, Capital and Consolidation: The Performance of De Beers Mining Company Limited 1880–89', *BHR* 61 (1987), pp. 3–42.
59 S. Marriner, 'Company Financial Statements', *BHR* xxii (1980), pp. 203–35; J. R. Edwards and K. W. Webb, 'The Influence of Company Law on Corporate Reporting Procedures', *BHR* xxii (1982), pp. 259–79.
60 Davis and Huttenback, *Mammon and the Pursuit of Empire*, pp. 106–10.

Table 3　Average annual rates of return as a percentage of capital invested in the UK, the Empire and foreign countries, 1860−1912

| | 1860−1884 | | | 1885−1912 | | |
	UK	Empire	Foreign	UK	Empire	Foreign
Firms engaged in commodity production	11.5	14.5	10.0	7.5	5.4	6.2
Equity capital alone	14.1	19.9	15.1	11.7	8.1	10.1
All claims on capital	5.8	9.7	5.8	5.5	3.3	5.3

Source: L. E. Davis and R. Huttenback, *Mammon and the Pursuit of Empire*, pp. 106−17.

the only evidence currently available for statistically based generalizations about the profitability of investing in the Empire before 1914.

Up to 1880 the numbers of imperial and foreign firms behind the rates of return cited in table 3 come to only 17 and 27 in each location respectively. But for all their deficiencies the estimates suggest that until that decade investments in the Empire yielded higher returns than domestic or foreign investments. Thereafter domestic investment turned out to be more profitable than either foreign or imperial investments. This hypothesis may eventually emerge as the accidental outcome of the data at the disposal of Davis and Huttenback. Imperial history is replete with the names of great capitalists. And buccaneering enterprises at new frontiers (when they succeed and thus spawn a hagiography of entrepreneurs) tend to record the fortunes made by adventurous men.[61] Although such highly profitable imperial enterprises can be found not only in archetypal pioneer sectors like mines and land speculation, they also show up in public utilities (gas, electricity and water companies) − presumably exploiting their privileges as local monopolies.[62] With the possible and less manifest exception of brewing, this data set does not reveal other lines of economic activity within the Empire which yielded relatively high rates of return for those who opted to invest there after 1880.

61　Davis and Huttenback, *Mammon and the Pursuit of Empire*, p. 106, fully recognize this point; Newberry, 'Capital and Consolidation', pp. 7−18; Chapman, 'Investment Groups in India and South Africa', p. 278.

62　Davis and Huttenback, *Mammon and the Pursuit of Empire*, pp. 87−104; R. V. Turrel and Y. J. Van Helten, 'The Rothschilds, the Exploration Company and Mining Finance', *BHR* xxviii (1986), pp. 62−79; R. V. Kubicek, *Economic Imperialism in Theory and Practice: The Case of South African Gold Mining Finance 1886−1914* (Durham, 1979).

28   *Patrick K. O'Brien*

Historians have recorded many examples where British investors were 'gulled' into anticipating supernormal profits. Private investors also derived reassurance from knowing that the presence of their troops and their officials provided some guarantee against debt crises, nationalization and fraudulent bankruptcies of the kind that came to afflict foreign investors from 1919–39 and again after 1979. (Although there is no evidence one way or another that before 1914 risks from default were any less in the Empire than elsewhere in the world economy.[63] Nevertheless, the growth of imperial sentiment and continued confidence in the Royal Navy created a climate that entered into the perceptions of otherwise 'rational' investors and lured their savings overseas and in growing proportion towards the dominions and colonies. In this sense the propaganda for an expanding Empire created illusions of security and false expectations that high returns would accrue to those who invested within its boundaries.[64]

This 'climate' of imperial sentiment must be analysed alongside other factors contributing to the long term decline of the British economy. But as emphasized in the previous section, the institutional framework of imperial systems of law, direct rule and defence were not necessary conditions for investment beyond the frontiers of the United Kingdom. The preservation and extension of the British Empire merely provided another source of encouragement for the massive and persistent drain of capital from the home economy which occurred from 1873 to 1914.

During that period somewhere between a quarter and a third of British funds invested overseas found their way to the Dominions, India, and other colonies.[65] Most of this money originated as the savings of investors, resident mainly in the home counties, who sought stable but somewhat higher returns than they could obtain from investments of comparable risk within the United Kingdom.[66] From their perfectly understandable point of view, the Empire (ostensibly strengthening and deepening its ties with the metropolis) provided satisfactory outposts for rentier capital, defensible and safe even from the emergent threat of trade unionism and the welfare state.[67] As recent research on probates and other evidence reveals, a majority of British investors preferred

63 C. Lipson, *Standing Guard: Protecting Foreign Capital in the Nineteenth and Twentieth Centuries* (Berkeley, 1985), chapters 2 and 3; Edelstein, *Overseas Investment*, pp. 128–30; Cairncross, *Home and Foreign Investment*, pp. 222–35.
64 J. M. Mackenzie, *Propaganda and Empire: The Manipulation of British Public Opinion* (Manchester, 1984); A. P. Thornton, *The Imperial Idea and its Enemies* (London, 1966), pp. 41–203; Hobson, *Imperialism*, pp. 3–13, 41–5 and 51–60; J. A. Schumpeter, 'Imperialism and Social Classes' in H. M. Wright (ed.), *The New Imperialism* (Lexington, 1961), pp. 47–61; B. Semmel, *Imperialism and Social Reform* (London, 1960), pp. 13–28.
65 See tables 1 and 2 and the commentary on this data in the text.
66 W. P. Kennedy, 'Foreign Investment Trade and Growth in the UK 1870–1914', *ExEcH* xi (1974), pp. 422–39.
67 P. Kennedy, *The Realities Behind Diplomacy* (London, 1981), pp. 43–51.

steady to volatile returns and were less inclined to hold the risky shares of domestic industrial companies, especially smaller-scale firms in industries using relatively untried technology or producing novel products.[68]

Their preferences are, moreover, explicable because the dominant modes of organization and managerial control favoured by British industry, namely smaller-scale family enterprises and private companies, hardly allowed for outside participation in the equity capital of either established or innovating firms.[69] Even the emergent corporate sector of business exhibited many of the closed and secretive features of more traditional forms of business organization. For example, the ordinary shares of limited liability companies remained concentrated in the hands of founding families or were retained by the rather exclusive social networks of people who continued to manage 'their' firms as they increased in scale, and gradually matured into fully fledged incorporated enterprises.[70] If and when such companies required funds for expansion, their boards of directors tended to favour the issue of preference or debenture stocks which left their control and profits to accrue mainly to founding families and their immediate business associates.[71] English company law, moreover, does not appear well designed to protect the interests of equity shareholders. Thus while the formation of limited liability companies became relatively simple under legislation enacted in 1855 and 1862, it was not until four decades later that annual audits and the filing of balance sheets became mandatory for all registered companies. Even then the presentation and disclosure of information to shareholders could be minimized and rendered opaque by directors determined to brook no outside interference with their authority to use and manage other people's money as they saw fit.[72] Long before 1914 the familiar divorce between the owners and controllers of equity capital was visible and effective.[73]

68 W. P. Kennedy, 'A Strategy for Measuring Efficiency in Services: The Special Case of Financial Intermediation — Notes on a Comparison of Britain and Germany' in P. K. O'Brien (ed.), *International Comparisons of Productivity 1750–1939* (Proceedings of 9th World Congress of Economic History, Berne 1986), pp. 24–9; W. P. Kennedy, 'Notes on Economic Efficiency in Historical Perspective: The Case of Britain 1870–1914' in P. Vselding (ed.), *Research in Econ. Hist.* ix (1984), p. 109.

69 Cottrell, *Industrial Finance*, chapters 4, 6 and 8; Kennedy, 'Notes on Economic Efficiency', pp. 109–41.

70 Cottrell, *Industrial Finance*, pp. 161–4; W. P. Kennedy, 'Institutional Response to Economic Growth: Capital Markets in Britain to 1914' in L. Hannah (ed.), *Management Strategy and Business Development* (London, 1976), pp. 151–83.

71 Cottrell, *Industrial Finance*, pp. 165–7; Kennedy, 'Institutional response', pp. 151–83.

72 L. Hannah, 'Takeover Bids in Britain Before 1950: An Exercise in Business Pre History', *BHR* xvi (1974), pp. 65–77; Cottrell, *Industrial Finance*, pp. 62–75; Kennedy, 'Notes on Economic Efficiency', pp. 109–41.

In contrast to Germany and the United States, entrepreneurial middlemen had not emerged to act as brokers in the marriage of British capital and enterprises.[74] In the United Kingdom, banks and other financial intermediaries did not see it as their business to conciliate the security-conscious mentality of typical investors with the need to increase the supply of funds for risky but potentially viable ventures in domestic industry and services.[75] Profitably occupied in dealing with the paper assets of colonial, dominion and foreign corporate enterprises, banks, insurance companies and the financial houses of the City came under no pressures to engage themselves more closely with the internal affairs of domestic limited liability companies. Before 1914 they also perceived no need to use their very considerable powers over the allocation of investible resources to bring about the restructuring and reorganization of established staple industries, let alone to involve themselves with supporting product and process innovations in new industries such as electrical engineering, chemicals, bicycles, and automobiles.[76] Not until the Great Depression of the 1900s did British financial institutions begin to assist in the restructuring of industry.[77] Banks that looked out for potentially profitable ideas from innovators with limited access to informal sources of finance took even longer to appear in the industrial regions.

For decades before the Great War at a time when British manufacturers came under intensified competition from European and American industry both at home and in their traditional markets abroad, British banks and other financial institutions continued to find the debentures, preference shares,

---

73 L. Hannah, *The Rise of the Corporate Economy* (London, 2nd edn, 1983), pp. 8–122; Cottrell, *Industrial Finance*, pp. 75, 162–7; Kennedy, 'Notes on Economic Efficiency', pp. 109–41; Chapman, 'British Based Investment Groups', pp. 243–5.
74 This thesis focused on the failure of financial intermediation in the UK has been fully developed by Kennedy, 'Institutional Response'; 'Notes on Economic Efficiency'; 'A Strategy for Measuring Efficiency in Services'. See also Cottrell, *Industrial Finance*, pp. 194–243; M. Best and J. Humphries, 'The City and Industrial Decline', in W. Lazonick and B. Elbaum (eds), *The Decline of the British Economy* (Oxford, 1986), pp. 223–9.
75 Kennedy, 'Notes on Economic Efficiency', pp. 109–41; W. P. Kennedy, 'Capital Markets and Industrial Structure' (unpublished Paper, London, November, 1986), pp. 2–3; Kennedy, 'Institutional Response', pp. 151–83.
76 Cottrell, *Industrial Finance*, pp. 211–44; Kennedy, 'Notes on Economic Efficiency', pp. 109–41; Cassis, 'Management and Strategy in English Joint Stock Banks, 1890–1914', *BHR* xxvii (1985), pp. 301–15.
77 Best and Humphries, 'The City and Industrial Decline', pp. 229–34; S. Pollard, *The Development of the British Economy* (London, 1933), pp. 145–9. There is, however, some controversy about the role played by banks in German industrialization and the debate is summarized in P. K. O'Brien, 'Do we have a Typology for the Study of European Industrialization in the XIXth Century', *JEurEcH* xv (1986), pp. 316–19.

equities and other claims issued by imperial and foreign firms and governments overseas secure and profitable enough for their rather myopic aspirations. Indeed an ever increasing supply of sound imperial and foreign assets maintained and strengthened an established style of financial intermediation — indifferent to domestic industry, especially to small-scale and younger firms.

On a priori grounds several consequences follow logically from a framework of company law that did not protect the interests of investors in domestic corporate enterprise and also from a tradition where banks found it unnecessary to assume that responsibility, or to take as active an interest in the future of the domestic economy as they did in the export of British capital overseas. Firstly, the overall rate of saving would remain depressed below its potential level. By failing to transform the risky claims on the fluctuating incomes and capital gains of domestic enterprises into more secure and less volatile ways of ensuring investors' wishes for safe and steady streams of income, banks, by default, discouraged savings and investment in the domestic economy.[78]

Secondly, as Hobson observed at the turn of the century, by facilitating the export of capital to the Empire and elsewhere Britain's financial institutions depressed money wages which restricted the development of a mass domestic market for the products of new consumer goods industries.[79] To some extent that effect was counteracted by imports of cheaper food and by the stimulus imparted to the British commodity exports. That stimulus was, however, concentrated upon old staple industries, destined to decline after the war.[80] Kennedy, who has attempted to estimate the scale of the general effects, positive and negative, of the export of capital, shows that 'feedbacks' imparted to plant, machinery and other new engineering goods were far weaker from foreign compared to domestic investment.[81] Meanwhile, infant industries (chemicals, electrical engineering, automobiles and machine tools) came under increasingly competitive pressures on a home market kept open and unprotected, in part to assist the nation's competitors to service their debts to British investors.[82]

78 For the theoretical underpinnings of this argument see Kennedy, 'A Strategy for Measuring Efficiency in Services', pp. 3–16; Kennedy, 'Foreign Investment Trade and Growth', pp. 415–44; Edelstein, *Overseas Investment*, pp. 20–5, 32–3, 171–95.

79 Hobson, *Imperialism*, pp. 41–5, 81–93; Cain, 'J. A. Hobson', pp. 567–73; Kennedy, 'Notes on Economic Efficiency', pp. 109–41; Wood, *British Economists*, pp. 237–8, 243–6.

80 Pollard, 'Capital Exports', pp. 507, 513; McCloskey's arithmetic warns against exaggerating the gains from trade: McCloskey, *Enterprise and Trade*, pp. 145–51; Hobsbawm, *Industry and Empire*, pp. 123–7; Cairncross, *Home and Foreign Investment*, pp. 103–208, 222–46.

81 Kennedy, 'Notes on Economic Efficiency', pp. 109–41.

82 P. J. Cain and A. G. Hopkins, 'The Political Economy of British Expansion Overseas', *EcHR* 2nd ser., xxxiii (1980), pp. 481–9.

Thirdly, small firms in need of risk capital found the transactions costs of raising money relatively high and the types of securities they could offer on British capital markets were 'crowded out' and their prices depressed by ever growing supplies of safer assets emanating in large part from outside the United Kingdom and in growing proportion from the Empire.[83] Britain's financial institutions were integrated into the City of London dominated by an increasingly 'aristocratic and cosmopolitan elite' which became socially as well as geographically remote from industry and technical innovation.[84] By 1911 when *The Economist* commented that 'London was more concerned with Mexico than the Midlands' it was clear that neither 'listening' nor 'action' banks had appeared on the scene to lend British industry the support accorded by its well developed network of financial institutions to the Empire and to its foreign competitors overseas.[85] Such support was becoming more rather than less important with the appearance of London-based multinational companies, interlocking mercantile enterprises and other forms of business operating on a global scale and divorced from the long-term future of local industry and the creation of domestic employment.[86]

Institutional sclerosis (the hereditary disease of industrial and commercial success) has now replaced entrepreneurial failure at the centre of modern historiography concerned with origins of the long-term decline of the British economy.[87] The 'penalties of an early start' and the continued commitment to the institutions, practices and technology that served the economy well for more than a century before 1873 but thereafter hampered its adaptation to the imperatives of the second industrial revolution, have re-emerged to dominate current historical debate.[88] In the context of this debate the legacy of empire

83 Cottrell, *Industrial Finance*, pp. 183–90, 269–70; Kennedy, 'Capital Markets and Industrial Structure', pp. 4–6; Kennedy, 'Notes on Economic Efficiency', pp. 109–41; Edelstein, *Overseas Investment*, pp. 47–72.

84 Y. Cassis, 'Bankers in English Society in the late Nineteenth Century', *EcHR* 2nd ser., xxxviii (1985), pp. 210–12, 224–9; J. V. Beckett, *The Aristocracy in England* (1986), pp. 105–6; P. J. Cain and A. G. Hopkins, 'Gentlemanly Capitalism', pp. 3–14; W. D. Rubinstein, 'The Victorian Middle Class: Wealth Occupation and Geography', *EcHR* 2nd ser., xxx (1977), pp. 609–12, 619–23.

85 Pollard, 'Capital Exports', p. 500; G. Ingham, *Capitalism Divided: The City and Industry in British Social Development* (London, 1984), pp. 45, 122–7, 136–9, 145–51, 166–9.

86 Hertner and Jones, *Multinationals Theory and History*, pp. 1–19, 96–109; Nicholas, 'British Multinational Investment Before 1939', pp. 605–30; Chapman, 'British Based Investment Groups Before 1914', pp. 230–47.

87 M. Olson, *The Rise and Decline of Nations* (London, 1982), pp. 77–9. On entrepreneurial failure see Floud and McCloskey, *The Economic History of Britain Since 1700*, ii, and the debate between the two approaches in *JEcH* xlii (1982), pp. 87–133.

88 Lazonick and Elbaum, *The Decline of the British Economy*.

and attempts to cash in on that legacy from Joseph Chamberlain to Winston Churchill appears as a major and costly delusion.[89]

Imperial Budgets and Strategic Necessities

If it is the case that trade with and investment in the Empire turns out in the cold light of history to have been neither necessary, nor 'socially' profitable for the metropolis, why were the rather considerable tax burdens contingent upon imperial defence and rule not curtailed long before 1914? The sharp answer is that ministerial perceptions and public opinion were not based upon the balance sheets of costs and benefit of the kind now being produced by economic historians long after the British Empire has passed away.[90] Although taxpayers' money allocated to maintain the apparatus of imperialism preoccupied Gladstonian liberals occasionally and the Treasury at all times, it seemed inordinately difficult for contemporaries to separate military expenditures into those necessary for the security of the realm and the protection of its commerce on the one hand from revenues required simply to maintain the framework of imperial rule on the other.[91] Politicians and officials were, in other words, unsure as to how much money could be left to fructify in private pockets and flow into the economy if successive British governments had cut and concentrated expenditure simply on the defence of its own territory and specific trading interests.[92] Furthermore, entirely inconclusive arguments about the cultural, psychic and other gains that accrued to Englishmen from the possession of vast areas shaded red on maps of the world may still legitimately 'muddy' this vulgar materialistic argument.[93] Nevertheless, recent research into the

89 B. Porter, *Britain Europe and the World*, pp. 57–81; B. R. Tomlinson, 'National Decline and Loss of Empire', *JICH* xi (1982), pp. 58–72; C. Barnett, *The Collapse of British Power* (New York, 1972), pp. 71–83; C. Barnett, *Strategy and Society* (The Spencer Wilkinson Memorial Lecture, Manchester, 1975).

90 R. Hyam, *Britain's Imperial Century 1815–1914* (London, 1976), pp. 99–134, 373–791; Thornton, *Imperial Idea and its Enemies*, pp. 1–49, 103–7; S. R. Stembridge, *Parliament the Press and the Colonies 1846–80* (London, 1982), pp. 107–19; P. Kennedy and A. Nicholls (eds), *Nationalist and Racialist Movements in Britain and Germany* (Oxford, 1981), chapters 1, 2, 10, 11; Fieldhouse, *Economics and Empire*, pp. 63–76.

91 P. Kennedy, *Strategy and Diplomacy* (London, 1953), p. 204; D. C. Gordon, *Dominion Partnership and Imperial Defence 1870–1914* (Baltimore, 1965), pp. 1–97.

92 P. Kennedy, *The Rise and Fall of British Naval Mastery* (London, 1983), pp. 156, 171; Benians (ed.), *Cambridge History of the British Empire*, iii, pp. 186, 232, 581–7; P. Kennedy, *Realities Behind Diplomacy*, pp. 33–6; P. Crowhurst, *The Defence of British Trade, 1689–1815* (Folkstone, 1977), pp. 15–93.

93 Kennedy, *Realities Behind Diplomacy*, pp. 51–65; Thornton, *The Imperial Idea and its Enemies*.

Patrick K. O'Brien

finances of states does offer some illuminating comparisons of taxation and
defence expenditures across large samples of countries which bring into relief
the relative position of the imperial government and domestic taxpayers.[94]

Taxes collected by the British Government were used basically to defray
military expenditure and to pay interest on a national debt which had accumulated as a consequence of past wars fought to acquire and defend the Empire.[95]
Table 4 indicates that from 1860 to 1914 the absolute levels of taxation and
military spending funded by residents of the United Kingdom stood above the
levels incurred by taxpayers in the rest of Europe, and by a considerable
margin. Unfortunately the data are not available in a form which allows us to
contrast the shares of national income collected as taxes and allocated for
military purposes over this period.[96] Since the British people enjoyed incomes
per capita above other Europeans (but not Americans) their relative tax and
defence burdens were certainly not as high as these figures might at first sight
suggest. But on any plausible hypothesis about the shares of income appropriated
as taxes and used to defray expenditures on defence Britain would remain way

Table 4   Average taxes and expenditure by central governments in £ per head,
1860–1914

	UK	Foreign States[a]	Dominions	Colonies	India
Taxes raised	2.41	0.96	1.65	0.34	0.17
Defence spending	1.14	0.42	0.12	0.02	0.10
Military Defence spending (% of budget)	37	32	4	6	33
Payments on govt. debt	0.7	0.26	0.59	0.01	0.04
Interest (% of budget)	27	19	19	2	13

[a] Incorporating most of Western Europe, Russia, USA and Japan, after 1900.
Source: Initially published by L. E. Davis and R. Huttenback, 'Public Expenditure and Private
Profit: Budgetary Decisions in the British Empire', *AmEcR* lvii (1977), and revised in their book
Mammon and the Pursuit of Empire, pp. 160–5.

94 The data were initially published by L. E. Davis and R. Huttenback, 'Public Expenditure and Private Profit: Budgetary Decisions in the British Empire', *AmEcR*
lxvii (1977) and are revised in their book *Mammon and the Pursuit of Empire*,
pp. 160–5.
95 P. K. O'Brien, 'The Political Economy of British Taxation, 1600–1815', in *EcHR*
2nd ser., xli XLI (1988), pp. 1–32, and 'Accounts of the National Debt', *Parliamentary Papers 1857* (xxxiii).
96 But the data is now being collected and processed. See P. Flora, *State Economy
and Society in Western Europe 1815–1975* i (London, 1983); J. Kohl, *Staatsausgasen
in Westeuropa: Analyses zur langfrilizers Entwicklung der offentilichen Finanzers*
(Frankfurt, 1985); N. F. R. Crafts, 'Gross National Product in Europe 1870–
1910: Some New Estimates' *ExEcH* xx (1983), pp. 387–401.

out at the top of international league tables from 1860 to 1914.[97] Indeed, recent estimates suggest that by 1910 French and German incomes per capita amounted to at least 70 per cent of British levels and their military expenditures per capita to only 48 per cent. Furthermore, the argument (formulated in a nuclear age when far higher shares of national income are allocated to defence) that before 1914 Britain ran her Empire 'on the cheap' is a *non sequitur*. It was not cheap because such funds have an opportunity cost. They might have been spent in ways that maintained the economic hegemony of the British economy, in relation to the economies of its rivals.[98]

Despite the Treasury's persistent efforts to ensure that all regions of the Empire contributed as much as possible towards their own defence, only for India (the Jewel in the Crown) was that policy implemented to the letter. Indian taxpayers underwrote direct military costs on their sub-continent and even funded some, but a disputed part, of the costs of Indian regiments stationed in other parts of the Empire.[99] Citizens residing in the white dominions of Canada, Australia, New Zealand, South Africa and Newfoundland secured a particularly good deal from the imperial connection. Although their taxes were high, expenditures by their governments on defence amounted to only 10 per cent of the levels assumed by their kith and kin who remained in the mother country. Furthermore, these affluent dependants of British largesse also enjoyed favoured access to loans on the London capital market, occasional grants in aid, cheap services from the Crown Agents and subsidies from the imperial communications network.[100] All these transfers allowed dominion (and also colonial) governments to allocate high proportions of their own revenues for public works, for health and education and for the enforcement of systems of free-enterprise property rights. India apart, residents of the dominions and the colonies derived tangible economic benefits from expenditures by their governments on local 'development' that were lavish by

97 A. Maddison, *Phases of Capitalist Development* (Oxford, 1982), pp. 7−9 and apps. A and B.

98 N. F. R. Crafts, 'Patterns of Development in Nineteenth Century Europe', *OEP* xxxvi (1984), p. 440. On the so-called 'cheapness of Empire' see M. Chalmers, *Paying for Defence* (Sydney, 1985), pp. 5−8. Even so military expenditure reached 6 per cent of GNP during the Boer War.

99 B. R. Tomlinson, *The Political Economy of the Raj* (London, 1979), pp. 104−18, 114−15 apparently is not impressed with the contribution India made to imperial defence, especially in the First World War. The subject is also treated cursorily in H. H. Dodwell (ed.), *The Cambridge History of India*, vi, (Cambridge, 1932), pp. 330−2, 401, 482−4.

100 Davis and Huttenback, *Mammon and the Pursuit of Empire*, pp. 166−88. But some historians are inclined to draw attention to cross subsidization − see: R. M. Kesner, *Economic Control and Colonial Development: Crown Colony Financial Management in the Age of Joseph Chamberlain* (Westport, 1981), pp. 65−88, 195−227; A. Porter, 'Britain, the Cape Colony and Natal, 1870−1914', *EcHR* 2nd Ser., xxxiv (1981), pp. 555−77.

international standards of the time. Such generous levels of public support presumably would not have been afforded by independent governments compelled to pay in full for the defence of peoples and territories under their jurisdiction.

It is proving rather difficult to put even a rough figure to the nevertheless considerable *subsidy* that the Empire enjoyed from British taxpayers. For example, Davis and Huttenback have argued that if the Treasury had somehow managed to compel the dominions, India and the colonies to shoulder the defence burdens, commensurate with those assumed by the governments of fully independent countries, *at comparable levels of economic development*, then the level of British taxes might have been reduced by over 40 per cent. They also invite historians to assume that if the British government had relinquished the Empire and then spent only as much per capita as France or Germany on its military forces, taxes could have been reduced by roughly a quarter.[101] Their counterfactual arithmetic is illuminating to ponder but not conclusive as a measure of the differential burdens imposed on British taxpayers in order to defend the Empire, not least because several foreign powers conscripted their soldiers and sailors and Britain's professional forces were presumably paid something approximating to market wages for their services.[102] In effect, conscription implies that a large part of the costs of, say, the German and French armies fell on their young recruits and is not revealed in the budgetary records of these states. That element of 'taxation in kind' could in principle be measured as the differential between the money wage a typical French or German conscript might potentially have earned in the civil economy and the real wages received in money and subsistence while they remained under arms.[103] For economies like that of tsarist Russia or Italy, afflicted with underemployment, these wage gaps could be small, even negative.[104] Compared

101 Davis and Huttenback, *Mammon and the Pursuit of Empire*, pp. 161—5.
102 This is, however, not clear cut. Military historians emphasize that the British army recruited officers and men on the cheap. The former required private means to serve as 'gentlemen'. And the latter, recruited largely from the unskilled and underemployed, received wages in money and kind at about 60 per cent of the levels paid to agricultural labourers. See W. S. Hamer, *The British Army: Civil Military Relations, 1885—1905* (Oxford, 1970), pp. 17, 87—8; G. Harries-Jenkins, *The Army in Victorian Society* (London, 1977), pp. 4—8, 274—81; I. F. W. Beckett and K. Simpson (eds), *A Nation in Arms: A Social Study of the British Army in the First World War* (Manchester, 1985), pp. 9—10, 24, 45, 46—8, 98—125, 221—30.
103 L. Thurow, *Investment in Human Capital* (Belmont, 1970). Total expenditures per soldier on the establishment were definitely higher for the volunteer armies of the UK and USA than for the conscripted armies of France, Germany and Russia — *Whitaker's Almanack* (London, 1915), p. 105; Hamer, *The British Army*, pp. 111—14. But there were still constant complaints by the general staff about the poor pay and low quality of British soldiers — see A. R. Shelley, *The Victorian Army at Home* (London, 1977), pp. 181—92.

to more backward economies Britain's 'real' expenditures on defence were very large indeed.

Furthermore the Navy absorbed an increasingly large part of the outlay on imperial defence. Expenditures on the fleet were in principle determined first by the scale of rival fleets (for decades by the French but, after 1897, by the German navy) and secondly by the Cabinet's perception of the military capability required to protect Britain's trade and commerce with the rest of the world.[105] After mid-century, as the economy became increasingly dependent on imported food and raw materials, the Royal Navy stood prepared to keep the sea-lanes open in the event of war.[106] And (to reiterate a point pressed time and again against hard-nosed officials from the Treasury) even in peacetime British commerce derived competitive advantages from naval cruisers stationed along mercantile shipping routes and serviced from such colonial stations as Gibraltar, Malta, Singapore, Bermuda, Hong Kong and Alexandria.[107]

Without the overwhelming superiority exercised by the Royal Navy from 1815–97, the argument runs, the domestic economy would not only have been vulnerable to blockade in wartime but trade could have been afflicted with privateering and other kinds of insecurities associated with previous centuries of intermittent warfare – a stage in power politics which effectively ended with the establishment of Britain's naval hegemony at Trafalgar.[108] If 'mercantilist' conditions returned, the risks and therefore the transactions costs to shipping, insurance, banking and distribution would rise. Invisible earnings from such activities would decline as Britain's shipping and commercial enterprise became less competitive compared with services offered by rival European firms.[109]

Several new facts and one or two alternative scenarios might now be contrasted with this rather too well established set of assumptions. First (and

104 But this argument is not concerned to pursue the interesting question of the real or opportunity costs of taxes allocated to support troops. See P. K. O'Brien and G. Toniolo, 'Sull Arretratezza Qell' Agricoltura Italiana', *Estratto da Ricerche Economiche*, ii–iii (1986), pp. 266–85; O. Crisp, *Studies in the Russian Economy Before 1914* (London, 1976), pp. 19–22, 40–1, 52–5.

105 B. Ranft (ed.), *Technical Change and British Naval Policy 1860–1939* (London, 1977), pp. 1–37; Kennedy, *Rise and Fall of British Naval Mastery*, pp. 156–7; Benians (ed.), *Cambridge History of the British Empire*, iii, pp. 232–41, 570–5; Kennedy, *Realities Behind Diplomacy*, pp. 33–6.

106 B. Semmel, *Liberalism and Naval Strategy* (Winchester, Mass. 1986), pp. 85–7; Crouzet, 'Trade and Empire', pp. 215–17; A. Offer, 'The Working Classes British Naval Plans and the Coming of the Great War', *Past and Present*, cvii (1985), pp. 204–26; Kennedy, *Realities Behind Diplomacy*, pp. 18, 27.

107 Kennedy, *Strategy and Diplomacy*, p. 204; Kennedy, *Rise and Fall*, pp. 150–6.

108 Crowhurst, *Defence of British Trade*, pp. 15–93; Kennedy, *Rise and Fall of British Naval Mastery*, pp. 149–202; Kennedy, 'Finance, Geography and the Winning of Wars 1660–1815' (Unpublished paper, Yale, 1985); Ranft (ed.), *Technical Change and British Naval Policy*, pp. 1–32.

even when the Mediterranean fleet is included for purposes of calculation as part of home defence) it was the case that just over half of total military spending was voted by Parliament to sustain and equip sailors and troops located outside the United Kingdom and its territorial waters.[110] A not inconsiderable proportion of that allocation served, as everyone at the time recognized, to protect the dominions, India and other colonies from potential external aggression.[111] Otherwise how else can we make sense of the attitudes of little Englanders (Forster, Goschen, Rosebery and Bryce) towards the 'forward' and in their view costly commitments entered into by Disraeli, Salisbury, Chamberlain and other imperialists?[112] If the amount of public money at stake was small, what was the point of Carnarvon's commission appointed in 1879 to 'enquire into the defence of British possessions at home and abroad'?[113] Was the parsimony of the Treasury and the perennial round of discussions between dominion and British politicians on the theme of how the costs of imperial defence might be more equitably allocated between the metropolis and its Empire of merely political significance?[114] As table 4 shows, India apart, the dominions and colonies spent insignificant shares of their budgets on defence. Like the Americans, who had successfully rebelled against metropolitan taxes, their politicians and officials obviously regarded military expenditure as something 'colonials' should not be obliged to shoulder.[115] Despite all the placatory noises made by their statesmen at conferences in London, the

109 P. J. Cain and A. G. Hopkins, 'Gentlemanly Capitalism and British Expansion overseas ... New Imperialism, 1650–1945' *EC H R*, 2nd ser., xl (1987), pp. 3–11; M. de Cecco, *Money and Empire: The International Gold Standard 1890–1914* (Oxford, 1974), pp. 22–38; 76–126; D. French, *British Economic and Strategy Planning* (London, 1982), pp. 13, 51–5; G. Ingham, *Capitalism Divided? The City and Industry in British Social Development* (London, 1984), pp. 117–34.
110 Davis and Huttenback, *Mammon and the Pursuit of Empire*, pp. 164–5; Kennedy, *Rise and Fall*, p. 171.
111 B. Porter, *The Lions Share: A Short History of British Imperialism, 1850–1983* (London, 1984), chs iii–vi; Howard, *Continental Commitment*, pp. 12–30; Kennedy, *Rise and Fall of British Naval Mastery*, pp. 190–4; Tomlinson, *Political Economy of the Raj*, pp. 106–18, 138.
112 Benians (ed.), *Cambridge History of the British Empire*, iii, pp. 127–37; Thornton, *Imperial Idea and its Enemies*, pp. 50–107; Kennedy, *Realities Behind Diplomacy*, pp. 82–139; Hamer, *The British Army*, pp. 87–94; R. V. Kubicek, *The Administration of Imperialism: Joseph Chamberlain at the Colonial Office* (Durham, NC, 1969), pp. 154–73.
113 Benians (ed.), *Cambridge History of the British Empire*, iii, pp. 232–4.
114 Gordon, *Dominion Partnership and Imperial Defence*, pp. xi–xiv, 1–17, 98–108, 144–63, 295–6; Howard, *Continental Commitment*, pp. 24–7.
115 Howard, *Continental Commitment*, pp. 9–30; Gordon, *Dominion Partnership and Imperial Defence*, pp. 66–7, 83, 96, 134–6, 146, 153–63, 164–296; R. Preston, *Canada and Imperial Defense* (Durham, NC, 1967).

shares of dominion budgets devoted to defence stood from 1865 right down to 1910–12 firmly in the 3 per cent to 5 per cent range. Even for India the per capita burden declined over that period but the Indian budget share did remain around the relatively high 30 per cent mark. Dependent colonies contributed next to nothing towards their own defence.[116]

Finally, there is no evidence that the competitive lead already long-established at mid-century by British shipping, insurance, banking and other invisible exports waned when France, Germany, Russia, Japan and the United States built up fleets effectively to challenge the hegemony of the Royal Navy.[117] On the contrary, for at least two to three decades before the outbreak of war in 1914, the diffusion of sea power across several countries created a 'strategic equilibrium' in which world commerce flourished. From 1899 to 1913 the build up of battle fleets by several countries was accompanied by the greatest boom witnessed by the international economy before that extraordinary upswing from 1950 to 1973.[118] Are there hard reasons to back the supposition that a continuation of the supremacy enjoyed by the Royal Navy over the combined fleets of all other powers from 1859–83 (or any two powers thereafter) was a precondition for the continuation of a competitive edge enjoyed by the City of London? Did the increase in scale and capability of the British fleet do anything to boost commodity exports? Not really: and the magnitude and extension of British imperial power exhibited by its ships, bases and garrisons around the globe provoked France, Germany, Russia, even the United States, to build navies in order to share in the glory and mythical spoils of Empire.[119] As Churchill reminded his Cabinet colleagues; 'We have got all we want in territory, and our claim to be left in unmolested enjoyment of vast and splendid possessions, mainly acquired by violence, largely maintained by force, often seems less reasonable to others than to us.'[120]

116 Davis and Huttenback, *Mammon and the Pursuit of Empire*, pp. 121–3, 161; Tomlinson, *Political Economy of the Raj*, pp. 109–18; Benians (ed.), *Cambridge History of the British Empire*, iii, pp. 568–70, 586–7.
117 A. Imlah, *Economic Elements in the Pax Britannica* (Cambridge, Mass., 1958), pp. 73–5; Crouzet, *Victorian Economy*, pp. 359–60. But see C. Trebilcock, 'The City Entrepreneurship and Insurance' in N. McKendrick and R. B. Outhwaite (eds), *Business Life and Public Policy* (Cambridge, 1986), pp. 138–40.
118 W. W. Rostow, *The World Economy* (London, 1978), pp. 66–7; Maddison, *Phases of Capitalist Development*, pp. 64–85; H. Van der Wee, *Prosperity and Upheaval in the World Economy* (London, 1987), pp. 48–93.
119 P. Kennedy, *The Rise of Anglo-German Antagonism 1860–1914* (London, 1982), pp. 410–31; D. C. Watt, *Succeeding John Bull: America in Britain's Place, 1900–75* (Cambridge, 1984), pp. 158–63, 169–73; Semmel, *Liberalism and Naval Strategy*, pp. 152–71.
120 Cited by Kennedy, *Realities Behind Diplomacy*, pp. 69–70.

Can there be any doubt that a phased withdrawal from Empire (as advocated by nineteenth-century radicals) would still have left British citizens on the eve of the Great War with taxes anything like double the size of taxes carried by the nationals of other advanced countries in Europe and North America?[121] Could this 'Cobdenite' policy have failed to relieve them of a large part of the fiscal responsibility for maintaining an inflated military establishment and funding a national debt, which from the end of the Crimean War onwards accumulated largely in order to finance a succession of 'colonial' wars including an extremely expensive and futile conflict in South Africa?[122] British expenditure on 'defence' together with interest on money borrowed, largely to acquire, enlarge and hold onto an Empire, imposed burdens that amounted to two or three times the comparable military costs carried by the citizens of other major European countries and the United States.[123] Politicians and Treasury officials who thought cogently about the economics of direct imperial rule rarely doubted that the possession and extension of Empire cost British taxpayers significant sums of money, even if the precise magnitude now eludes measurement, except within rather wide bounds of plausibility.[124]

What is proving less difficult to estimate is the unequal distribution of both the tax burden and the material rewards, from the imperial connection. Benefits accrued disproportionately to the undertaxed white settlers of the dominions and colonies, and to those at the top end of the income and social scales in British society. But this suggestion about tax incidence must be qualified somewhat. From the 1870s onwards, as the share of current revenue derived from income and inheritance taxes rose from around 17 per cent to reach 44 per cent in 1910–12. Taxation certainly became less regressive.[125] Moreover, the proportion of revenue appropriated for central government in the United Kingdom which took the form of direct taxes was markedly different from the ratios observed for most other advanced capitalist societies.[126] These trends and comparisons in incidence may have given British taxpayers the illusion that the costs of Empire were becoming more equitably distributed.

---

121 Davis and Huttenback, *Mammon and the Pursuit of Empire*, pp. 222–5; and Davis and Huttenback, 'Political Economy of British Imperialism', pp. 122–6.

122 C. Trebilcock, 'War and the Failure of Industrial Mobilisation: 1899 and 1914' in J. M. Winter (ed.), *War and Economic Development* (Cambridge, 1975), pp. 139–61; Kennedy, *Strategy and Diplomacy*, p. 204. On costs of Boer War and its impact on British politics of the period see H. V. Emy, 'Financial Policy and Party Politics Before 1914', *HJ* xv (1972), pp. 114–16.

123 Davis and Huttenback, *Mammon and the Pursuit of Empire*, pp. 160–5; and Flora, *State, Economy and Society*, i, pp. 257–449.

124 H. Roseveare, *The Treasury* (London, 1969), pp. 183–210, 216, 227, 235–81; M. Wright, *Treasury Control of the Civil Service, 1854–74* (Oxford, 1969), pp. 329–51, 373; B. Chubb, *The Control of Public Expenditure* (London, 1952), pp. 42–108; Gordon, *Dominion Partnership and Imperial Defence*, pp. xi–xiii; R. M. Kesner, *Economic Control and Colonial Development* (Weaport, 1981), pp. 221–5.

That impression was not, however, based upon any real appraisal of the relevant statistics. As late as 1903—6, and long after the tax system had begun to move towards a less regressive basis, those with total earnings from property and work above £1,000 a year still transferred less than 8 per cent of their incomes to the state, a total amount which accounted for only 11 per cent of total tax revenue.[127] Among this elite (in receipt of up to 40—45 per cent of the national income) are to be found social and occupational groups who benefited most directly and tangibly from military and other governmental expenditures allocated to support imperial rule, to foster imperial trade and to mitigate the risks of private investment in the dominions and colonies.[128] Britain's 'gentlemanly capitalists', resident in large part in the home counties (financiers, bankers, merchants, shippers and other intermediaries involved in servicing commerce between the metropolis and the Empire) derived the largest gains (net of taxes) from military and other forms of imperial subsidy.[129] While the majority of English people cheerfully and even proudly shouldered a tax bill for an Empire from which they derived very little in the form of tangible pecuniary gains for decades before or decades after the Great War.[130]

A Retrospective Balance Sheet for Empire

Modern research in economic history turns away from traditional concerns with impulses behind imperialism in order to evaluate the costs and benefits for European nations most actively involved in the quest for Empire. Of course, questions comparable to those posed in this historiographical essay have long been debated in relation to parts of South America, Africa and Asia,

125 B. Mitchell and P. Deane, *Abstract of British Historical Statistics* (Cambridge, 1962), pp. 393—5; B. K. Murray, *The People's Budget, 1909—10* (Oxford, 1970), pp. 89—98, 169, 173, 293—5, 310—13; U. K. Hicks, *British Public Finances: Their Structure and Development* (Oxford, 1954), pp. 69—106; M. Freeden, *The New Liberalism: An Ideology of Social Reform* (Oxford, 1978), pp. 121, 131—3; F. Shehab, *Progressive Taxation* (Oxford, 1953), pp. 173—246. The politics behind these trends is discussed in Emy, 'The Impact of Financial Policy on English Party Politics', pp. 107—13.

126 B. Mitchell, *Abstract of European Historical Statistics 1750—1975* (London, 1975), pp. 733—69; Flora, *State, Economy and Society*, pp. 257—449.

127 Davis and Huttenback, 'Public Expenditure and Private Profit', pp. 282—7; Davis and Huttenback, *Mammon and the Pursuit of Empire*, pp. 244—52; Emy, 'Financial Policy and Party Politics', pp. 110—14, 119—24.

128 B. Supple, 'Income and Demand 1860—1914' in R. Floud and McCloskey (eds), *Economic History of Britain*, ii, pp. 125—6; Lee, *British Economy since 1700*, p. 29.

129 Davis and Huttenback, *Mammon and the Pursuit of Empire*, pp. 195—217, 250—2.

130 Thornton, *Imperial Idea and its Enemies*, pp. 50—152; Kennedy, *Strategy and Diplomacy*, pp. 203—7; Porter, *Lions Share*, pp. 135—7; C. Barnett, *Collapse of British Power*, pp. 71—83; D. Fieldhouse, *Economics and Empire*, pp. 69—76.

incorporated formally and informally into the empires of Britain, France, Holland, Spain and Portugal.[131] But the gains to metropolitan economies and societies as a whole from the conquest, settlement and retention of territory in other continents is more often asserted than investigated, let alone measured.[132]

One European nation, Britain, emerged at the Treaty of Vienna as the indisputable victor in the prolonged struggle for Empire that marked the mercantile era. An effective fiscal system, an outstanding navy and an expanding industrial economy (in that order) provided the British state with the means to acquire and to hold on to vast tracts of territory overseas.[133] Throughout the long nineteenth century its governing elite continued, with varying degrees of enthusiasm and commitment, to frame foreign and strategic policies on the assumption that the security and vitality of Britain's economy and society depended upon the retention, defence, and, whenever necessary, the extension of the Empire.[134] After the repeal of the Corn Laws in 1846, that assumption (first subjected to critical scrutiny by the *Wealth of Nations*) came under persistent attack, occasionally from within government circles, prominently from radicals in the House of Commons, and above all from the pens of liberal economists, historians and other polemicists for free trade and a Cobdenite vision of international relations.[135]

They predicted that money spent on the defence of an indefensible geographical entity would turn out to be extremely costly for the majority of British taxpayers. They argued that the framework of imperial rule and institutions did little to ensure high rates of return on British funds invested abroad; that the Empire was not a particularly productive location for capital or manifestly popular with migrants leaving this country; and finally that holding on to alien territory and resources was not required to ensure access to markets or to supplies of food and raw materials imported from beyond the kingdom's borders.

131 The history of underdevelopment is dominated by debates about the negative and positive effects of imperialism. The negative case has been vigorously challenged by P. Bairoch, 'Le bilan economique du colonialisme: myths et realites', *Itineranio* i (1980), pp. 29–41; and some of the major books are cited in P. K. O'Brien, 'The Third World in the International Economy', *Revista di Storia Economica* i (1984), pp. 164–74. See also T. Raychaudhuri, 'Historical Roots of Mass Poverty in South Asia, A Hypothesis', *EcPW* xx (1985), pp. 801–6.
132 But for an early excellent book see G. Clark, *The Balance Sheets of Imperialism* (New York, 1936) and the literature cited by A. G. Hopkins, 'Accounting for the British Empire', *JICH*, xv (1988).
133 O'Brien, 'The Political Economy of British Taxation', pp. 1–32.
134 Kennedy, *Realities Behind Diplomacy*, p. 17–139; Hyam, *Britain's Imperial Century*, pp. 99–102, 103–34, 373–4.
135 I. Beckett and J. Gooch (eds), *Politicians and Defence: Studies in the Formulation of British Defence Policy, 1845–70* (Manchester, 1981); Wood, *British Economists*; Semmel, *Rise of Free Trade Imperialism*; Semmel, *Imperialism and Social Reform*, pp. 128–33, 141–65, 188–215.

Perhaps this radical tradition in politics and intellectual life restrained dormant imperialistic impulses among the masses and their rulers and exercised some effect in holding down military and colonial expenditures to more manageable levels. Nevertheless, the 'Cobdenites' cried out for decades in the wilderness. And from 1883 through to the Great War they floundered against waves of resurgent imperialism, nationalism and the so-called *realpolitik* of strategic necessity.[136]

During the high tide of European imperialism, when the competitive lead long established by British industry and commerce on world markets was being eroded by the United States, Germany and other European powers, British statesmen, businessmen, bankers, merchants and investors turned more and more towards that huge and ostensibly underexploited national asset, the Empire.[137] Although Chamberlainite schemes for federation and imperial preference failed to solidify into national policy, trade and the emigration of labour and exports of capital became slowly but perceptibly more concentrated upon the Empire. Before 1914 that inefficient shift away from competitive towards safer markets was not, however, accompanied by anything other than token concessions by dominion and colonial governments to pressures from London for higher contributions towards ever mounting expenditures on imperial defence.[138]

A century later when historical accounts are being added up, the 'debits', so often and so clamorously emphasized by radicals begin to acquire statistical clothing. For example, the facts begin to reveal how heavily the fiscal burden for defence and other imperial commitments weighed on British citizens and their economy; and how inequitably the burden was distributed among domestic taxpayers as well as between metropolis and Empire.

Strategic 'necessities' are difficult for historians and economists to reconstruct and even more difficult to evaluate. There are no 'objective functions' to be maximized and it is rarely clear what statesmen are trying to achieve. Strategic policies always emerge as heavily conditioned by the shifting and essentially short-term perceptions of the day.[139] But has the time not arrived for diplomatic

136 Semmel, *Liberalism and Naval Strategy*, pp. 120–33; Kennedy, *Realities Behind Diplomacy*, pp. 68–73; The Cobdenite Programme is movingly described in E. Wallace, *Goldwin Smith Victorian Liberal* (Toronto, 1957), pp. 185–210; Beckett and Gooch, *Politicians and Defence*, pp. 1–20.
137 Hyam, *Britain's Imperial Century*, pp. 99–102, 103–34, 165–204; Porter, *The Lion's Share*, pp. 132–4; Kennedy, *Realities Behind Diplomacy*, pp. 28–32; Kennedy, *Rise and Fall of British Naval Mastery*, pp. 190–2.
138 R. F. Holland, *Britain and the Commonwealth Alliance* (London, 1981), pp. 206–9; Benians (ed.), *Cambridge History of the British Empire* iii, pp. 585–8; Kubiceck, *Administration of Imperialism*, pp. 155–78.
139 Ranft (ed.), *Technical Change and British Naval Policy*, pp. vii–xii, 108–10; Kennedy, *Realities Behind Diplomacy*, pp. 74–127. For some theory relevant to the evaluation of decisions in defence policy see R. N. McKean, *Efficiency in Government Through Systems Analysis* (New York, 1958).

and military historians to pay some attention to the possible validity of counterfactual scenarios for defence put forward by nineteenth-century 'troublemakers'
in opposition to the foreign and strategic policies actually pursued for, say, the
three decades down to 1907?[140] With hindsight might they not be prepared to
concede something to Liddell Hart's suggestion that before the Great War the
British Empire represented 'the greatest example of strategical overextension
in history'?[141] Admiral Fisher certainly made that assumption when he pulled
back the fleet to home waters after 1905.[142] After all, it was not only radicals
but some entirely 'respectable' strategic planners and politicians who recognized
very early on that the Empire was not a defensible entity without massive and
politically unacceptable increases in taxation.[143]

   With hindsight it is not difficult to see that responsibility for the defence of
territory and bases scattered around the globe obfuscated, delayed and in the
end increased the total cost of the diplomatic and strategic decisions eventually
taken by the British Government to defeat German ambitions in the First
World War.[144] Of course the manpower and resources of the dominions and
colonies also played their part in that tragic armed struggle from 1914–18.
Nevertheless, nearly 80 per cent of the casualties and 88 per cent of the
expenditure incurred by the empire to defeat Germany came from the United
Kingdom and from domestic taxpayers.[145]

   Given that the balance of power could not be restored in Europe without
curbing the military ambitions of Germany, the issue that now emerges in
retrospect is the scale of a gigantic misallocation of public money, disbursed

140 The phrase refers to A. J. P. Taylor's *The Troublemakers: Dissent over Foreign
    Policy, 1792–1939* (London, 1964), pp. 40–131.
141 Cited by Kennedy, *Strategy and Diplomacy*, p. 18; Kennedy, *Rise and Fall of British
    Naval Mastery*, pp. 209–32; Watt, *Succeeding John Bull*, pp. 158–73. Strategic
    overextension continued to be a feature of British policy for decades after 1914 –
    Barnett, *Collapse of British Power*, pp. 71–80; Holland, *Britain and the Common-
    wealth Alliance*, pp. 206–10.
142 Kennedy, *Rise and Fall of British Naval Mastery*, pp. 215–29; Kennedy, *Strategy
    and Diplomacy*, pp. 55–60.
143 Harmer, *British Army*, pp. 87–9, 91–4, 111–13; Beckett and Simpson (eds), *A
    Nation in Arms*, pp. 2–4; Semmel, *Liberalism and Naval Strategy*, p. 91; Ranft
    (ed.), *Technical Change and British Naval Policy*, pp. 78–81; Benians (ed.), *Cam-
    bridge History of the British Empire*, iii, p. 128 cites an observation of Sir William
    Harcourt's on the Empire: 'if you give the heart too much work to do by extend-
    ing the limbs and the frame beyond measure you enfeeble its constitution and it
    succumbs.'
144 Howard, *Continental Commitment*, pp. 9–73; Semmel, *Liberalism and Naval
    Strategy*, pp. 85–7, 141–9; Beckett and Simpson (eds), *A Nation in Arms*,
    pp. 2–4, 12; French, British Economic and Strategic Planning, pp. 7–16; Porter,
    Britain, Europe and the World, pp. 61–79.
145 Kennedy, *Realities Behind Diplomacy*, p. 167; G. Hardach, *The First World War,
    1914–18* (London, 1977), pp. 152–5.

over many years in pursuit of those conjoined chimeras: imperial defence and hegemony at sea. How much money might have been saved by politicians with enough strategic sense to appreciate just when the empire became indefensible; when maintenance on the cheap of a *Pax Britannica* became redundant, pretentious and provocative? Could the nation's military expenditures from say 1897 to 1919 have been significantly reduced by statesmen with sufficient foresight to make explicit and effective their country's commitment to contain German militarism where it was eventually defeated — on the battlefields of Europe?[146]

Yet some imperial historians are still inclined to argue that the empire successfully prolonged Britain's status as a great power and was a profitable investment which cushioned the long-term decline of its economy.[147] Indeed the tendency of the 'official mind' to believe that the empire could both prop up an ailing economy and sustain Britain's role in international affairs persisted long after the Treaty of Versailles. That unprofitable mode of thought was reinvigorated by the Great War and solidified in the inter-war years into formal agreements on imperial tariffs, sterling areas and defence plans.[148] Although Britain survived as a great power down to 1945 the notion that the Empire made any positive long-term contribution to the health of the domestic economy is unlikely to survive systematic economic analysis and statistical testing. Modern research in economic history now lends rather strong statistical support to Cobdenite views of Britain's imperial commitments from 1846 to 1914. Only conquests of loot and pillage of the kind maintained by King Leopold of Belgium in the Congo seem capable of providing metropolitan traders and investors with supernormal profits. In this sense the British Empire can be plausibly represented, in Adam Smith's words, as 'a sort of splendid and showy equipage, not an empire but the project of an empire, not a gold mine but the project of a gold mine'.[149]

Clearly the Empire was an enormous fact which imperial historians will continue to puzzle over and explain. For not inconsiderable numbers of English people (outside and inside some very powerful social groups) the Empire paid. What has been argued in this chapter is that massive public expenditure upon the apparatus of imperial rule and defence was neither sufficient nor necessary for the growth of the economy from 1846 to

146 These counterfactual speculations are prompted by my reading of: Howard, *Continental Commitment*, chs 1–3; Kennedy, *Rise and Fall of British Naval Mastery*, chs 7–9; Kennedy, *Strategy and Diplomacy*, chs 1–3; Kennedy, *Rise of Anglo-German Antagonism*, chs 21–2; Porter, *Britain, Europe and the World*, ch 3.

147 Porter, *Lions Share*, p. 364 for attitudes of the British elite towards the Empire; Watt, *Succeeding John Bull*, pp. 32–81 and Hyam, *Britain's Imperial Century*, pp. 373–8.

148 I. M. Drummond, *British Economic Policy and the Empire, 1919–1939* (London, 1973), pp. 17–142; Holland, *Britain and the Commonwealth Alliance*, pp. 206–10; Porter, *Britain, Empire and the World*, pp. 82–110.

149 Cited by Wallace, *Goldwin Smith*, p. 187.

1914. Thereafter Hobson's analysis of 1902 that the Empire represented an increasingly costly alternative to social reform and to structural changes within the domestic economy can be accepted as entirely percipient.[150] Eight decades later that 'splendid and showy equipage' begins to appear in the flat prose and statistics of the economist, more and more like a redundant ship of the line drifting away from the Kingdom's shores on the ebb-tide of twentieth-century history.

150 Hobson, *Imperialism*; A. Offer, 'Empire and Social Reform: British Overseas Investment and Domestic Politics 1908–14', *HJ* xxvi (1983), pp. 119–38; Emy, 'Financial Policy and Party Politics', pp. 103–12, 117, 128–9.

3

The Dynamism of the British Economy in the Decades to 1914 – Change of Direction or Failure of Nerve?

Sidney Pollard

The performance of the British economy in the hundred years or so to 1873 has received little but praise in the literature; indeed it has frequently been taken as the standard of excellence against which other countries were to be measured. At different times France, Germany, Belgium and even the United States have tended to emerge from the comparison as lagging imitators at best. From the industrial revolution to the mid-Victorian boom all seemed to be right with the British economy.

Thereafter, the picture changes with remarkable rapidity. Growth, it appears, slows down. What had formerly been the basis of economic strength, the staple industries, and the industrial sector generally, turn into a source of weakness. Other countries now make the running to 1914. It is scarcely possible to consult any modern account of the period (accounts written up to the early 1960s tend to be different)[1] without encountering phrases like 'decline' or 'climacteric',[2] intermingled with numerous explanations of Britain's disappointing performance. The erstwhile success story had turned to a paradigm of failure.

Did this rapid change of fortunes from the early 1870s onward really take

---

1 E.g., J. H. Clapham, *An Economic History of Modern Britain*, vol. 2, *Free Trade and Steel* (Cambridge: 1932), vol. 3, *Machines and National Rivalries* (Cambridge: 1938); William Ashworth, *An Economic History of England 1870–1939* (London: 1960).

2 E.g., M. W. Kirby, *The Decline of British Economic Power since 1870* (London: 1981); E. H. Phelps Brown and S. J. Handfield-Jones, 'The Climacteric of the 1890s', *OEP*, 4 (1952); D. J. Coppock, 'The Climacteric of the 1890s: a Critical Note', *Manchester School of Economic and Social Studies*, 24 (1956).

place? Why had it not been noticed before the 1960s? How can it be defined and measured? The first part of this paper will concern itself with some attempts to measure and characterize the record of British economic growth in those years. The second will deal with some explanations. In the third part, some international and historical parallels will be briefly examined. Some conclusions are attempted in the final section.

British Economic Growth 1870–1914: Characteristics and Measurements

Given the widespread acceptance of a marked slowing down of growth, if not actual decline, in our period, it is rather remarkable that there is no agreement on the timing of the change in tempo. Coppock, in a well-known paper, opted for the early 1870s. This would coincide with the onset of the world-wide 'Great Depression', but it was his view that while the rest of the developed world recovered its momentum in due course, the British growth rate stayed down. A similar turning point is supported by Hoffmann's statistics of industrial growth, and appears also to be in line with the views of Arthur Lewis.[3] Aldcroft and Richardson opt rather for the end of the 1870s.[4]

Against this, Phelps Brown and Handfield-Jones put the climacteric into the 1890s. They were influenced above all by the poor showing of the older staple industries, while the new industries were yet too small to make much impact.[5] The very last year of the nineteenth century was favoured by Matthews, Feinstein and Odling-Smee, whereas McCloskey believed the change, if any, to have occurred later still, at the beginning of the twentieth century: until then, he maintained, British productivity increases were comparable to those of the USA and not much below those of Germany.[6] Others

3 D. J. Coppock, 'The Causes of the Great Depression 1873–96', *Manchester School*, 29 (1961); and 'British Industrial Growth during the "Great Depression" (1873–96): a Pessimist's View', *EcHR*, 17 (1964–5); W. A. Lewis, *Growth and Fluctuations, 1870–1913* (London: 1978), chapter 5.

4 Derek H. Aldcroft and Harry W. Richardson, *The British Economy 1870–1914* (London: 1969), pp. 126–9.

5 Phelps Brown and Handfield-Jones, 'The Climacteric of the 1890s'; E. H. Phelps Brown and Margaret H. Browne, *A Century of Pay* (London: 1968), pp. 116–18, 190–4.

6 Donald N. McCloskey, 'Did Victorian Britain Fail?', *EcHR*, 23 (1970), and *Enterprise and Trade in Victorian Britain* (London: 1981) pp. 94–110; McCloskey, 'Victorian Growth: a Rejoinder', ibid. pp. 115–19; R. C. O. Matthews, C. H. Feinstein and J. C. Odling-Smee, *British Economic Growth 1856–1973* (Oxford: 1982), pp. 23, 31, 172, 381–2; C. H. Feinstein, R. C. O. Matthews, J. C. Odling-Smee, 'The Timing of the Climacteric and its Sectoral Incidence in the U.K., 1873–1913', in C. P. Kindleberger and G. di Tella (eds), *Economics in the Long View: Essays in Honour of W. W. Rostow* (1981), p. 169.

could discern no clear turning point at all. The late Victorian or Edwardian climacteric, they judged, was a myth.[7]

It is, of course, possible for the change in tempo to have been so gradual that no break can be discerned, yet to have been nonetheless real enough. Alternatively, given the existence of cycles of varying length and import which were superimposed on the secular trend, it might well be that a change in direction of the latter would be swamped by short-term fluctuations in the statistical series. Sophisticated statistical techniques should be able to isolate these various influences from each other, though it is precisely these which may have made a break in this period disappear from view altogether.

Perhaps it is time to look at some of the data themselves: tables 1 and 2 give views of annual rates of growth from 1856 to 1913. Total output figures are affected to some extent by changes in the rate of growth of population or working population. Table 2 compares some of the best available per capita series using the same reference cycles.

In both tables, there are considerable differences between the estimates, sometimes exceeding the differences between the cyclical growth rates. It is not entirely surprising that some of the statistics tend to confirm the views of their authors, e.g. Aldcroft's thesis of a general decline, or McCloskey's of a

Table 1 Annual rates of growth of GDP, UK 1856–1913 at constant prices or constant factor costs

Years[a]	Aldcroft %	Feinstein %	Lewis %	Greasley %
1856–65	2.1[b]	2.0	2.0	1.8
1865–74	2.2	2.1	2.1	2.2
1874–83	1.8	1.7	1.7	1.8
1883–90	2.2	1.9	1.8	1.9
1890–1901	1.9	1.8	1.8	2.0
1901–07	1.7	1.5	1.4	1.2
1907–13	1.5	2.1	2.2	1.9

[a] Start-years and end-years are averages of three, of which they are the middle ones, except for 1913, and excluding Aldcroft.
[b] 1859–65
Source: Based on D. H. Aldcroft, 'McCloskey on Victorian Growth: a Comment', *EcHR* 27 (1974), pp. 272–3; C. H. Feinstein, *National Income, Expenditure and Output of the United Kingdom 1855–1965* (Cambridge: 1972), TT. 24–5; W. A. Lewis, *Growth and Fluctuations*, pp. 260–4; Greasley, 'Growth', pp. 429, 438–9.

7 Steven Broadberry, 'ESRC Quantitative Economic History Study Group 1985 Conference', *JEurEcH*, 15 (1986), pp. 386–90; David Greasley, 'British Economic Growth: the Paradox of the 1880s and the Timing of the Climacteric', *ExEcH*, 23 (1986).

Table 2   Annual rates of growth of real output per head, UK 1856–1913

	Feinstein GDP per head[a]	Mitchell/ Feinstein NNI per head[a]	Feinstein Output per worker		McCloskey Productivity
1856–65	1.19	1.97	0.85	1856–66	1.090
1865–74	1.42	1.26	1.53	1867–74	1.390
1874–83	0.75	0.69	1.28	1874–83	0.693
1883–90	1.52	3.52	0.90	1884–90	1.090
1890–1901	1.01	1.11	0.91	1891–1900	0.717
1901–07	0.37	0.07	0.63	1901–13	0.233
1907–13	1.18	0.76	0.53		

[a] Start-years and end-years are averages of three, of which they are the middle ones, except for 1913.
Source: Based on Feinstein, *National Income*, TT. 42, 51–2; B. R. Mitchell and Phyllis Deane, *Abstract of British Historical Statistics* (Cambridge: 1962), pp. 367–8; Donald N. McCloskey, 'A Rejoinder'.

decline only in the twentieth century. Nowhere, however, is there a clear change in direction visible, particularly if we bear in mind that the years leading up to the great boom of 1870–3 or 1870–4 were years of exceptionally fast growth even by the standard of the earlier nineteenth century and therefore not a fair basis of comparison. The early years of the twentieth century were undoubtedly years of slow growth, visible more clearly on a per capita basis, but there was a rapid recovery in the immediate pre-war years, and we cannot be certain that, had the war not intervened, the upswing would not have continued.

Much of the literature, however, is concerned not so much with total national income, as with the secondary sector or with manufacturing, and it is frequently asserted that it was there that the loss of momentum had made itself felt above all. 'Manufacturing' is not perfectly definable, and there are problems of international comparability, but the statistics of industrial productivity per head should provide a measure of some validity of the alleged loss of the growth dynamic.

In table 3, the slowing down after c.1874, and the further slowing down, amounting almost to a standstill, in the early years of the twentieth century, are more obvious. Yet the differences between the two sets of estimates, and the extremely fast growth in the years just before 1913 in one series, are more obvious still. Total factor productivity, a better indicator of efficiency than output per head, though more difficult to measure accurately, has been calculated to have declined only from a growth rate of 0.9 per cent a year in 1856–73 to 0.6 per cent a year in 1873–1913 in manufacturing; against this,

Table 3   Annual rates of growth of industrial output per head, UK 1854–1913

	Feinstein Industrial Production[a] (%)		Coppock Industrial Productivity[b] (%)
1856–65	2.5	1854/60–1861/5	0.6
1865–74	1.5	1861/5 –1866/74	2.2
1874–83	1.1	1866/74–1875/83	1.0
1883–90	1.1	1875/83–1884/9	0.5
1890–1901	1.3	1884/9 –1890/9	0.1
1901–07	−0.8	1890/9 –1900/07	0.2
1907–13	2.9	1900/07–1908/13	−0.1

[a] Start-years and end-years are averages of three, of which they are the middle ones, except of 1913.
[b] Corrected for unemployment.
Source: Based on Feinstein, *National Income*, TT. 24–5, 120–1; D. J. Coppock, 'The Climacteric', p. 7.

it fell in mining, strongly affected by the working out of the better coal seams, from a positive rate of 1.4 per cent a year in the first period to a negative rate of −0.1 per cent a year in the second period,[8] and this tended to exert a considerable downward pull on all indices.

Particularly worrying for contemporaries, who lacked these modern measures but had other indices pointing in the same direction, was the fact that this apparent secular stagnation was not a world-wide phenomenon, but on the contrary seemed to be confined to the United Kingdom alone. In table 4, Britain's snail's pace is compared with the vigorous growth of the two economies that were considered her chief rivals, Germany and the USA.

The British attitude to these two countries showed considerable differences, though there were phases of fear over the economic threat from both.[9] While the United States was seen as a country still largely developing its own vast territory, the German competition appeared to be more dangerous, since it made itself felt in Britain's traditional export markets and even on her home ground. Moreover, while the rising per capita output of North America could be explained at least in part by her richer natural resources and more fortunate circumstances, Germany's resources were so similar to Britain's that

8   Matthews, Feinstein and Odling-Smee, *British Economic Growth 1856–1973*, pp. 229, 378.
9   R. H. Heindel, *The American Impact on Britain* (Philadelphia: 1940); Ross J. S. Hoffman, *Great Britain and the German Trade Rivalry 1875–1914* (New York: 1964, reprint of Philadelphia 1933).

Table 4 Annual rate of growth of industrial output in three countries, 1870−1913

	Hilgerdt: Manufacturing production			Lewis: Industrial production[a]		
	UK (%)	USA (%)	Germany (%)	UK (%)	USA (%)	Germany (%)
1870−80	2.1	5.4	2.9	2.3	5.7	5.9
1880−90	1.9	5.4	5.5	2.5	5.6	4.6
1890−1900	1.5	3.4	5.0	2.1	3.1	3.9
1900−13	2.1	5.2	3.9	2.1	5.4	4.4

	Hilgerdt: Manufacturing output per head of population		
	UK (%)	USA (%)	Germany (%)
1871/5−81/5	0.6	2.7	1.7
1881/5−96/1900	0.9	2.1	3.9
1896/1900−1911/13	0.7	3.2	2.5

[a] Excluding construction

Source: Based on Folke Hilgerdt, *Industrialization and Foreign Trade* (League of Nations 1945), pp. 56, 132; W. A. Lewis, *Growth*, pp. 248−50, 269, 271, 273.

her successes could not but be seen as evidence of British failure. America's overtaking of Britain was thus accepted with greater equanimity than the German catching-up process. At the same time, despite all the British qualms and the German crowing, the Reich was still a long way from having caught up on the British industrial performance by 1913 (see table 5).

As shown in table 6, even in the most sensitive area, the area most commonly cited by contemporaries, namely the export of manufactured goods, Germany had failed to match the British achievement even by 1913, despite her much larger population, though the rapid decline of Britain from her overwhelmingly dominant position in the 1870s was real enough.

The differences between the series are explained in part by different estimates of total 'world' trade, and partly by different definitions of what constitutes manufactures, but the trends are similar. The decline of the British share was drastic by any standards, but the United Kingdom was still the strongest manufacturing and exporting economy in Europe at the end of the long peace.

The evidence, then, is equivocal: some distinct slowing down, especially in the manufacturing sector, but no clarity as to whether the recovery in the last pre-war years betokened a revival or only a brief respite. A relative decline of this ambiguous kind could mean one of two different things. It could reflect a deceleration, perhaps only temporary, of the possibilities of technological

Table 5   Comparative economic performance, selected countries, *c.*1913

	Per capita product, 1910 US$ of 1970 (Crafts)	*GDP per man-hour 1913 US$ of 1970 (Maddison)*	*GNP per capita 1913 US$ of 1960 (Bairoch)*	*Manufacturing per capita 1913 US = 100 (Lewis)*
UK	1302[a]	1.35	965	90
Belgium	1110	1.26	894	73
Denmark	1050	1.00	862	46
Switzerland	992	1.01	964	64
Germany	958	0.95	743	64
Netherlands	952	1.23	754	44
France	883	0.90	689	46
Austria	802	0.90	681	31
Sweden	763	0.83	680	50
Italy	548	0.72	441	20
USA		1.67		100

[a] Great Britain

Source: Based on W. A. Lewis, *Growth*, p. 163; Angus Maddison, *Phases of Capitalist Development* (1982), p. 212; idem, 'Long-Run Dynamics of Productivity Growth', *Banca Nazionale di Lavoro Quarterly Review* 32 (1979), p. 43; Paul Bairoch, 'Europe's Gross National Product 1800–1975', *JEurEcH* 5 (1976), pp. 286, 307; idem, *Commerce extérieur et développement économique de l'Europe au XIXe siècle* (Paris 1976), p. 292; N. F. R. Crafts, 'Gross National Product in Europe, 1879–1910: Some New Estimates', *ExEcH* 19 (1982).

Table 6   Shares in the world's manufactured exports, UK and Germany, 1872–1913

	Saul/ Tyszynski		*Buchheim*		*Lewis/ Phelps Brown*	
	UK	*Germany*	*UK*	*Germany*	*UK*	*Germany*
1872			45.5	12.6		
1880	41.4	19.3				
1883			36.5	18.7	37.1	17.2
1890	40.7	20.1	34.6	18.8	35.8	17.2
1899	32.5	22.2	29.4	21.0	28.4	19.5
1913	29.9	26.4	26.8	24.4	25.4	23.0

Source: Based on H. Tyszynski, 'World Trade in Manufactured Commodities, 1899–1950', *Manchester School* 19 (1951), p. 286; S. B. Saul, 'The Export Economy', *Yorkshire Bulletin of Economic and Social Research* 17 (1965), p. 12; Christoph Buchheim, 'Aspects of XIXth Century Anglo-German Trade Rivalry', *JEurEcH* 10 (1981), p. 276; W. Arthur Lewis, 'International Competition in Manufactures', *AmEcR* 47 (1959), p. 579; E. H. Phelps Brown, 'Then and Now: The British Problem of Sustaining Development, 1900s and 1960s', in M. Peston and B. Corry (eds), *Essays in Honour of Lord Robbins* (1972), p. 196.

innovation for the country at the technical frontier, while the other economies
which were in process of catching up could still expand faster until they,
in turn, reached that frontier with its slower growth opportunities: in that
case, Britain would be matched, but, except for countries with better natural
endowments like the USA, not overtaken. Alternatively it could reflect the
onset of real failure, inability to keep up with the best and the latest productive
methods pioneered elsewhere: in that case, Britain would be overtaken and
left behind even by economies no better endowed than her own.

Our macroeconomic data do not permit a clear choice between these two
developments. Nor are the detailed paths of individual industries any more
conclusive. Undoubtedly there were industries in which Britain made a poor
showing: these included the organic chemical industry, in some sectors of
which the Germans were responsible for 85 per cent of world output before
the war[10], and the electrical engineering industry, in which technical innovation
was in the hands of the Americans or the Germans, and the relatively
underdeveloped British industry consisted largely of branches of American or
German firms.[11] But against this, Britain still built well over half the world's
ships, and a much higher proportion, if the tonnage built abroad only because
of subsidies or legal restrictions, is deducted.[12] Similarly, 60 per cent of the
world's cotton goods exports still originated in Britain[13] and 50 per cent of its
coal exports[14] in the years before the First World War.

There was an undoubted tendency for Britain to do better in traditional
branches than in newer, 'high tech.' sectors as well as a tendency to be rather

10   J. J. Beer, *The Emergence of the German Dye Industry* (Urbana, Ill.:1959), pp. 96,
     114; L. F. Haber, *The Chemical Industry During the Nineteenth Century* (Oxford:
     1958), p. 108; H. W. Richardson, 'The Development of the British Dye-Stuffs
     Industry Before 1939', *Scottish Journal of Political Economy*, 9 (1962), pp. 110–11;
     Fritz Redlich, *Die volkswirtschaftliche Bedeutung der deutschen Teerfarbenindustrie*
     (Munich/Leipzig: 1914), pp. 44ff., 77ff.; Paul M. Hohenberg, *Chemicals in Western
     Europe 1850–1914* (Chicago: 1967), p. 39.
11   Thomas Parke Hughes, 'British Electrical Industry Lag: 1882–1888', *Technology
     and Culture*, 3 (1962); T. Sakamoto, 'Technology and Business in the British
     Electrical Industry, 1880–1914', in Akio Okochi and Hoshimi Uchida (eds),
     Development and Diffusion of Technology (Tokyo: 1980), pp. 68–9; S. B. Saul,
     'The American Impact on British Industry 1895–1914', *Business History* 3 (1960),
     pp. 31–5; R. A. S. Hennessey, *The Electrical Revolution* (Newcastle upon Tyne:
     1972), pp. 26ff.; I. C. R. Byatt, *The British Electrical Industry 1875–1914* (Oxford:
     1979), pp. 143–7, 161ff.; J. H. Clapham, *Economic History*, vol. 3, p. 136.
12   S. Pollard, 'British and World Shipbuilding, 1890–1914: A Study in Comparative
     Costs', *JEcH*, 17 (1957); S. Pollard and Paul Robertson, *The British Shipbuilding
     Industry, 1870–1914* (Cambridge, Mass.: 1979), pp. 25, 44–5; Edward Lorenz
     and Frank Wilkinson, 'The Shipbuilding Industry, 1880–1965', in B. Elbaum
     and W. Lazonick (eds), *The Decline of the British Economy* (Oxford: 1986),
     pp. 109–34; James Mackinnon, *The Social and Industrial History of Scotland*
     (1921), pp. 93–104.

slower than other leading economies in introducing the latest technology into all industries, old and new. Yet here, also, the issue is not clear-cut. Thus the alleged technical backwardness in such major sectors as iron and steelmaking, coal mining and cotton spinning and weaving, frequently deplored in the traditional British literature, has in recent researches, largely when carried out by American or German scholars been shown to have been sensible and rational in the circumstances, a symptom not so much of backwardness as of differences in the costs of factor supplies or in market structure.[15] It may even be that it was a sign of British maturity not to chase after every innovation, but rather to wait until it had proved itself before installing it. Certainly, British industry remained highly profitable.

How, then, are we to judge the British performance? How does it fit into the world picture of development?

Explanations

Much writing on the subject, having taken the decline for granted, has associated it with an alleged long-standing *malaise* of British society, brought

13   R. Robson, *The Cotton Industry in Britain* (London: 1957), pp. 358−9; R. E. Tyson, 'The Cotton Industry', in D. H. Aldcroft (ed.), *The Development of British Industry and Foreign Competition 1875−1914* (London: 1968), p. 118; Balfour Committee on Industry and Trade, *Survey of Textile Industries* (Parl.P. 1928), pp. 10, 156; Departmental Committee on Textile Trades after the War, *Report* (Parl.P. 1918), p. 8.

14   Roy Church, *The History of the British Coal Industry*, vol. 3, *1830−1913: Victorian Pre-Eminence* (Oxford: 1986), pp. 3, 759, 772−3, 779; J. H. Clapham, *Economic History*, vol. 3, p. 125; H. Stanley Jevons, *The British Coal Trade* (London: 1915), pp. 676−8; A. J. Taylor, 'The Coal Industry', in Aldcroft, *Development*, pp. 38−9.

15   E.g. Church, *British Coal Industry*, pp. 356−7, 429−30, 770−1; Barry T. Hirsch and William J. Hausman, 'Labour Productivity in the British and South Wales Coal Industry, 1874−1914', *Economica* 50 (1983), pp. 154−5; William Lazonick, 'Competition, Specialization and Industrial Decline', *JEcH*, 41 (1981); Lazonick, 'Industrial Relations and Technical Change: The Case of the Self-Acting Mule', *CJE*, 3 (1979); Lazonick, 'Factor Costs and the Diffusion of Ring Spinning in Britain Prior to World War I', *QJE*, 96 (1981); Lazonick, 'Production Relations, Labour Productivity and Choice of Technique: British and U.S. Cotton Spinning', *JEcH*, 41 (1981); Lars G. Sandberg, 'Movements in the Quality of British Cotton Textile Exports', *JEcH*, 28 (1968); Gary R. Saxonhouse and Gavin Wright, 'New Evidence on the Stubborn English Mule and the Cotton Industry, 1878−1920', *EcHR*, 37 (1984); debate between Lazonick, Saxonhouse and Wright in *EcHR*, 40 (1987), pp. 80−94; D. N. McCloskey, 'Productivity Change in British Pig Iron, 1870−1939', *QJE*, 82 (1968); McCloskey, *Economic Maturity and Entrepreneurial Decline: British Iron and Steel, 1870−1913* (Cambridge, Mass.: 1973); Ulrich Wengenroth, *Unternehmensstrategien und technischer Fortschritt. Die deutsche und die britische Stahlindustrien 1865−1895* (Göttingen 1986).

forth, or worsened, by the early start in the industrialization process, and becoming effective in the later years of the reign of Queen Victoria. The British, or at least the English, it is said, always preferred the country to the town, unlike the elites of other European countries, and they never abandoned that predilection even in the industrial age. They hankered after a landed, aristocratic style of life and after gentlemanly ideals, both of which were inimical to industrial success, and as soon as they had made some money, they left production for leisure, draining industry of its best talents. Manufacturing and money making had but low public esteem, and this bias was fostered and increased by a unique system of education in the public schools and the ancient universities. Further, the openings available in a huge Empire were destined to make governing rather than producing the preferred careers for ambitious men. To all this was added the third generation syndrome, compared with the vigour of the self-made pioneers of contemporary Germany and America.

Some of these ideas have recently been re-stated with great elegance and plausibility by an American author in a book which enjoyed a remarkable success among the British public.[16] It seemed to express on the national scale what many had felt to have been the case in their own circle of observation, and was certainly backed by much of the contemporary literature. At the same time it is not unlikely that at least part of the resonance which it called forth was due to its convenient role as an explanation of the undoubted British economic decline since the Second World War. It offered a ready-made excuse for those who bore some of the responsibility for the failures after 1945, since a decline which began before 1914 clearly cannot be laid at their door. Beyond this, it also flattered the British public as a whole to think that Britain's poor performance was due not to inferiority or incompetence, but rather to holding to more elevated ideals than the lesser breeds abroad.

Many professional historians, on the other hand, remained unimpressed by Wiener's arguments.[17] This was not merely because of technical weaknesses, such as the biased selection of quotations, but because the picture drawn of British society seemed to contradict much of what was known of the essential character of the period.

For one thing, the British aristocratic tradition was anything but averse to money-making. Britain's agriculture had been market-oriented earlier than most others, and her landlords accustomed for many centuries to take their tribute in money rents. This was augmented by the development early on of other estate resources, such as coal or iron ore, by the use of locational advantages such as exorbitant charges for land used by railways, and by the

---

16 Martin J. Wiener, *English Culture and the Decline of the Industrial Spirit, 1850–1980* (Cambridge: 1981).
17 E.g. reviews by William Ashworth in *EcHR*, 34 (1981), p. 659 and Jose Harris in *EHR*, 98 (1983), pp. 921–3.

development of urban sites. The speeches of the landed and titled members of both houses of Parliament in the nineteenth century were as mercenary as those of grocers and ironmasters, and in Victorian novels, as in the Georgian novels before them, men and heiresses of the upper echelons of society are valued by the size of their annual incomes. Even the 'public school ethos did not discourage money-making, only technological and scientific professionalism'.[18] Whatever the gentlemanly ideal had become, it was certainly not unworldly or incapable of reacting to the market.

In the world of finance, the late Victorian and Edwardian economy reached its apogee. Never before or since has London held such an overwhelmingly important place in the world's financial network. Even if the original causes of the rise of the City as a major provider of financial services, must be sought at least in part in the success of British producers in making goods which were saleable abroad, and in the success of British merchants in selling them and in linking British markets with those of the rest of the world, it is clear that the drive, as well as the skills, to be found in the Square Mile had greatly contributed to the success in building on the foundations thus laid.

In part, the hegemony of the London money market was based on specialization which in turn derived from its size and early development. Only in London were men in the Stock Exchange divided into brokers and jobbers; only there could the seeker after finance find bill brokers, merchant banks and Acceptance Houses, City Banks and offices of huge provincial branch banks, offices of foreign banks and of British banks operating mainly abroad, beside many others.[19] Unlike most other centres, there were no privileges in London, with the exception of the Bank of England, and competition was keen. Perhaps most astonishing of all for a centre claiming to be the financial hub of the world, this enormous activity which depended to a remarkably large extent on international links, was managed on a tiny gold reserve which yet succeeded in keeping the pound sterling throughout on an undisturbed and unquestioned parity with gold: in 1881 the Bank of England's bullion reserve was only 14.3 per cent of the reserves of the British, French, and German central banks and the American Treasury combined, and this had dropped to 9.2 per cent in 1885.[20]

18 E. J. Hobsbawm, *Industry and Empire* (Harmondsworth: 1977), p. 185; also David Spring, *The English Landed Estate in the Nineteenth Century* (Baltimore: 1962); A. Offer, *Property and Politics 1870–1914* (Cambridge: 1981); D. Cannadine, 'The Landlord as Millionaire: the Finances of the Dukes of Devonshire c.1800–1926', *Agricultural History Review* 25 (1977), pp. 77–9.

19 E.g. H. Withers, *The Meaning of Money* (London: 1909); C. A. E. Goodhart, *The Business of Banking 1891–1914* (London: 1972); Hamish McRae and Frances Cairncross, *Capital City* (London: 1973); W. T. C. King, *History of the London Discount Market* (London: 1936); F. Lavingon, *The English Capital Market* (London: 1921).

20 Alfred Marshall, evidence to Royal Commission on the Precious Metals, *Fourth Report* (Parl.P. 1888), QQ. 10198–10201; W. A. Lewis, *Growth*, p. 56.

Britain's active, pushful and successful entrepreneurship in the sphere of finance was matched by her equally dominant position in the world's insurance business. Where international competition was possible, particularly in the field of marine insurance, London was the centre, determining the world's rates. The world's leading produce exchanges were likewise to be found in London or Liverpool.

Shipping deserves a special mention. On the one hand, the shipping industry is the originator of one of the most mobile services, easily available on an international basis with minimal transport costs: technically, there was here a truly competitive international market. At the same time, for that very reason but also because of the military potential of shipping, there were few countries (not excluding Britain)[21] which did not in one form or another subsidize their shipping and shipbuilding or disadvantaged foreign tonnage in their ports. Moreover, British shipping legislation was among the strictest in the world, which gave shipping under some other flags the opportunity to survive with the help of laxer safety and manning regulations. It is therefore all the more remarkable that even at the outbreak of war, 40 per cent of the world's shipping fleets measured in gross tons, sailed under the United Kingdom flag, compared with only 33 per cent in 1880. In terms of age as well as quality, of steam and steel, the British share of carrying capacity was larger still. Thus in 1900, 77.5 per cent of the British tonnage was steam as against 51.5 per cent in the rest of the world, and in 1913 it was 97.7 per cent against 87.7 per cent; indeed, a not inconsiderable part of the rest of the world's tonnage consisted of second-hand ships from Britain.[22] It need hardly be stressed that on those terms, much of the British merchant fleet maintained itself in completely open competition without subsidy in trades between third countries. Nevertheless, trade from and to Britain continued to form the base for the overwhelming superiority of the British shipping industry. Britain, as table 6 shows, was not only the world's largest manufacturing exporter; she was also by far the most important importer of goods by sea. Her overseas trade showed no signs of decline or even deceleration, though it was subject to wide fluctuations, both in quantity and price. In terms of volume, exports (1880 = 100) stood at 140 in 1900 and at 239 in 1913, while imports stood at 166 and 220, and re-exports at 128 and 183 respectively, at those two dates. In terms of values, on the same basis, exports were 131 and 235, imports 127 and 187, and re-exports 100 and 173.[23] The tremendous growth in exports, particularly after the turn of the new century, increasing at the annual rate of 4.2 per cent in volume and 4.6 per cent in value, seems to refute any possible notion of failure in terms of international comparison. What more could have been expected of a mature economy of moderate size?

21 S. Pollard, 'Laissez-Faire and Shipbuilding', *EcHR* 5 (1952).
22 William Woodruff, *Impact of Western Man* (1966), pp. 255–6; Pierre Léon (ed.), *Histoire économique et sociale du monde*, vol. 4 (Paris: 1978), pp. 169–70.
23 B. R. Mitchell and Phyllis Deane, *Abstract*, pp. 283–4, 328–9.

Innovation and enterprise were to be found, however, not only in the services: even the much-maligned productive sector had some success stories to record. These were to be found not so much in the basic sectors, such as steel or coal or cotton, in which nations were wont to measure their progress; and, arguably, there was little more dynamic to be had, little extra demand to be filled in those industries in an advanced economy at that time before new technical breakthroughs, such as motor cars, would again furnish mass demands for steel, glass or rubber. The innovative, entrepreneurial spirit was to be seen, not entirely surprisingly, in consumer goods industries as well as in consumer services. Britain had, simultaneously with the USA, become the first mass consumer society.

Let us look at some of them. Soap was a typical product, combining some technical innovation with an elastic market with rising incomes. Output rose from about 90,000 tons a year in the 1850s to *c.*260,000 tons in 1891 and 366,000 tons in 1910. Most of this was for the expanding home market, but about one quarter was exported, and British firms led in world exports.[24] It is not without significance that, contrary to the widespread acceptance of the view that the British made inventions which others then proceeded to exploit, the technical breakthrough in soap making and in related techniques such as the production of glycerine and caustic soda, came largely from Germany, while the commercial exploitation was led by British firms. William Lever was the outstanding entrepreneur in the industry, revolutionizing it with his innovative ideas on advertising, packaging, organizational control and capital expansion. While he experimented in Port Sunlight with new ideas on factory layout and workers' housing, his plantations and branches abroad made his company one of the earliest multinationals. Meanwhile Crosfields' expanded on the basis of the new chemistry, before being merged with Lever's firm in 1919.

Sugar refining and sugar confectionery also experienced rapid growth. Cadbury's, at Bournville, were another pioneering firm in the matter of workers' housing, while Rowntree's experimented successfully with improvements in working conditions. The differences in approach between Taylor's American 'scientific management', which in its basic inhumanity was rejected even by British employers, and the quite different motivations to greater output devised in British Quaker chocolate factories, do possibly reflect the differences between an economy satisfied with its achievements, and one still on the make. The British were also unbeatable in other similar products such as biscuit making, where Huntley & Palmer were the world's leading exporters.[25]

24 A. E. Musson, *The Growth of British Industry* (London: 1978), p. 221; Musson, *Enterprise in Soap and Chemicals: Joseph Crosfield and Sons Limited 1815–1965* (Manchester: 1965); Charles Wilson, 'Economy and Society in Late Victorian Britain', *EcHR*, 18 (1965), p. 187; Wilson, *The History of Unilever* (1968).
25 Musson, *British Industry*, pp. 134–5, 234; T. A. B. Corley, *Quaker Enterprise in Biscuits: Huntley & Palmer's of Reading 1822–1972* (London: 1972).

Very similar was the innovative activity of the Wills family in the tobacco trade, then, be it noted, in its fourth generation, thus having successfully withstood the notorious third generation syndrome. After pioneering, not unlike William Lever, novel methods of packaging, advertising and sales increase via the retailer, they then went on to lead in the use of the Bonsack cigarette packaging machine, transforming the country's smoking habits in the process, and to fight off successfully the assault of one of America's biggest trusts by carrying the war into the enemy's camp.[26]

Considerations of space forbid a more detailed treatment of only marginally less flamboyant, but similarly successful innovative and growing enterprises among producers of such things as patent medicines, prepared foods, ready made clothing, boot polish and Reckitts Blue. The cheap, sensational, mass-produced newspaper for a new readership was another field of action for the new type of 'tycoon'. In retail distribution, frequently combined with a growing manufacturing potential, Paris may have pioneered the department store, but it was in Britain that branch retailing first took root on a large scale, from W. H. Smith's railway station bookshops to Lipton's, Boots' and the embryonic Marks & Spencer.[27]

Last, but not least, the rise of dormitory suburbs with their networks of urban transport, and the growth of seaside holiday towns should be recorded. The latter, depending as they did on the growing leisure for working men which was one of the gains derived from British economic success, are among the many aspects of Victorian achievements which normally do not appear in the statistical accounts. Both represented heavy investment in buildings, railways, tramways, piers and promenades[28] which could, no doubt, have been used to enlarge the output of 'productive' industry had it been decided to switch them to that purpose. They were among the areas in which the tendency of the late Victorian economy to choose consumption rather than investment is most clearly evident.

Virtually all these activities are partly or wholly omitted by the standard statistics. Even the majority of the manufacturing activities listed here are generally missing, apart from some specific recent studies, for lack of reliable output data. Hoffmann's study of industrial growth[29], still the base for more recent estimates, tended to use raw material input data for final goods, thus

26 B. W. E. Alford, *W. D. & H. O. Wills and the Development of the U.K. Tobacco Industry, 1786–1965* (1973).
27 J. B. Jefferys, *Retail Trading in Britain 1850–1950* (London: 1954); Asa Briggs, *Friends of the People* (London: 1956); Stanley Chapman, *Jesse Boots of Boots the Chemists* (London: 1974); William Ashworth, 'Changes in the Industrial Structure, 1870–1914', *Yorkshire Bulletin of Economic and Social Research*, 17 (1965).
28 William Ashworth, 'The Late Victorian Economy', *Economica* 33 (1966); J. K. Walton, 'The Demand for Working-Class Seaside Holidays in Victorian England', *EcHR*, 34 (1981).
29 Walther G. Hoffmann, *British Industry 1700–1950* (Oxford: 1955).

hiding the very additions to the value created by the manufacturing process which it was meant to describe. Suspicions about the thesis of decline, which assail most of those who are familiar with the era, are thus strengthened by suspicions about the very statistics themselves.

Yet a nagging doubt remains. Technical lags in key industries cannot be argued away, tending to belie the mere disadvantage of being on the technical frontier. Britain was better at the old than at the new. Home capital formation was lower than elsewhere. Can it be that Britain opted for high consumption 'too early'?

Britain was not the first, and is evidently also not the last, country to feel the drawbacks of being in a position of economic leadership. Whatever the advantages of that position may be, there are at least three sorts of danger that will face the leading economy in a competitive world.

The first is the tendency to hold to a policy of free trade, even if other countries turn increasingly protectionist. The reason for this attitude is the assurance, derived precisely from the inherited leading position, that given a fair fight and no favours, one's own industries would gain at the expense of the others. After all, a free trade policy on the part of the lead economy has the task not only of allowing in imports to pay for the industrial exports, but also of persuading others that it is a desirable kind of policy. Moreover, the rising trading and financial sectors are certain to favour the abolition of obstacles to trade.

Great Britain formed a classical example of this syndrome. So strong were her free-trade convictions, that she held on to her principles even after the rest of Europe had abandoned them (the USA never having embraced them) and was using the tariff and other restrictions to preserve agriculture at home and build up those industrial sectors that were deemed particularly desirable − usually at the expense of British imports. The resulting structural shifts enforced on Britain are precisely what one would expect in those circumstances: a relative loss, if only marked by declining growth, in those industries favoured abroad by foreign tariffs, as British exports became possible only into the shrinking unprotected world, where they had to compete against rising competition from the newly industrializing economies; uncertainty about further investment in Britain in those industries; a continuing boom in 'sheltered' British industries not affected by foreign protection and dumping; and a higher standard of living, based on cheaper imports, at any given level of home productivity compared with protectionist foreign countries. This latter was, of course, a main argument for free trade.

The second problem arises from the stream of capital exports almost inevitably associated with economic leadership. They tend to originate in part in the trading or payments surplus achieved in the years of true industrial hegemony, and in part in the fact that the richest country also has the largest accumulations of capital. Since it is also likely to be the country with the highest wages combined with low interest rates, there will be a strong incentive for capital owners in the lead country to seek investment opportunities abroad.

There are, no doubt, some advantages in thus being the world's rentier, and these are stressed adequately in the literature, but there are also hidden dangers. One, noted frequently enough, is that capital exports will help to build up rival industries abroad, earlier than would otherwise be the case. Even if the capital is sent into a complementary, rather than a competing economy — say, to a colony or a South American country — complementary economies have a nasty habit of turning into competing ones. But beyond this, capital exports give rise to a more acute danger. For a stream of foreign investments will in due course create a stream of in-payments in the form of profits and interest, which sooner rather than later will equal, and then exceed, the outward annual stream of original investments. If capital exports then cease, in order to stop the foreign debt mountain from growing, the debtor country is frequently unable to service its debt, to the direct loss of lender. But if the foreign debtor is able to pay a net sum yearly on capital account, this can be absorbed by the initial lending country only by either curbing its exports, thus harming its export industries, or by accepting a stream of unrequited imports, thus harming employment in its home industries. Precisely that was the position reached by Britain before 1914. In the last years of peace, the inward payment stream was such that, given a general balance on current goods and services account, vast new investments had to be made every year before the foreign account could be balanced; or, putting the same equation differently, given the annual stream of capital exports, payments inflows, and services sold abroad, Britain had to accept a vast import surplus on goods trade to balance the accounts, with negative effects on home employment and industrial progress.[30]

The third problem arises from the fact that the leading country is also likely to have the highest wages and the best social services, and to have imposed other expenses, such as consumer protection, ahead of the rest. This arises not only because, being richer, it can afford more, though this generally may have been the original cause of the difference; it also arises because the economy in the lead, pioneering the way, will have moved more slowly and thus will have given the social system more time to adjust to the higher economic capability. The followers, reaching their target more quickly, have less time to adjust socially, so that their wages and social costs are, at least temporarily, not only absolutely, but also relatively lower, at any given level of productivity, than those of the leading country. This will mean that the leader will lose all those industries whose products enter into international competition in which his higher wages and other costs are not fully compensated by a productivity lead.

This dynamic relationship has been termed the product cycle in the twentieth-century world, but it is applicable to our period also, though not necessarily, as in the modern version, as a shift *within* multinational firms.

30 S. Pollard, 'Capital Exports, 1870–1914: Harmful or Beneficial?', *EcHR*, 38 (1985), p. 511.

Alfred Marshall saw the issue clearly at the very beginning of the twentieth century:

> The very perfection of the textile and other machinery by which England has won her industrial leadership, has enabled it to be worked fairly well by backward races... Modern machinery 'which does most of the thinking by itself' puts England at a growing disadvantage with places where there are abundant supplies of low-grade labour... England will not be able to hold her own against other nations by the most sedulous practice of familiar processes... England's place among the nations in the future must depend on the extent to which she retains industrial leadership. She cannot be *the* leader, but she may be *a* leader... Sixty years ago England had the leadership in most branches of industry. The finished commodities and, still more, the implements of production, to which her manufacturers were giving their chief attention in any one year, were those which would be occupying the attention of the more progressive of Western nations two or three years later, and the rest from five to twenty years later.[31]

The assumption of the modern theory is that innovations will arise first in the leading country, for a variety of reasons, such as the availability of capital, entrepreneurship and skilled, highly mobile personnel, as well as the existence of a rich market. At first the product may be a luxury product, made in small quantities, possibly without standardization. As its technology improves, its costs will come down and its market will widen, to broader groups in the lead country and to some groups in those countries following close behind. At this point production may well be transferred there, to capture the lower labour and other costs. As costs fall and markets widen further, while the technology is once more improved and simplified, production will be moved further out, into even less developed countries with still lower costs at the same technology.

---

31 Alfred Marshall, 'Memorandum on Fiscal Policy of International Trade' (1903), in *Official Papers* (1926), pp. 403–5; also Raymond Vernon, 'The Product Cycle Hypothesis', *OBES*, 41 (1979); Vernon, 'International Investment and International Trade in the Product Cycle', *QJE*, 80 (1966); Vernon, *Sovereignty at Bay: The Multinational Spread of U.S. Enterprises* (New York: 1971); Seev Hirsch, 'The Product Cycle Model of International Trade', *OBES*, 37 (1975); Hirsch, *Location of Industrial and International Competitiveness* (Oxford: 1967); H. Frankel, 'Industrialisation of Agricultural Countries', *EJ*, 53 (1943); M. V. Posner, 'International Trade and Technical Change', *OEP*, 13 (1961); Gary Hufbauer, *Synthetic Materials and the Theory of International Trade* (Cambridge, Mass.: 1966); Paul Krugman, 'A Model of Innovation, Technology Transfer and the World Distribution of Income', *JPE*, 87 (1979); Robert Gilpin, *U.S. Power and the Multinational Corporation* (New York: 1975); James R. Kurth, 'The Political Consequences of the Product Cycle: Industrial History and Political Outcomes', *International Organization*, 33 (1979); Michael Claudon, *International Trade and Technology: Models of Dynamic Comparative Advantage* (Washington: 1977), pp. 1–6.

By this time they may well be in a position to export the product to the leading country where it was first tried out.

It is a process which has contributed enormously to the economic welfare of some of the less developed countries, advancing both their techniques and the absorptive capacity of their home markets; but it puts the leading economy under constant threat. It can only maintain itself, and in particular only maintain its high standard of living, if it is continuously a step ahead of everyone else, that is to say, if a constant stream of innovations perpetually renews its always temporary income from quasi-rents. Such dynamic is difficult to maintain over a long period, and there were several reasons why Britain failed to maintain it in a number of key industries in the years before the First World War.

However, there are some sectors in which the pressure from the followers-on is far weaker, or, in other words, in which the original lead remains an advantage for much longer. These are (beside possibly the high quality sectors of most industries) the services, and in particular the trading and financial sectors. The early build-up of improved transport facilities, such as harbours and ships, the earlier accumulations of capital, the international know-how and the personal connections are much easier to hold, much harder to break into from the outside. In the international division of labour, the former leading country can thus keep its specialisation in these fields far longer, while conversely the high earnings in these sectors help to lift the general income level in the country to a point at which it becomes difficult to hold on to internationally competitive manufacturing industries. Britain, in our period, still enjoyed its undisputed dominance in invisible exports; it is no accident that it was precisely there that much of her skill, enterprise and initiative was concentrated.

International and Historical Parallels

The discussion, on these last problems, has been conducted largely in general terms, but it will be evident that these generalizations are derived directly from the British experience. Are we justified in the suggestion that some of the problems and weaknesses were not specific to the British economy of those years but bore at least an element of inevitability, being part of the syndrome arising from the very success as the leading industrializing economy over the course of the preceding century? Is it the fate of all leading economies to fall victim, after a period of glory, to industrial senescence in the way described in the British case?

It is not too difficult, *mutatis mutandis*, to see some very similar symptoms in the American economy, so overwhelmingly strong only twenty years ago, in relation to the Far East today. Better still than speculating about the future is trying to learn from the past. We shall therefore look, all too briefly, at two actual historical examples, the Italian cities and the Dutch Republic in their heyday, to test our assumptions.

In the high Middle Ages, the cities of Central and Northern Italy represented the economic centre of the European world, wealthy, technically advanced and highly productive. Because the area was polycentric, its decline is not easy to date with precision. Its industrial power declined first, but even at the beginning of the seventeenth century, with the Dutch in the ascendant, the region could still be described as 'one of the more highly developed regions of Western Europe, with an exceptionally high standard of living for that time'.[32]

The original lead was based solidly on the productive skills to be found in the Italian cities, particularly in textiles. This provided an initial export surplus. At the same time, her lucrative international trade, with which she linked up the European world, and even more her spectacular financial transactions, increased the wealth of Italy:

> Even at the end of the sixteenth century, as in previous centuries, the economic prosperity of Italy was fundamentally dependent on massive exports of manufactured articles (chiefly textiles), and on a huge volume of invisible exports such as banking and shipping services. The entire economic structure of the country depended on being able to sell abroad a large proportion of the goods it manufactured and of the services it could provide. 'At one time', it has been said, 'Venice was the greatest industrial power in Europe. The cinquecento was the heyday of Venetian manufacturing.'[33]

It was precisely in the manufacturing sector that the Italian position was undermined first. Fundamentally, Italian goods were priced out of foreign markets by their high cost structure. Other troubles supervened also: plagues, wars, the shift of trade out of the Mediterranean, and it is by no means easy to distinguish cause and effect. Yet the key mechanism was the price of internationally traded goods.

Why were Italian prices too high? The original cause was a series of technical innovations elsewhere, which the Italians would not or could not copy, and the reason for that, in turn, was a set of guild restrictions and regulations, or, at least in the case of Lombardy, of state-enforced constraints. Additionally, craftsmen's guilds kept wages unduly high, and were content, for a time, to concentrate on the luxury end of the market at which old skills still counted, until it was too late to modernize. Moreover, Italian taxes were

32 Carlo M. Cipolla, 'The Economic Decline of Italy', in Cipolla, *The Economic Decline of Empires* (1970), p. 196, also in Cipolla, *Before the Industrial Revolution*, 2nd edn (London: 1971), p. 253.
33 Cipolla, 'Economic Decline', p. 202; Richard Tilden Rapp, *Industry and Economic Decline in Seventeenth-Century Venice* (Cambridge, Mass.: 1976), p. 6. Also Fernand Braudel, *The Perspective of the World* (New York: 1984), p. 136.

higher than those elsewhere, and were collected in an inefficient and costly manner.[34]

It is a familiar tale. What had once been elements of strength became causes of weakness, derived from Italy's 'early start'. Early success caused rigidities in the face of innovation: earlier prosperity had created a floor of incomes and taxes higher than those of competitors. Familiar also is the survival of banking and finance later than industrial power, and the flow of capital into agriculture after industry had declined.[35]

The story of Dutch economic leadership and its loss shows even more affinity with the British experience than the Italian. At the same time, many of the chief phenomena found in Italy were repeated here also.

To begin with, the Dutch supremacy, their 'golden age' centred on the seventeenth century, was based solidly on productive efficiency at home, and shipping abroad. There were the 'traffics' — transforming imported products like the boiling of sugar, tobacco curing, and oil pressing. But there were also 'native' industries, such as working up timber, potteries, breweries and distilleries, but above all the textile trades and shipbuilding, which had reached a high level of standardization methods.[36] Power and heat were provided mainly by an immense array of windmills, and by local peat. The high level efficiency

34 Cipolla, passim; Domenico Sella, 'The Rise and Fall of the Venetian Woollen Industry', in Brian Pullan (ed.), *Crisis and Change in the Venetian Economy in the Sixteenth and Seventeenth Centuries* (1968); Brian Pullan, 'Wage Earners and the Venetian Economy, 1550–1630', in *Crisis and Change*, pp. 164–5; Ralph Davis, 'England and the Mediterranean 1570–1670', in F. J. Fisher (ed.), *Essays in the Economic and Social History of Tudor and Stuart England in Honour of R. H. Tawney* (Cambridge: 1961), pp. 123–4, 134; Immanuel Wallerstein, *Modern World System* (London: 1974), pp. 219–21; Charles H. Wilson, 'Trade, Society and the State', *Cambridge Economic History of Europe*, iv (Cambridge: 1967), pp. 491–2; Rapp, *Industry*, pp. 139–40; Domenico Sella, 'Les mouvements longs de l'industrie lainière à Venise aux XVIe et XVIIe siècles', *Annales E.S.C.* 21 (1957), pp. 39–41; Sella, *Crisis and Continuity, The Economy of Spanish Lombardy in the Seventeenth Century* (Cambridge, Mass.: 1979), pp. 62ff., 79–105.

35 Rapp, *Industry*, pp. 154–9; Braudel, *Perspective*, pp. 162–73; E. J. Hobsbawm, 'The Crisis of the Seventeenth Century', in Trevor Ashton (ed.), *Crisis in Europe 1560–1660* (1965), pp. 19–20; Frederic C. Lane, 'Recent Studies in the Economic History of Venice', *JEcH*, 23 (1963), p. 333; Ludwig Beutin, 'Der wirtschaftliche Niedergang Venedigs im 16. und 17. Jahrhundert', *Hanseatische Geschichtsblätter*, 76 (1958), pp. 54, 69; I. Wallerstein, *Capitalist World Economy* (Cambridge/Paris: 1979), p. 38; Giuseppe Felloni, *Gli investimenti finanziari genovesi in Europa* (1971).

36 Jan de Vries, *The Dutch Rural Economy in the Golden Age 1500–1700* (New Haven: 1974), pp. 186–7; Angus Maddison, *Phases of Capitalist Development* (Oxford: 1982), pp. 30–1; Richard W. Unger, *Dutch Shipbuilding Before 1800* (Assen/Amsterdam: 1978).

and productivity reached in the fisheries, in shipping itself, and in agriculture[37] should also be mentioned in this connection.

Together with the invisible exports of shipping and gradually also of financial services, these industries provided the foreign payments surplus out of which the enormous capital exports of the later seventeenth and of the eighteenth centuries were financed.[38] Exactly as in the Italian case earlier and the British case later, these took on increasing importance just as the industrial lead was being lost and Dutch industry began its long period of stagnation around the second quarter of the eighteenth century. Thereafter the Netherlands led a rentier existence, lasting almost two centuries, against a background of stagnating industry and specialized agricultural exports.

What was responsible for the Dutch industrial 'decline', or at any rate stagnation? Fundamentally, Dutch goods were being priced out of their markets by foreign, above all British, competition. The list of causes for this will by now cause no surprise. There were the high wages, derived from the earlier high productivity, but maintained, even after that had gone, by rigid urban regulations and generous social security payments, funded by local taxation and private charitable foundations:

The inheritance of the golden age to the Dutch economy of 1800 consisted of an income distribution in which wages were substantially higher than elsewhere on the Continent.[39]

There were the costs of empire – including high taxes and the loss of up to one-fifth of the adult male population in migration and deaths in the East Indies.[40] There was the dominance of the financial and trading sector which prevented any form of protection for Dutch industry while countries like

37 A. R. Mitchell, 'The European Fisheries in Early Modern History', *Cambridge Economic History of Europe*, v (Cambridge: 1977), pp. 148–53; J. H. Parry, 'Transport and Trade Routes', ibid. IV (Cambridge: 1967), pp. 210–16; Violet Barbour, 'Dutch and English Merchant Shipping in the Seventeenth Century', *EcHR*, 2 (1930); J. C. Boyer, 'Le capitalisme hollandais et l'organisation de l'espace dans les Provinces-Unies', in Maurice Aymard, *Dutch Capitalism and World Capitalism* (Cambridge/Paris: 1982), pp. 13–22; Pierre Jeannin, 'Les interdependences économiques dans le champ d'action européen des Hollandais (XVIe-XVIIIe siècle)', ibid., p. 162; B. H. Slicher van Bath, 'The Economic Situation of the Dutch Republic during the Seventeenth Century', ibid. p. 30; van Bath, 'The Rise of Intensive Husbandry in the Low Countries (*ca.*1600–1800)', in J. S. Bromley and E. H. Kossman (eds), *Britain and the Netherlands* (1960), pp. 130–53; C. H. Wilson, *The Transformation of Europe 1558–1648* (1976), pp. 17–18.
38 C. H. Wilson, *Anglo-Dutch Commerce and Finance in the Eighteenth Century* (Cambridge: 1941, repr. 1966), pp. 198–200; James C. Ridley, *International Government Finance and the Amsterdam Capital Market 1740–1815* (Cambridge: 1980).

Great Britain and France enjoyed protection and subsidies of various kinds. Industrialists

> were not strong enough to force their claims for tariffs and subsidies against the traditional ideas and interests, the accumulated wealth and prestige of the old merchants... The capital which should have been absorbed at home was driven abroad to find higher rates of interest.[41]

Thus the industrial supremacy was undermined:

> The weakest point in the Dutch economy (sc. in the eighteenth century) was the absence of a large export industry which could form the backbone of a sold export trade and provide a real channel for home investment.[42]

Interestingly enough, a decline in entrepreneurship, in a society which had only a short while earlier been the European epitome of robust commercialism, has also frequently been made at least partly responsible just as in the case of Britain later. Dutch entrepreneurs were accused of 'risk averseness, technical ineptitude, leisure preference, and general perfunctory and complacent attitudes'. Alternatively,

> those who made a fortune, or even a comfortable living, from industry or craftsmanship were apt to change over to a merchant's calling as soon as they had enough capital to do so.[43]

39 Joel Mokyr, *Industrialization in the Low Countries, 1795–1850* (New Haven: 1976), p. 201; idem, 'The Industrial Revolution in the Low Countries in the First Half of the Nineteenth Century', *JEcH*, 34 (1974), pp. 381 ff.; Wilson, *Anglo-Dutch Commerce*, Preface; idem, 'The Historical Study of Economic Growth and Decline in Early Modern History', *Cambridge Economic History of Europe*, V, p. 27; Kristof Glamann, 'The Changing Patterns of Trade', ibid., p. 253; C. H. Boxer, 'The Dutch Economic Decline', in Cipolla, *Economic Decline*, pp. 240–5; Jan de Vries, 'The Population and Economy of the Preindustrial Netherlands', *Journal of Interdisciplinary History*, 15 (1985), pp. 672–4; idem, 'The Decline and Rise of the Dutch Economy, 1675–1900', in Gary Saxonhouse and Gavin Wright (eds), *Technique, Spirit and Form in the Making of Modern Economies* (Greenwich, Conn./London: 1984), pp. 178–82; idem, *Dutch Rural Economy*, p. 200; Jan A. van Houtte, 'Economic Development in Belgium and the Netherlands from the Beginning of the Modern Era', *JEurEcH*, 1 (1972), pp. 110–12.
40 Jan de Vries, 'The Population', pp. 667ff. For Spain, see Wilson, *Transformation*, p. 154; J. H. Elliott, 'The Decline of Spain', in Cipolla, *Economic Decline*. For the UK see Lance E. Davis and Robert A. Huttenback, 'The Political Economy of British Imperialism: Measures of Benefits and Support', *JEcH* 42 (1982) p. 127.
41 C. H. Wilson, 'Economic Decline', pp. 260, 268; Mokyr, *Industrialization*, p. 220.
42 C. H. Wilson, *Anglo-Dutch Commerce*, p. 187.
43 Mokyr, *Industrialization*, p. 215; C. R. Boxer, 'The Dutch Economic Decline', p. 261.

The drain of talent to merchanting and finance was paralleled by the drain of capital: the Dutch capital market was simply not accessible to home manufacture, and capital exports were thus said to have starved Dutch industry of capital. But conversely, it could be argued that capital exports were the most effective reply to the high tariffs levied abroad to keep out Dutch goods – precisely as in Great Britain later.[44] Meanwhile, the large annual interest inflows had a deflationary effect on the productive side of the economy.[45]

In the heyday of Dutch leadership, other countries enticed away Dutch skilled workers and technicians: a law of 1752 forbidding the emigration of skilled workers had little effect. Thereafter, however, the Dutch workman was accused of being badly trained as well as slovenly.[46]

Every one of these factors, including the switch to trade and later still to finance as a leading sector, may be put down to the Dutch 'early start'. In turn, these were responsible for the peculiar role and attitude of Government (if that is the right term for the Dutch political authority), dominated as it was by mercantile, colonial and financial interests. It failed to protect and subsidize industry, it failed to ensure adequate technical training, and it failed to add to the infrastructure after the canals and harbours of the golden age had been built.

Given the enormous differences in circumstances, in technology, in the position of the rest of Europe and the world which obtained in their periods, the parallels between these cases, to which possibly the Spanish case may also be added[47] are truly striking. It is difficult to believe that these are all pure coincidences: too many of the later signs of decline are logically derivable from the 'early start', that is to say, the earlier economic leadership itself.[48] Obviously, the more the ills and weaknesses of each society in relative decline are derived from its earlier successes, the less the responsibility that is borne by the contemporaries.

---

44 C. H. Wilson, *Anglo-Dutch Commerce*, p. 18; de Vries, *Dutch Rural Economy*, pp. 243–8, 266–71; Maddison, *Phases*, p. 33; W. P. Klein, 'Stagnation économique et emploi du capital dans la Hollande des XVIIIe et XIXe siècles', *Revue du Nord*, 52 (1970), p. 36.

45 Mokyr, *Industrialization*, p. 214; Maddison, *Phases*, p. 34.

46 Boxer, 'Dutch Economic Decline', pp. 256–9; Mokyr, *Industrialization*, pp. 215ff.

47 Elliott, 'Decline of Spain'; Henry Kamen, 'The Decline of Spain: A Historical Myth?', *Past and Present*, 81 (1978), and debate in ibid. 91 (1981), pp. 170–85; also Henry Kamen, 'The Decline of Castile: The Last Crisis', *EcHR* 17 (1964–5).

48 But see Maurice Aymard, *Dutch Capitalism*, p. 5, also Wallerstein in *Capitalist World Economy*, pp. 63, 96: the pattern, according to the latter, 'seems marvellously simple. Marked superiority in agro-industrial productive efficiency leads to dominance in the sphere of commercial distribution of world trade... Commercial primacy leads in turn to control of financial sectors of banking... and of investment.' Also Terence K. Hopkins and Immanuel Wallerstein, *World Systems Analysis* (Beverley Hills: 1982), p. 118.

Sidney Pollard

Conclusions

It is not necessarily a disaster for a country to decline from a previous position of dominance. There is, in fact, a lot to be said for leaving the costs of pioneering, the false starts, and the experimentation to others, as well as the costs of empire, of gunboats, and of acting as the world's policeman. While it may not be easy for a country to decline elegantly, relative decline, in comparison with others, may not involve actual falls in the standards of life. Possibly Italy, and certainly the Netherlands remained wealthy as well as stable societies even after they ceased to be in the front rank. Switzerland, to cite another example, maintained efficient manufacturers even after she had changed to an economy exporting mainly services.

In the British case it is not clear that an actual decline had set in in the four or five decades to 1914. There were some signs of senescence, and far more signs that the path from the productive to the trading and financing stage had been entered. But the British economy was still extremely efficient by contemporary standards, that is, within the realms of what was technically possible at the time.

Even if we accept that there is a kind of inevitability about the decline after a phase of world economic leadership, there can be no certainty about the time scale of that process. The period of British leadership, involving the pioneering of modern industrialism and the opening out of the rest of the world to European progressive capitalism − truly remarkable achievements on a world scale − lasted well over a century. If others now began to carry the burden of innovation, it was still too early to diagnose a climacteric. It will not do to seek the causes of the undoubted failures after 1945 in the late Victorian and Edwardian ages.

4

Britain's Decline: Some Theoretical Issues

Andrew Gamble

The Problem of British Decline

Britain's loss of great power status and its relative economic decline during the twentieth century have often been analysed and debated as though these were problems peculiar to Britain. Britain's experience, however, raises a number of major theoretical issues which have wider interest for any explanation of socio-economic change. The literature on British decline is extensive, and the debates on its causes stretch back to the turn of the century. It is hard to think of a major theoretical perspective that has not been employed at some time to explain the reasons for Britain's performance.

One of the difficulties in making sense of the literature on decline is that such different levels of analysis incorporating very varied time horizons are encountered. Henk Overbeek, in an important recent overview of the whole debate which utilizes the categories of Braudels's historiography, has pointed out the different conceptions of time that are involved in various theories.[1] British decline can be analysed in terms of very long-term structural factors, reaching back to the seventeenth century; or primacy can be given to structural changes in the last one hundred years; or the focus can be placed on very recent events and trends. All three approaches may possess validity, and Overbeek has argued that for a full understanding of the causes and implications of British decline it is necessary to combine all three. Britain's crisis in the 1970s was created by an amalgam of factors, some of which were short-term, some medium-term and some long-term. It was the coming together of all these different factors which made the crisis both so explosive and apparently so intractable.

1 Henk Overbeek, *Global Capitalism and Britain's Decline* (University of Amsterdam, 1988).

The extent to which a process like decline is inexorable and pre-ordained is a vital question for political analysis. The fatalism that is involved in some accounts of Britain's decline is deeply unwelcome to politicians, who need to believe that political will and judgement can make a difference. They therefore prefer conjunctural analyses or, at most, medium-term analyses, which suggest that remedies to present problems are available and that existing trends can be turned round if necessary.

At the other extreme are those analyses which, by emphasizing long-term trends and structures, suggest that the scope for remedial action by politicians is slight because the constraints on their decisions are so tight. The trends are so well established that nothing politicians can do will alter their direction very much. What may be important here is whether the trend is conceived as cumulative or cyclical. If it is a cycle then there is little possibility of escape — human agents must reconcile themselves to performing the roles that are appropriate at each stage of the cycle. If, however, the trend is unilinear, there is the possibility that the buildup of tension may be such that at some point there is a major rupture and discontinuity. What is to count as such a rupture, and how much of the social order it affects becomes a key question.

Faced with the perils of fatalism and voluntarism on either side it is hardly surprising that many analysts pursue a middle course, sceptical of the explanatory value of long-term trends and structures, but also aware of the limitations of explanations that focus on immediate events and circumstances.

Some of these different explanations will be reviewed in this chapter, although the focus will be mainly on long-term and medium-term explanations, partly because these accounts contain the greatest theoretical interest and partly because a phenomenon like British decline, which has lasted for such a long time, and which has successfully resisted so many attempts to reverse it, cannot be adequately explained in terms of very recent events.

There are two fundamental questions in the study of British decline; firstly the loss of great power status by Britain in the first half of this century. Could this have been averted or was it inevitable? Secondly, the relative economic decline that has accompanied it. Was this part of the legacy of Britain's great power status? Or was it due to quite separate and identifiable causes?

Debates on these questions have raged fiercely at different times. The decline is not a single phenomenon, but has passed through several phases. This chapter will discuss three such phases, each characterized by its own particular debate on decline. What mark off one phase from another are changes to Britain's position within the world order. As the world economy has changed so the political perceptions of the problems confronting Britain, and the remedies for them, have shifted also.

The first phase was between 1880 and 1914. The growing challenge to the military and economic position of the British Empire from rising powers triggered a wide-ranging debate on national efficiency and whether Britain had fallen seriously behind its main rivals.

The second phase lasted from 1917 until the 1970s. During this period of the debate Britain's hegemonic role in the world system was ceded to the United States, and Britain shed its colonial empire and its world power. Awareness of American industrial and commercial superiority launched a major debate on what Britain needed to do to modernize its institutions to match the Americans.

The third phase runs from the 1960s up to the present. It was marked by the erosion of American hegemony in the world system and the new situation this created for all states. The collapse of the international monetary order that had guaranteed financial and trading stability accelerated the trends towards greater interdependence and internationalization. The focus of debate on decline shifted to the institutions and policies of British social democracy — its shortcomings, its adequacy, its resilience, and the alternatives to it.

Arising out of these debates many different theses have emerged as to the cause of British decline. Four major theses are analysed in this chapter. They are chosen because they allow some of the key theoretical issues to be posed quite sharply. The four theses may be termed the imperial thesis, the cultural thesis, the corporatist thesis and the class thesis. Two other important theses not discussed in this chapter are the market thesis, which receives a strong statement in Mancur Olson's chapter in this book, and the constitutional thesis, which focuses on the organization of the political system.[2]

The Phases of Decline

1880–1914: The challenge to empire

The first phase of decline resulted from the increasing challenge from Germany and the United States to the exceptional position of military and economic strength which Britain had built up in the nineteenth century. British capital, technology, and expertise had been important in promoting industrialization in other parts of the world, and Britain greatly benefited from this, but at the cost of losing the lead in productivity and the market dominance that had characterized British industry in the middle decades of the nineteenth century.

Awareness that Britain was becoming vulnerable both militarily and economically grew rapidly after 1880 and culminated in the vigorous debates on national efficiency after 1900. What concerned many observers was Britain's lack of preparedness for a major military contest with one of its challengers, and this was increasingly traced to the shortcomings of British economic performance, and to the inertia of Britain's traditional liberal, *laissez-faire*

---

2   These additional themes are analysed in Andrew Gamble, *Britain in Decline* 3rd edn (London: Macmillan, 1989).

policy regime. The lack of organization and planning of British resources and the British national effort was frequently cited by Social Imperialists, New Liberals, and the new breed of state socialists as the basic problem that had to be remedied.[3]

The performance of other nations forced the British to acknowledge that they lagged behind in the development of new products and new industries; that costs were now lower in a number of industries; and that the techniques of marketing and selling goods and services were much more advanced in other countries, particularly the United States. The spectre of Germany and the United States leap-frogging over Britain in industrial output and productivity had become a real possibility.

The consequences of the changing balance of economic power in the world economy for the political and military balance were instantly apparent. Britain was perceived as especially vulnerable because of the small land base and therefore limited physical and human resources of the British Isles itself compared to the unlimited potential of the continent-sized economies.

Britain ruled over a greater population and a greater land area than any other power in 1900, but the British Empire was a highly diverse and fragmented political entity. It compared unfavourably with the concentration of resources and territory enjoyed by both Germany and the United States. It was impossible for Britain to extend its immediate heartland, and indeed even part of that — Ireland — was seriously disaffected.

These facts gave rise to the geopolitical theories of Halford Mackinder and the Social Imperialists, which pin-pointed Britain's strategic dilemma. The solutions of the Social Imperialists were twofold. Firstly Britain needed much more positive public policies to remedy deficiencies in education, health, housing and social security. Secondly the British Empire had to be welded into a much more cohesive political and economic bloc. British industry would be partially safeguarded from competition by the imposition of a tariff, the proceeds of which would pay for new public spending programmes. The physical and human resources of the Empire would be much more consciously organized to promote increasing integration and common purpose.

Like earlier dreams of a Greater Britain embracing the Anglo-Saxon white Dominions, the plans of Chamberlain and Milner were never realised. Welding the British Empire into a single state was never a plausible prospect, given its heterogeneous character and the unwillingness of even the white Dominions to contemplate it. But it did define quite accurately the nature of Britain's problem. In the new age of organized mass production, only powers with access to vast physical and human resources could aspire to be leading military and political powers. If Britain could not secure access to such resources it would inevitably become subordinate to more successful powers.

---

3 Bernard Semmel, *Imperialism and Social Reform* (London: Allen & Unwin 1960).

Mackinder argued that the contest between a sea-based power and the land-based power of the state that could dominate the Eurasian landmass would be critical for determining the course of twentieth-century history.[4] He expected the sea-based power to be Britain, but this depended on the British industrial base being dramatically deepened and extended. In retrospect it was always more likely that this role would be taken by the United States which could back its naval power with a continent-sized industrial base.

1917–1970s Modernization

The long-drawn out struggle between England and Germany in the First World War was eventually broken by the entry of the United States on England's side in 1917. Both England and Germany were severely weakened by the war, while American power and influence were enormously enhanced. After 1917 it soon became clear that Britain's traditional naval predominance would never be restored, that her financial strength had been significantly undermined, and that it was no longer possible for Britain singlehandedly to perform state functions for the world economy in the 1920s and 1930s as had been the case when Britain's hegemonic position was undisputed. The events of 1931 were finally to confirm this.

After 1917 there was a long period of often uneasy relations between Britain and the United States during which British political opinion eventually became reconciled to the assumption by the United States of many of the roles which Britain had once performed. This was very slow at first because of the desire in Britain to hold on to its empire for as long as possible, and because of the isolationist feeling in the United States.

In both countries influential groups emerged who saw an Anglo-American link as indispensable to the future security of both countries. Such attitudes were held particularly strongly in Britain.

The key period for the debate on the transfer of hegemony was the 1940s. This involved not merely the renewal of the military alliance in the Second World War, but the political and financial negotiations which took place during the war and after it, and which saw the undisputed emergence of the United States as the leading world power after 1945, with Britain in a subordinate although still important role. This transfer was by no means smooth, and Britain continued to resist American leadership. But in retrospect the trend of policy is extremely plain. By 1950 a consensus in Britain on the importance of the alliance with the United States as the cornerstone of British policy had been firmly established.[5]

---

4 Halford Mackinder, *Democratic Ideals and Reality* (London: Constable 1919). See also Geoffrey Parker, *Western Geopolitical Thought in the Twentieth Century* (London: Croom Helm, 1985).

5 Kees van der Pijl, *The Making of an Atlantic Ruling Class* (London: Verso 1984); Richard Gardner, *Sterling-Dollar Diplomacy* (Oxford: Clarendon 1956).

This phase of decline saw repeated attempts to modernize British industrial structure and to change the nature of state–industry relations and the character and extent of state intervention. The first phase of decline had also been associated with debate on British industrial shortcomings. What was different after 1918 was that the various crises and deep-seated social conflict that had beset Britain between 1880 and 1920 gave way to a period of stability, and the emergence of a domestic compromise on policy between capital and organized labour which laid the basis for the legislative programmes of the governments of the 1940s.

Britain attempted to modernize by emulating the institutions and practices of other economies which were forging ahead more rapidly, particularly the United States. It was the industrial, social, and political system which has become known as Fordism which Britain increasingly tried to copy. This system involved the need for mass production, large production units, the development of new industries and new technologies, the provision of infrastructure and adequate social spending, the extension of citizenship rights, and the undertaking by governments to enlarge domestic demand. It came to be broadly accepted that the state must have an expanding role in providing the conditions under which a successful industrial economy could survive and compete.

None of these changes was accomplished without considerable effort and political struggle. In Britain the analysis and prescriptions of Keynesianism were not accepted until the 1940s. The trend however towards more corporatist arrangements in industry was already visible in the 1930s. The provision of infrastructure, the encouragement of domestic industries, the enlargement of the domestic market, the merger of many companies, saw the adoption of Fordist methods of industrial relations and work organization in many key industries, and the emergence of British firms in the new leading sectors of the world economy.

Domestic modernization assumed greater importance as Britain adjusted to the transfer of hegemony and the diminution of its own power, since it became clear that Britain must find its way and maintain its economic security in a world order whose shape and direction was determined by other states. This was why the accumulating evidence by the end of the 1950s that the British economy was growing more slowly than other advanced capitalist economies renewed the debate on modernization all over again. It was apparent that the efforts that had been made were not enough. The modernization and reconstruction of the 1930s and 1940s had still not produced an economy that was internationally competitive.

The perception that Britain was still performing less well than comparable economies became a dominant issue in British politics in the 1960s and produced a great deal of diagnosis and many new policies and spending programmes aimed at remedying the deficiencies and closing the gap. But the issue was debated within the framework and assumptions that the leaderships of both main parties had accepted since at least 1945 and in some aspects since the 1920s.

1960s: Social democracy

The most recent phase of the decline includes the turbulent decades of the 1970s and 1980s, which saw the British political order confronted by a series of crises on a scale unmatched since the first three decades of the century. The relative failure of British Governments to push through successful modernization programmes and the resulting weakness of the British economy in relation to other OECD economies loomed much larger with the onset of world recession in 1974. The breakdown of post-war stability brought not a retreat into protectionism but an acceleration of the pace of internationalization. Responding to this new world forced reassessment of the priorities and feasibility of national economic management and the relations between governments and their economies. In Britain the focus of the debate on decline became the social democratic order that had earlier supplanted liberalism. The accommodation between organized labour and capital which had sustained the British polity for more than forty years broke down.[6]

The catalyst for these events was the failure of the social democratic regime to deliver the modernization that it promised. As it was the very high levels of economic prosperity in the 1950s and 1960s helped make bearable the increasingly evident downgrading of Britain's world status. But the inability to arrest the relative economic decline and the increasingly serious impact of this on inflation, unemployment, and living standards weakened the authority of governments in the 1970s and for a time unhinged the party system and brought a deep-seated crisis of legitimacy.[7]

These events were accompanied by a much more polarized and wide-ranging debate on decline than at any time since the issue had been starkly posed as a choice between the preservation of capitalism and its replacement by socialism. Even then, the debate on the future of the British Empire had generally excluded the socialists. Those who participated in it, whether Free Traders or Tariff Reformers, shared the assumption that the empire should be preserved. The debate on modernization had taken for granted the structure of British Government, the role of the private sector, the scope of government intervention, and the role of the trade unions that had emerged in the 1940s settlement.

What occurred in the 1970s was a polarization of political argument, the revival of a socialist critique of British capitalism on one side, and the revival of anti-collectivist arguments on the Right. Both the liberal and the conservative wings of the New Right which emerged in Britain rejected many aspects of the 1940s settlement and sought radical changes in the relationship of government to the economy and the society. Britain's faltering economic performance

6 Mary Langan & Bill Schwarz (eds), *Crises in the British State 1880–1930* (London: Hutchinson 1985).
7 Anthony Birch, 'Overload, ungovernability, and delegitimation', *British Journal of Political Science*, 14: 2 (1984), pp. 135–60.

and increasing public disorder were identified as the problems of the social democratic regime. Economic revival demanded policies that would greatly reduce the role of government in the economy, while strengthening its authority and its ability to remove obstacles to the workings of free markets. The New Right therefore advocated both a free economy and a strong state.[8]

On the Left there was a restatement of the case for public ownership and planning. It took the form of an 'alternative economic strategy' which, although it had many variants, generally advocated some form of economic protectionism in order to rebuild Britain's industrial base. The more radical versions envisaged a major break in Britain's foreign economic policy − withdrawal from the European Community as well as from NATO − and the subordination of finance to industry. What was wrong with the social democratic regime was that it had produced a stalemate between labour and capital which was increasingly debilitating.[9]

Four Theses on Decline

The imperial thesis

This thesis argues that British decline is a result of the over-extension of British power. It focuses attention primarily on Britain's imperial experience, the reasons why the empire broke down, and the legacies it left behind. The key structural relationships that are explored are those between the nation state and the world economy. These are seen as imposing powerful constraints on national policy, but those in charge of national policy retain a degree of autonomy. The process of historical change is viewed through the structures and institutions of the state.

The imperial thesis in relation to Britain has received a recent forceful restatement by Paul Kennedy.[10] He argues that although it is foolish to search for invariant cycles, there are certain broad features which occur in the history of states which have risen to the position of great powers. There is a trade-off between economic security and military security, and the fate of great powers is that they progressively lose the ability to maintain the balance and fall victim to rising powers who can afford to be more single-minded in their pursuit of economic success.

Kennedy's book is a sustained development of the insight that in the long

8   This is analysed at much greater length in Andrew Gamble, *The Free Economy and the Strong State* (London: Macmillan 1988).
9   See the readings in David Coates & John Hillard (eds), *The Economic Decline of Modern Britain* (Brighton: Wheatsheaf 1986).
10 Paul Kennedy, *The Rise and Fall of the Great Powers* (London: Unwin Hyman, 1988).

run political and military power depend on economic strength. The problem confronting governments is threefold:

> simultaneously to provide military security...for its national interests, *and* to satisfy the socioeconomic needs of its citizenry, *and* to ensure sustained growth, this last being essential both for the positive purposes of affording the required guns and butter at the present, and for the negative purpose of avoiding a relative economic decline which could hurt the people's military and economic security in the future.[11]

Kennedy argues that achieving all three of these objectives is extremely difficult for any state because of the uneven pace of technological and commercial change and the 'unpredictable fluctuations in international politics'. But if a state should achieve the first two without the third it will suffer relative economic decline, which in turn will lead inexorably to relative eclipse as a great power. This he notes has been the fate of all slower-growing societies that 'failed to adjust to the dynamics of world power'. England is the most striking example in the last two hundred years, a country which lost its position as the world's undisputed industrial leader in 1880 without ever being defeated in a major war.

Kennedy explains England's eclipse as the result of the effort devoted to safeguarding Britain's position as a world power. This has been a constant theme in the literature on decline – the consequences of attaching greater priority to 'grandeur' rather than growth, and the illusions this has created as to Britain's real position and real interests.[12]

Much of the writing on the part played by Britain's status as a great power has emphasized mistakes of state policy. Two different arguments are prominent. The British state is faulted both because it gave too little priority to the empire when Britain was still a great power, and because it clung to the empire and the illusions of great power status when the basis for them had disappeared. The first theme is evident in the writings of the Social Imperialists and restated in Corelli Barnett's book *The Collapse of British Power*.[13] The second was a prominent theme during the debates on modernization, and has been forcefully argued in relation to British foreign economic policy by Stephen Blank.[14] It is also a major theme of Corelli Barnett's most recent book *The Audit of War*.[15]

For the Social Imperialists the issue was whether Britain could break with

11 Kennedy, *Rise and Fall*, p. 446.
12 Andrew Shonfield, *British Economic Policy Since the War* (London: Penguin, 1958).
13 Corelli Barnett, *The Collapse of British Power* (London: Methuen, 1972).
14 Stephen Blank, 'The Politics of Foreign Economic Policy', *International Organisation*, 31: 4 (1977), pp. 673–722.
15 Corelli Barnett, *The Audit of War* (London: Macmillan, 1986).

free trade and *laissez-faire* policies and organize its domestic base and its empire as an integrated unit which could sustain the military commitments and the rate of economic growth that were considered necessary to resist the challenge of other empires. Once that possibility no longer existed and Britain was embarked on the transfer of its hegemonic role in the world system to the United States, the issue from this perspective became whether Britain could rapidly disengage itself from its imperial role and reorganize itself for a new role within a world order in which it was no longer a leading force.

Many of the contributions to the imperial thesis appear to believe in the capacity for political decision-making to make a difference. The decline was not pre-ordained. Even those who accept that the Social Imperialist project was a fantasy and that Britain's retreat from empire was inevitable can still argue that the adjustment of Britain to its new role and status could have been much smoother and more successful if Britain had not been burdened by the costs of sustaining its former role and blinded by the illusions which this still created. Barnett's views here are typical. He regards the failure of Britain's rulers of all parties to adjust to the collapse of British power in the Second World War as crucial. They were resolved, he argues, to restore and perpetuate Britain's traditional world role:

> The pursuit of this hallucination in the next quarter of a century was to cost Britain in defence expenditure up to double the proportion of GNP spent by European industrial competitors who limited themselves to contributing to the non-nuclear defence of the North Atlantic Treaty Area. It was to impose a heavy deadweight on Britain's sluggish economy and on her fragile balance of payments, suck away from exports scarce manufacturing resources in advanced technology, and continue the wartime concentration of much of Britain's even scarcer R and D resources on defence projects.[16]

The important theoretical question which the imperial thesis raises is how far state policy is autonomous and how far it can make a difference. It is possible to cast the imperial thesis in a much more determinist mould, as tends to be done by world system theorists. The search for invariant cycles in historical development implies the impossibility of one state sustaining a position of leadership and dominance indefinitely. Kennedy is much more cautious in his judgements. He notes the constraints and the difficulties that a great power encounters when it tries to retain its position of dominance. But he does not rule out the possibility. In Britain's case, however, the dominance the country enjoyed in the middle of the nineteenth century was always exceptional. As Kennedy puts it:

> the geographical size, population, and natural resources of the British Isles would suggest that it ought to possess roughly 3 or 4 per cent of the world's

16   Barnett, *Audit of War*, p. 304.

wealth and power, *all other things being equal*; but it is precisely because all other things are *never* equal that a peculiar set of historical and technological circumstances permitted the British Isles to expand to possess, say, 25 per cent of the world's wealth and power in its prime; and since those favourable circumstances have disappeared, all that it has been doing is returning down to its more 'natural' size.[17]

What this leaves out are the insights contained in the world system literature which insists on looking at the world politics as a system rather than focusing so exclusively on the nation states that compose it.[18] What makes the history of British decline of wider interest for theories of social and economic change is the light it throws on the problem of the creation and maintenance of political order in the world system. Such a perspective suggests that the constraints on national policy-making are tighter and the illusions more real than proponents of the imperial thesis often suppose.

The cultural thesis

At the core of the cultural thesis is the identification of an anti-industrial or anti-enterprise culture as the fundamental cause of Britain's problems. This has proved to be the most popular and readily accepted explanation of Britain's shortcomings. Important recent versions of the thesis have been contributed by Martin Wiener and Corelli Barnett.[19]

The cultural thesis places greatest importance on the climate of ideas in shaping behaviour and determining socio-economic change. In most versions of the thesis much more attention is paid to the ideas of elites than to those of the people. Decline has come about primarily because of the values and attitudes embraced by the elites rather than the masses. The people may as a result have become inert, unenterprising, deeply conservative and inflexible, but the fault for this lies with the elites rather than with the masses. If the elite changed its attitudes and behaviour this would be the catalyst for transforming mass attitudes.

The greatest difficulty faced by the cultural thesis lies in explaining why there should be any growth at all if the anti-industrial culture in Britain is so strong. It must also explain why an enterprise culture flourished earlier in the nineteenth century. How can the same national culture be responsible for such different sets of attitudes and values?

The answer given by proponents of the cultural thesis like Martin Wiener is that the anti-industrial culture was always ambivalent. The political elite, he

---

17 Kennedy, *Rise and Fall*, p. 533.
18 I. Wallerstein, *The Modern World System* (New York: Academic Press, 1980); *The Politics of the World Economy* (Cambridge: Cambridge University Press, 1984).
19 Martin Wiener, *English Culture and the Decline of the Industrial Spirit* (Cambridge: Cambridge University Press, 1981).

argues, 'like the social and cultural elite of which it was part, both desired and feared technical advance and economic growth'.[20] The anti-industrial culture was a culture of only partial resistance to industry and technology, but it was powerful enough frequently to frustrate and delay industrial and economic change, but never to prevent it altogether. What the anti-industrial culture enshrined was a set of values which were disdainful of modern industry yet parasitical upon it. Wiener summarizes this argument as follows:

> social prestige and approbation were to be found by using the wealth acquired in industry to escape it. This...both diverted talent and energies from industry and gave a particular 'gentry' cast to existing industry, discouraging commitment to a wholehearted pursuit of economic growth.[21]

This kind of analysis has directed attention to the British status system, and the institutions like the public schools, the collegiate universities, and the professions, which have been so important in preserving and fostering an anti-industrial culture for the elite.

Some attention to prevailing ideas and particularly to the culture of the elite is common in all theories of decline. The cultural thesis is noteworthy for the weight and the primacy it attaches to it. The main critics of the cultural thesis have argued that cultures in highly differentiated societies like modern Britain are much more fragmented, diverse and permissive than the cultural thesis appears to allow. Evidence for anti-industrial attitudes is plentiful, but there is always a question about its representativeness. It is often possible to explain the phenomena explored by cultural theories in other ways. As Hobsbawm puts it: 'Economic explanations of economic phenomena are to be preferred if they are available.'[22]

Nevertheless the appeal of cultural explanations is very great. When the authors of the Brookings study on the British economy despaired of finding economic explanations of why British productivity was comparatively so poor they suggested that the answers lay 'deep in the social system'.[23] This notion that behind the surface phenomena of economics and politics lies a more permanent world of values remains a very powerful orthodoxy.

Cultural perspectives have been employed by analysts with very different approaches. The early version of the New Left Review thesis was heavily culturalist in orientation, and offered an account of British history which emphasized the role of ideology, and the failure of the rising industrial bourgeoisie ever to supplant the ideology and the institutions of the aristocracy. Instead they were co-opted into the aristocrats' world. In this way Britain

20 *Ibid.*, p. 126.
21 *Ibid.*, p. 127.
22 Eric Hobsbawm, *Industry and Empire* (London: Penguin, 1969), p. 187.
23 R. Caves & L. B. Krause (eds), *Britain's Economic Performance* (Washington: Brookings, 1981) p. 19.

never experienced a thoroughgoing modernization of the kind experienced by other European countries.[24]

Barnett also indicts the culture of the ruling elite as the main cause of the decline. It is the reason why the opportunities for strengthening the empire were never taken, and why in the 1940s a coherent strategy of industrial regeneration was never devised. Barnett launches a bitter polemic against what he calls 'The New Jerusalemists'. The archetype of this group is Beveridge. Barnett charges that it was the religious and social ideals which animated large sections of the Establishment and the upper class, and whose main although not exclusive vehicle was the Labour Party, which caused all the attention in post-war reconstruction to be placed on redistribution and the remedying of past injustices instead of tackling the urgent problems of inadequate training, industrial backwardness, and poor industrial relations. The chances of economic revival were thrown away.[25]

The corporatist thesis

The corporatist thesis contends that the causes of Britain's decline lie in the incomplete and flawed character of the Fordist regime of accumulation that was established in Britain. British experience is judged against the experience of other countries whose Fordist regimes have enjoyed greater success.

This kind of analysis places the emphasis firmly upon state–economy relations. It encourages detailed historical and comparative institutional analysis of the state bureaucracy, the business community, and organized labour, and the interrelations of all three. Decline is viewed as a problem of institutional failure, although the nature of this failure remains a matter of dispute since there is disagreement as to which institutions have most importance in influencing economic performance. The picture is complicated because there is no single model of successful Fordism, but several distinct national variants. The applicability of these models to Britain has always been contentious, and leaves plenty of room for ideological argument.

Fordism has come to be the label for what is elsewhere defined as organized capitalism.[26] It signifies the dominance of a particular kind of production process, the assembly line and mass production, which institutionalizes continual technological advance and the de-skilling of large parts of the workforce in the search for rising labour productivity. The generalization of this regime of accumulation across all industrial sectors implies the development of new forms of industrial relations and state involvement. In particular the need to ensure that there is a mass demand commensurate to the capacity of the

24 Perry Anderson, 'Origins of the Present Crisis', *New Left Review* 23 (January–February 1964).
25 Barnett, *Audit of War*.
26 Scott Lash & John Urry, *The End of Organised Capitalism* (Cambridge: Polity, 1987).

factory production lines requires either the creation of a mass domestic market or access to external markets. The industrial struggles to win collective bargaining rights helped achieve and maintain the high wages that were necessary to generate a mass internal market; so too did the political struggles to extend public responsibilities and programmes in welfare, education, health, economic management, the provision of infrastructure, and defence.

The two key requirements of a Fordist regime of accumulation, firstly avoiding large fluctuations in demand and maintaining a steady expansion of markets, and secondly ensuring competitiveness through rising productivity and efficiency, both implied an active interventionist role for the state. Intervention however could be developed in a number of ways.

The debate on modernization was about how a viable Fordist regime could be established in the UK, and how best-practice techniques, policies, and institutions could be imported from elsewhere and adapted to British conditions. Britain's institutional peculiarities were seen as the main obstacles. The most important were considered to be (1) the lack of integration between the industrial and financial sectors; (2) the Treasury–Bank–City nexus which was much more influential in determining economic policy priorities than manufacturing industry or organized labour; (3) poor industrial relations and poor management, as shown by strikes, restrictive practices, and low productivity; (4) the character and style of state intervention in Britain.[27]

British experience in all these areas often contrasted sharply with experience in other countries. Perry Anderson has listed four different national models of successful Fordism, all of which have exhibited what he calls a regulative intelligence, all of which were lacking or only partially achieved in Britain. The four types of regulative intelligence he identifies are (1) the state technocracy in France; (2) the banking system in West Germany; (3) the combination of interventionist bureaucracy and banking system in Japan; and (4) the organized labour movement in Sweden.[28]

What is highlighted in these accounts is the extent to which Britain, by failing to become a developmental state, failed to renew its economic dynamism. This is explained in terms of British institutions – the character of the British civil service, the British banking system, or the British labour movement. In each case these institutions are seen as less well adapted for the task of economic modernization than institutions in other countries.

The class thesis

A fourth thesis which emerges from the debates on British decline focuses on the character of British capitalism. One of the most well-known of all interpretations of British decline is the analysis developed in *New Left Review* by

27 Peter Hall, *Governing the Economy* (Cambridge: Polity, 1986).
28 Perry Anderson, 'The Figures of Descent' *New Left Review* 161 (January–February 1987), pp. 20–77.

Perry Anderson and Tom Nairn.[29] They argued that the British bourgeois revolution was premature and therefore unfinished, and that the consequences of this, both for the capitalist class and the industrial proletariat that eventually emerged, were profound, and created legacies which were eventually to become crucial handicaps for the British economy in competition with economies whose modernization had been later and more radical.

The value of Anderson and Nairn's long historical perspective was that it provided a framework for interpreting many particular aspects of British decline such as the role of the City, the character of Labourism, the anti-industrial culture of the ruling groups, and the failure of modernization programmes. Their work has stimulated a great deal of research by authors such as Colin Leys, Geoffrey Ingham, and Frank Longstreth on the precise nature of the divisions within British capital.[30] The thesis of the unfinished revolution has in this way become the thesis of divided capitalism with more emphasis being placed on the social and economic character of the division rather than on its ideological features.

Anderson and Nairn's work has been extremely influential and has often tended to eclipse other perspectives. Many of its emphases are however contested by two older interpretations of British capitalism. The first of these places much greater weight on the struggle between classes, and specifically on the defensive ability of the British working class to resist the pressures from capital for rationalization and higher productivity. The labourism of the British trade union movement is viewed more positively than in Anderson and Nairn's account. Instead of being a symptom of the incorporation of the Labour movement into the British *ancien régime*, it reflects instead the stalemate between capital and labour in Britain, which neither side was powerful enough to break. Some socialist accounts of the strength of organized labour came close to endorsing the argument that it was the strikes and restrictive practices of the labour movement which were the major cause of Britain's low pro-ductivity.[31] The policy conclusions that were drawn from this were however very different from those of the New Right.

The second emphasis has been to dispute the significance and the extent of the split between industry and the City. Britain is viewed in the context of

29 Perry Anderson, 'Origins of the Present Crisis', *New Left Review* 23 (1964), pp. 26–53; Tom Nairn, 'The Twilight of the British State', in *The Break-up of Britain* (London: New Left Books, 1981).
30 Colin Leys, *Politics in Britain* (London: Verso, 1986); 'Thatcherism and British Manufacturing', *New Left Review* 151 (1985), pp. 5–25; Geoffrey Ingham, *Capitalism Divided* (London: Macmillan 1984); Frank Longstreth, 'The City, Industry, and the State', in C. Crouch (ed.), *State and Economy in Contemporary Capitalism* (London: Croom Helm 1979), pp. 157–90.
31 Andrew Glyn & Bob Sutcliffe, *British Capitalism, Workers, and the Profits Squeeze* (London: Penguin, 1972). See also Bernard Stafford, 'Theories of Decline' in Coates and Hillard (eds), *The Economic Decline of Modern Britain*, pp. 334–48.

global capitalism. The international orientation of British capital is explained not by the ascendancy of finance over industry but by the greater opportunities for profitable accumulation for all sections of capital outside Britain than within it. The turning away of capital from development within Britain can therefore be presented as an entirely rational course of action for British firms. The mistake, it is argued, is to treat British capital as though it were a national capital instead of part of international capital. It is the increasing autonomy of all sections of capital from the British economy which then stands out.

These arguments were deployed in the past by Eric Hobsbawm amongst others, and have recently been pressed vigorously by Michael Barrat Brown in a wideranging critique of the *New Left Review* thesis.[32] Barratt Brown argues that Britain has declined as a national economy not because British capital is backward, but because the pressure to modernize and reorganize the British economy has always been diluted and diverted by the success of British capital in operating internationally.

The class thesis gives most importance to classes defined in relation to the process of production rather than in terms of status. The disputes concern the identification of these classes, their interests, and how these interests are represented. Shifts in the balance of power between classes and between factions within classes are held to be crucial for explaining how policy agendas emerge and the nature of the eventual policy outcomes.

Assessment: Decline and Recovery

In the 1980s the long-running debate on British decline appeared to have reached another turning point with the election of a government in 1979 which was not only pledged to reverse decline but by 1987 was confidently proclaiming that the recovery in the economy since 1982 was evidence that it had achieved its aim.

The claims and counter-claims for British economic performance raise important questions for the analysis of socio-economic change. If a trend so well established as British relative economic decline can be reversed very rapidly in a few years by an active state policy, it suggests either that the obstacles to modernization identified in the various debates were insubstantial or that the general context had changed in such a way as to make the obstacles less important. It will be argued here that in so far as the claims that 'Britain is back' are correct, it is likely to be for the second reason.

The British recovery can be assessed in relation to each of the four theoretical perspectives discussed above. This chapter concludes with a preliminary survey of some of the evidence and points that might be considered.

32   Michael Barratt Brown, 'Away with all the Great Arches: Anderson's History of British Capitalism', *New Left Review* 167 (1988) pp. 22–51.

The imperial thesis

Britain's imperial experience is now firmly in the past. The Falklands war was an echo of that past rather than a sign of renewed imperial vigour. Nevertheless many of the burdens imposed on Britain by the over-extension of its power have still not been removed. The Falklands War itself is one illustration of this. It was preceded and in part triggered by a determined British effort to negotiate with the Argentinians for the dilution and eventual surrender of British sovereignty over the islands. It ended with a much larger and much more costly permanent commitment to the defence of the islands by Britain.

The Thatcher Government, although it did not sanction the kind of arms build-up that took place in the United States, was nevertheless a leading protagonist in the new cold war, and Britain re-established itself as America's closest ally in Europe. The parts of the British state and the British economy that had expanded as a result of Britain's world role were boosted, not contracted, during the 1980s. From the standpoint of the imperial thesis therefore there is still considerable scope for retreat from the illusions and pretensions of Britain's former world role. Britain has further adjustments to make. Defence spending is too high, defence commitments are too many, and the defence sector of British industry is too large, too protected, and consumes too much of Britain's available resources for R & D.

The legacy of Britain's former world role still affects Britain's relationships with the European Community. Britain has been an obstructive and difficult member, and has often resisted the development of common European policies. Britain's attitude has been expressed both in actions – such as the repeated refusal to join the European Monetary System – and by words, most notably by Margaret Thatcher's Bruges speech in 1988. From the perspective of the imperial thesis, with its emphasis upon the close connection between economic resources and military and political power, there would be considerable advantages to Britain's domestic economy of rapid integration of the Community in economic, defence, and political institutions and policies. It might finally release the British economy from the burdens and roles it continues to sustain only at considerable cost to other objectives.

The cultural thesis

The Thatcher Government has given strong support to the development of an enterprise culture in place of a culture of welfare and dependency. Much of the New Right critique of social democracy from which Thatcherism derived so much of its inspiration can be seen as a cultural critique, both of the values and attitudes of workers, and of professional elites, towards markets and enterprise.

The measures to foster enterprise have involved substantial cuts in direct taxation for high income groups to the point where the progressive character of the income tax has been greatly reduced; the privatization of state assets, in part to raise revenue, in part to encourage the development of personal ownership of shares and other assets (popular capitalism); the use of state agencies like the Manpower Services Commission and the Urban Development Corporations to encourage the development of entrepreneurial attitudes and improve skills; and attacks upon the privileges, status, and ethos of major institutions and professions, including the television media, the Anglican Church, and the Universities.

The policies hardly amount to the cultural revolution that is sometimes talked about. Certain changes are evident, but there has been no radical reshaping so far of key institutions like the civil service (although plans do exist). Even the education reforms look timid compared to what would be required if the Government were to take seriously Corelli Barnett's thesis.

If attitudes to work and success are as deep-rooted as the cultural thesis suggests, then it would be remarkable if the Thatcher Government had been able to effect more than very marginal changes. The government is also handicapped because while Thatcherite Conservatives have attacked the traditional status system in Britain and openly poured scorn on the old Establishment and the 'grandees' of the Tory party, many of the most visible expressions of that status system such as the House of Lords and the honours system have been unscatched. The radicalism and populism of the leaders of the Thatcher Government in this field is more a matter of personal distaste and rhetoric rather than a coherent programme of policy.

Nevertheless, although the Thatcher Government has done little to bring it about, there is considerable cultural change currently taking place in Britain, mainly because of the sudden acceleration in the decline of traditional manufacturing and the working class communities and ethos associated with it. This re-making of the working class by occupational and technological changes may have a more long-term effect upon Britain's anti-industrial culture than the slow reform of Britain's elites.

The corporatist thesis

Whatever else the Thatcher Government has done it has not established a successful Fordist regime in Britain, if only because the conditions for the establishment of such a regime now seem to have passed. The era of 'post-Fordism' and 'disorganized capitalism' have arrived. What the Thatcher Government set out to do was to dismantle many of the structures of the Fordist regime that previous governments had struggled to create. This was most evident in the field of industrial relations, where tripartite structures, particularly at the national level, were abolished. The trade unions were largely excluded from any share in national decision-making, and their freedom of action was severely curtailed by a succession of new labour laws, which altered the legal balance firmly in favour of management.

Privatization of public enterprises gathered momentum, and the government also struggled (with only partial success) to contain public spending. The various policies of the Thatcher Government reflected its increasingly confident belief that it was no longer necessary to conciliate the interests of organized labour. Some have viewed the programme that emerged as wholly destructive, dismantling the previous policy regime but putting nothing in its place. Others have pointed to a growing coherence between the different parts of the government's programme.[33]

Many economists still point to the technology gap, the training gap, and the investment gap which exists between Britain and similar economies, and have argued that the boom between 1982 and 1988 has been underpinned by oil revenues and promoted by the expansion of the world economy and a rapid growth of credit. The real test for the changes that the government claims to have introduced will be how resilient the new business sectors prove when the economy turns down, and what measures prove necessary to tackle the structural deficit in Britain's balance of payments which the government has allowed to re-emerge.

The class thesis

From a class perspective the Thatcher Government has been assessed in a number of ways. Its early monetarist period when it helped precipitate an extremely severe recession and shakeout of labour was seen by some as either a highly irrational strategy, because so many industrial companies were wiped out, or as a policy which reflected the continuing dominance of the City over industry. Others, however, believed from the outset that the main purpose of the government was to precipitate a showdown with organized labour, whatever the short term cost.[34]

The latter explanation certainly offers a plausible explanation for the Thatcher years. The series of defeats suffered by organized labour, most notably the miners' strike in 1984–5, contributed to the mood of confidence in political and business circles and facilitated the restructuring of British industry and the raising of productivity. Evidence on how far the class balance at the point of production has been shifted still appears inconclusive, however. The trade union movement has suffered defeats but given the scale of the recession it is perhaps surprising it has not been broken further. The withering away of unions or even the development of a new business unionism are still far from achieved.

The reduction in influence of the trade unions, however, and the scale of the world recession did create a space in which new experiments could be made, and the Thatcher Government, more through good fortune than design,

33 Martin Holmes, *The First Thatcher Government 1979–1983* (Brighton: Wheatsheaf 1985); Grahame Thompson, *The Conservatives' Economic Policy* (London: Croom Helm, 1986).
34 I have explored these interpretations further in *The Free Economy and the Strong State* (London: MacMillan, 1988).

did succeed in developing a new accumulation strategy that fitted well the new technological, social and political conditions that had emerged as a result of the big structural shifts in the world economy and world politics in the 1970s. This strategy played to the particular strengths of the British economy, in particular the international orientation of the leading sectors of British business, while dismantling and abandoning sectors, communities, and institutions that had failed or only partially succeeded in the post-war period. The Thatcher Government encouraged the complete internationalization of the British economy by removing virtually all controls on inward and outward investment, privatizing state assets, reducing programmes of state support for both industry and welfare, and bypassing the structures of the local state. It was rewarded by a surge of growth and prosperity in the South and East, which made it politically possible to ignore the increasing poverty of marginal groups and declining areas.

As internationalization proceeds one of the key questions becomes how far national models of economic development are still relevant. The very lack of a successful Fordism may in this respect be an advantage to the British Government, since it is much easier to dismantle institutions that have plainly failed, and to experiment with new and more flexible policies. Britain enjoys certain advantages in comparison to other countries in becoming a successful site for international accumulation by multinational companies. The state has been used very effectively to clear the ground and 'free' the economy. A new form of accumulation is gradually emerging. But the consolidation of this regime of accumulation may require a renewed emphasis on state intervention, although this time with less trade union influence or participation. Many of the historical perspectives on British decline also suggest that a lasting British recovery may also require at some stage a more determined *perestroika* of the state itself.

5

Is Britain the Wave of the Future?
How Ideas Affect Societies[*]

Mancur Olson

How important are ideas as compared with organized interests as influences on societies? John Maynard Keynes argued in the peroration of his *General Theory* that, in spite of the allegation that vested interests largely determine what happens, the world is ruled by ideas and by little else. But Keynes's conclusion has not, so far as I know, ever been adequately tested. Nor have the channels by which ideas exert any influence they may have on societies ever been satisfactorily delineated. The task of systematically testing Keynes's assertion about ideas is so huge that it could not be encompassed within a single paper, and even mapping all the channels by which ideas could influence social outcomes is beyond the scope of the present essay. The purpose here is instead only to set out some problems and paradoxes that have to be understood before an adequate study of the role of ideas can be designed, and to make some casual suggestions about the routes by which ideas influence public policies. The paper is motivated by the hunch that ideas about economics and public policy have a larger role than is often realized in explaining what happens to societies.

Readers who have a *faint* knowledge of my prior writings will probably be astonished that I should have this hunch. I have written a good deal about organized interests and the decisive influence they have had on many societies (and especially on Great Britain), but I have never written anything systematic on the influence of ideas on societies. In fact, my emphasis here on the role of ideas and my suggestions on the routes by which they affect social ideas arise directly out of my previous work on collective action and vested interests: the inherent nature of collective action not only explains some problems that socially useful ideas have to overcome and some powerful forces that oppose

*© Copyright by the author. By prior arrangement, this paper has been published elsewhere.

their implementation, but also why there are special circumstances in which ideas can play a large role and why widely accepted ideas can sometimes overcome the strongest organized interests. Moreover, in this account of the influence of ideas, as in my prior work on the impact of collective action by organized or collusive interests on economic performance, there will be a special focus on Great Britain, on the grounds that British society has been prototypical with respect to the role of collusive and organized interests and especially instructive in terms of the history of economic ideas as well.

Unfortunately, a major problem with the argument that I offer here is that it is fully meaningful only to the few who have a precise knowledge of two of my books, *The Logic of Collective Action* and *The Rise and Decline of Nations*. I shall accordingly offer here some brief, incomplete, and unrigorous evocations of certain *parts* of these books. The hope is that these evocations may make the argument here semi-comprehensible, or ideally even persuade a few readers of this essay to study those books.

There is fairly widespread agreement among the historians of economic thought that a very large proportion of the most important economic thinkers were British. A mere listing of the names that are given the most attention in such histories – names such as Adam Smith, T. R. Malthus, David Ricardo, John Stuart Mill, Stanley Jevons, Alfred Marshall, and John Maynard Keynes – makes this clear. Perhaps smaller societies such as Austria and Sweden did better on a per capita basis than Britain in generating giants of the history of economic thought. And it is certainly true that British economists in the time of Marshall and Keynes greatly exaggerated the extent of the British leadership in economic thought and gave much less attention to foreign economists such as Knut Wicksell than they should have. Nonetheless, even if the British lead was exaggerated, it remains true that Britain has had more of the giants of economic thought than any other country.

Unfortunately, I know of no systematic cross-national surveys in earlier times of public opinion, or even of elite opinion, that would quantitatively establish whether this historic British preponderance in original economic thought implied a better understanding of economics by the British public or by British elites outside of the economics profession. But almost certainly general elite opinion and broad public opinion in Britain were influenced more by intellectual advances in economics than in most other countries. In the continental European countries, the reception of new economic ideas was slowed by differences in language. The writings of the leading British economists were, by contrast, widely and fairly promptly propagated in Britain. Some of the original economic thinkers, such as Adam Smith and Alfred Marshall, had an extraordinary capacity to explain their theoretical advances to relatively broad audiences, and others, such as John Maynard Keynes, had a special gift for attracting attention to their conclusions.

Consider also the widespread conflation of economic thinking in the first century and a half after Adam Smith with classical liberal ideology. Unfortunate as the comingling of intellectual discoveries with popular ideologies and political movements was, it helps us judge the impact of economic thinking from Adam Smith to Alfred Marshall on public opinion. Most of the great early economists, and certainly men like David Ricardo and John Stuart Mill, were classical liberals. Some of their conclusions and prejudices if not their technical discoveries were popularized by people like Cobden and Bright. Almost everyone concedes that classical liberalism was more popular in nineteenth-century Britain than in most other countries, and certainly more popular in Britain than in most countries of continental Europe.

The economists' emphasis on the advantages of free international trade also appears to have had a wider audience in Britain than in Europe or North America during most of the nineteenth century and until at least the 1930s. For reasons that have been spelled out elsewhere and that will be sketched impressionistically later in this paper, we cannot simply infer public opinion directly from public policy choices, so we cannot conclude that there was a more widespread appreciation of the advantages of free trade in Britain than in other countries simply because Britain had free trade and other countries did not. But there is quite a bit of independent evidence that the shortcomings of protection were better understood in nineteenth-century Britain than in most other countries. At that time, a belief in free trade was taken to be a "British" notion. I can recall having read British writing published before World War I in which the author pointed to his familiarity with protectionist arguments by saying that he had lately traveled in the United States and talked about trade policy with many people there, and in such a way that it was obvious that the author took it for granted that his audience shared his belief that protectionist beliefs were incomparably more common in the United States than in Britain.

What are the implications of this historically large British role in economic thought for economic policy and economic performance in Britain? Though I won't fully answer this question, I shall later suggest that British economic policy and British economic performance have been *improved* by the relatively advanced state of economics and economic understanding in Britain.

Obviously, if ideas were the overwhelming influence on economic performance, then Britain should be the richest or at least one of the very richest nations on earth. As everyone knows, it is not. Indeed, during almost all of the time since the last years of the nineteenth century Britain has suffered from the "British disease" of slow growth.[1] The British disease is certainly not

---

1 The naive reader might even suppose that a greater grasp of the ideas of the giants of economic thought was harmful to economic performance, and perhaps conclude that these giants were largely wrong. An analysis of this naive supposition would require a long digression, so I shall not go into the matter here, except to say that a general cross-national comparison of the level of economic understanding and the level of economic performance would by no means support the naive supposition that has just been mentioned.

explained by the observation that Britain has had an exceptionally large role in the development of economic understanding.

This point is underlined by a comparison of Britain and West Germany in the first quarter century after World War II. There is no doubt that the general level of economic understanding in Britain was higher than in Germany. German universities and intellectual life, especially in economics and the social sciences, had been devastated by Hitler's repression of free debate and by the emigration of leading intellectuals. Even before Hitler, German contributions to economics had been relatively modest, perhaps because of the influence of the now-defunct German historical school of economics. Yet the economy of the Federal Republic of Germany performed incomparably better than the British economy did after World War II.

So we need something besides the level of economic understanding to explain economic performance. I therefore turn to an evocation or promotion of the argument about the British disease contained in some parts of my book on *The Rise and Decline of Nations*. This argument will also help us develop a framework for understanding the role of ideas. There is, of course, some controversy about whether the British disease has lately been cured under the government of Margaret Thatcher or whether it has been especially severe since she took office, but the argument here does not depend on which way that argument is settled. Thus the reader may as he pleases suppose either that the argument in the next section relates to Britain before the first Thatcher Government or also to Britain now.

The British Disease

Many commentators, British as well as foreign, claim that the slow growth of the British economy is due to some endemic trait of the British people or to one or another of its social classes. Britain, they allege, has been growing slowly because the British are inherently inclined to take it easy, or because the British working class is naturally unruly, or because the primordially class-conscious middle and upper classes are prejudiced against business careers and lacking in entrepreneurial drive.

These allegations, even if true, cannot provide an adequate explanation of the British disease, for they do not explain why the alleged traits emerged. They also overlook the fact that for nearly a century Britain was the fastest-growing country in the world; the source, indeed, of the industrial revolution which started all modern or rapid economic growth. If in the late eighteenth and early nineteenth centuries British workers had been less energetic or cooperative than those in other countries, and the British class system less open to rising talents, and British attitudes more antagonistic to business pursuits, and British entrepreneurs more tradition-bound, then modern or rapid economic growth would presumably not have begun in Britain.

It follows that no explanation of the relatively slow growth of the British economy today can *possibly* be correct unless it finds the cause in some change, however gradual, in British society *since* the eighteenth or early nineteenth century, or (conceivably) in some change conducive to growth that occurred in *other* developed countries but not in Britain.

As soon as we realize that the explanation of Britain's relatively slow growth in the twentieth century logically has to be found in some change or evolution since the industrial revolution, it is natural to ask what traits of character and social structure were most often observed in eighteenth-century Britain. Intriguingly, we find that the stereotypes were exactly the *opposite* of those alleged to be characteristic in recent times. It is a commonplace in economic history texts that, by comparison with Continental Europe, eighteenth-century Britain was distinguished by a greater interest in commercial and industrial pursuits, by a lesser attachment to tradition, by more daring innovators, and by an uncommon social mobility. Continental critics found Britain relatively lacking in respect for aristocratic tradition and feudal order; Napoleon was not alone in referring to Britain as a "nation of shopkeepers."

It is obvious on reflection why we must also look at growth rates in other countries to understand British growth. A medical researcher would not conclude that cabbage caused cancer because a patient with the disease ate an unusual amount of cabbage; he would probably want to check many people to see whether the incidence of cancer increased with the consumption of cabbage. Similarly, we can not determine the cause of any "British disease" without at least looking at several countries or regions to see whether some alleged retardant to growth is present in the slow growing and absent in the fast growing. As Dr. Johnson said, he who knows only England, knows not England.

In particular, we must look at the examples of the fastest growth in the developed democracies since World War II, that is, at West Germany, Japan, and Italy in the first quarter century after World War II, to see the ways in which these countries in this period contrasted most sharply with England and other countries that have in this century grown relatively slowly. We must also look at France, because in view of the instabilities and invasions that country has suffered, and the corresponding hazards for the long-run investments needed for economic growth, France's postwar growth has at times also been remarkable. It is also instructive to look at the United States, not so much because it has grown nearly as slowly as Great Britain as because its size, diversity, and its division into different states with distinctly different histories and policies give us evidence from a larger number of "patients" or "natural experiments." Why are many American states in decline, while many others, mainly in the West and the South, grow rapidly? Why is the United States doing so badly in the industries in which it pioneered mass-production, such as in automobiles, steel, and consumer appliances, yet at the same time doing relatively well in new, high technology industries?

The different rates of growth in different periods and places that I have described can be understood only if we look at "distributional coalitions," or special-interest organizations and collusions; that is, organizations of firms or individuals that combine to increase the price of what they sell, or to influence the government, or to do both. The professional association, the trade union, the farm organization, the trade association, and the "oligopolistic" collusion are the leading examples of these "cartelistic" and lobbying organizations.

To understand distributional coalitions, we must first think through what I call the logic of collective action. If any individual or firm in a cartelistic or lobbying organization should act in the interest of his group, the benefits of this action are inevitably shared with the others in the group; the higher price or wage will be enjoyed by everyone who continues to sell the cartelized good or labor; the favorable government action will benefit everyone who shares the special interest. The result of action in the collective interest is a "collective good" available to everyone in the relevant group whether he has contributed or not. All else equal, the larger the group, the smaller the share of the gain to the group that goes to an individual trying to produce the collective good, and the less incentive the individual has to act in the group interest. It follows that groups with a common interest will not automatically act to serve that interest, and that if a group is sufficiently large we can be confident that voluntary, self-interested behavior will *not* lead to collective action.

The collective interest of large special interest groups can be served only if there is coercion, such as in a picket line, or some reward apart from the achievement of the collective good, such as social prestige in the group, that is offered in return for the group-oriented action. Collective action is accordingly extremely difficult to organize, and for large groups it is available only to those that can arrange coercion or positive individual incentives for group action. Workers who must enter a given factory or mine may be accessible to coercion, but scattered consumers are not; socially interactive groups may respond to social rewards and pressures, but groups without a common social life cannot. Even when coercion or other selective incentives are potentially available, organizing them for the first time is difficult and requires good leadership and favorable conditions.

The foregoing argument should lead us to expect that no country will have a uniform or symmetrical organization of all its constituent groups; some large groups, such as consumers, taxpayers, the unemployed, and the poor will not be represented by mass organizations. This in turn rules out the possibility that the leaders of all of the major groups in society might bargain together until they agreed on some efficient, growth-oriented policy, and then divide up the gains in a way that left every group better off.

The fact that collective action is problematic leads us to expect that stable societies with given boundaries will accumulate more distributional coalitions as time goes on. Since collective action, especially for large groups, requires favorable conditions, few groups will be able to organize until their time has come, and more of them will be organized the more time has passed.

Most distributional coalitions, whether cartelistic or oriented to the lobbies of power, are harmful on balance to efficiency and growth. One reason is that organizations that try to raise prices or wages through collective action can only do this by restricting entry into the industry or occupation they control, and these barriers to the mobility of resources greatly reduce the speed at which an economy can adapt to changing demands and new technologies. Another is that the special-interest legislation sought by lobbies encourages resources to move into areas in which (though privately profitable) the resources produce less value to society. There are also many other ways in which distributional coalitions are harmful to economic growth, but these are discussed elsewhere and I shall not consider them here.

In a few cases, particularly in Scandinavia and West Germany, a special-interest organization encompasses a substantial proportion of the population or resources of a society. It follows from the same logic that makes small groups easier to organize than large ones, that these organizations will have an incentive to try to maintain the efficiency of the society of which they are a part. Their members will bear a significant share of the losses from any inefficient policies, so their organizations will try to get a large slice of the pie without wasting any in the process.

If what I have said so far is correct, the rapid growth of West Germany, Japan, and Italy since World War II is no longer surprising. Their totalitarian governments did away with most independent organizations, including all of those on the left, and the Allied occupiers finished off those that had been implicated with the defeated regimes. The new organizations that were created after the war were as inclusive as their promoters (often occupation authorities) could make them. Thus special-interest organizations in Germany, Japan, and (to a lesser extent) Italy after World War II were relatively sparse and those that existed were often relatively encompassing.

My argument also helps to explain why France, in spite of the discouragement to long-run investment from the upheavals and invasions it has suffered, should have grown so rapidly in the last couple of decades. Distributional coalitions accumulate in *stable* societies with *given* boundaries. France has not always been stable. There has been time for organizations of the handfuls of big firms in particular industries to form, since small groups are easier to organize than large ones. These business lobbies made France a highly protectionist country that sheltered many inefficient industries, but in *this* respect the society had changing boundaries: the power to set tariffs shifted with the Common Market and this deprived the French trade associations of most of their protection and political power.

We may now ask what society should be at the opposite extreme from those just discussed? What industrial country has had stable freedom of organization and borders that have held fast against invasion for the longest? The answer is so well known it need not even be stated.

Twentieth-century Britain has, moreover, had exactly the slow growth rate that our argument would lead one to expect.

We mustn't draw any conclusions, however, until we see whether the country in question has the historical pattern of economic growth and the powerful pattern of special-interest organizations and collusions that my argument implies. Britain has indeed only gradually become one of the slowest-growth developed countries. It also has the dense and powerful network of special-interest organizations, and these again have accumulated gradually. It is not only the labor unions; think also, for example, of the unique, and cartelistically imposed separation of barristers and solicitors, or of the farmers' union, or of the business organizations or collusions in nearly every industry.

Note that, though Britain had in the eighteenth century a reputation for greater social mobility and a more commercial and entrepreneurial mentality than its continental neighbors, in the twentieth century everyone emphasizes other traits. This apparent shift in the relative degree of class-consciousness and enthusiasm for entrepreneurship has not been adequately explained, but it is precisely what the argument here predicts. Organizations and collusions can only raise prices or wages by restricting the supply and by keeping out other suppliers — that is, through some form of *exclusion*. As we remember, a special-interest organization will be strengthened by the social rewards it can give to those who cooperate and the pressures it can put upon those who do not; these social incentives apply only to those who interact socially, so that the special-interest organization has an incentive to maintain social homogeneity. There are other countervailing forces that have tended to increase social mobility in Britain in recent centuries, but (especially in making historical comparisons with Continental Europe) we must remember that accumulating organizations and collusions can make what looks like a "nation of shopkeepers" into a land of clubs and pubs.

My argument further suggests that older industries in the United States, especially in concentrated industries that are especially susceptible to collusion and cartelization, ought to be growing less rapidly than relatively new industries in which there has been less time for coalitions to develop, such as those built on new technologies. This is in fact the case. Since most manufacturing industries in a country like the United States can move to areas that were settled only in the late nineteenth century, or were disrupted by the American Civil War and the century of racial conflict and instability that followed it, and accordingly have relatively low unionization, we should expect that less union-ized states of the United States are growing more rapidly. They are. As Peter Murrell has shown, Britain has also done relatively badly in old, concentrated industries, at least in comparison with Germany.[2]

Other developed democracies that have relatively long records of stability and immunity from invasion, yet unusually high per capita incomes, tend to have unusually encompassing organizations, or special constitutional restraints which constrain lobbies, and these factors alleviate the institutional sclerosis that has been described.

2   Peter Murrell, "The Comparative Structure of the Growth of the West German and British Manufacturing Industries," in *The Political Economy of Growth*, ed. Dennis C. Mueller (New Haven, Connecticut: Yale University Press, 1983), pp. 109–31.

The fact that my argument is broadly consistent with the growth experience throughout developed democracies since World War II, and with the historical pattern in at least the country that has been industrialized the longest, does *not* however mean that we have achieved a monocausal explanation of economic growth. Reality is awesomely complex and *many* factors are undoubtedly involved.

Even if what I have said so far is found to be compelling, that would not justify one *supposed* policy implication of the theory that is sometimes suggested by those with a taste for superficial wit. This is the alleged implication that unsuccessful wars and violent revolutions every so often are desirable. This makes about as much sense as recommending pestilence or war as a cure for overpopulation: it recognizes the gain, but overlooks even the colossal costs.

The real policy implications of my argument are very different, and indeed will eventually take us back to the role of ideas in societies and the ways in which it might be possible to overcome or get around the obstacles that vested interests place in the way of ideas that would improve a society's performance. But we must first find out why, in the case of Britain in the twentieth century (and, it turns out, in many other societies too), economic ideas do not automatically or straightforwardly keep the vested interests from doing harm. We have to figure out why, in dramatic contrast to Keynes's view, vested interests do a very much better job than the level of economic thought does in explaining the pattern of relative growth rates. In order to see the reasons why Britain's relatively high standing in the history of economic thought has by no means spared it from institutional sclerosis, we need to analyze the single most important factor limiting the diffusion and political potency of better ideas: rational ignorance.

The Rational Ignorance of the Typical Citizen

Consider a typical citizen who is deciding how much time to devote to studying the policies or leadership of his or her country. The more time the citizen devotes to this matter, the greater the likelihood that a vote will be cast in favor of rational policies and good leadership. This typical citizen will, however, get only a small share of the gain from the more effective policies and leadership: in the aggregate, the other residents of the country will get almost all the gains, so that the individual citizen does not have an incentive to devote enough time to fact finding and to thinking about what would be best for the country. Each citizen would be better off if all citizens could be coerced into spending more time finding out how to vote to make the country better serve their common interests.

This point is most dramatically evident in national elections. The gain to a voter from studying issues and candidates until it is clear what vote is truly in his or her interest is given by the difference in the value *to the individual of the "right" election outcome, multiplied by the probability a change in the individual's vote will alter the outcome of the election.* Since the probability that a typical voter will change the outcome of the election is vanishingly small, the typical citizen, whether he is a physician or a taxi driver, is usually rationally ignorant about public affairs.

Sometimes information about public affairs is so interesting or entertaining that acquiring it for these reasons alone pays; this situation appears to be the single most important source of exceptions to the generalization that *typical* citizens are rationally ignorant about public affairs. Similarly, individuals in a few special vocations can receive considerable rewards in private goods if they acquire exceptional knowledge of public goods. Politicians, lobbyists, journalists, and social scientists, for example, may earn more money, power, or prestige from knowledge of public affairs. Occasionally exceptional knowledge of public policy can generate exceptional profits in stock exchanges or other markets. Withal, the typical citizen will usually find that his or her income and life chances will not be improved by the zealous study of public affairs or even of any single collective good.

This fact — that the benefits of individual enlightenment about public goods are usually dispersed throughout a group or nation, rather than concentrated upon the individual who bears the costs of becoming enlightened — explains many other phenomena as well. It explains, for example, the "man bites dog" criterion of what is newsworthy. If the television newscasts were watched or newspapers were read solely to obtain the most important information about public affairs, aberrant events of little public importance would be ignored, and typical patterns of quantitative significance would be emphasized; when the news is, by contrast, for most people largely an alternative to other forms of diversion or entertainment, intriguing oddities and human-interest items are in demand. Similarly, events that unfold in a suspenseful way or sex scandals among public figures are fully covered by the media, whereas the complexities of economic policy or quantitative analyses of public problems receive only minimal attention. Public officials, often able to thrive without giving the citizens good value for their taxes, may fall over an exceptional mistake that is simple and striking enough to be newsworthy. Extravagant statements, picturesque protests, and unruly demonstrations that offend much of the public are also explicable in this way: they make diverting news and thus call attention to interests and arguments that might otherwise be ignored. Even some acts of terrorism that are described as senseless can from this perspective be explained as effective means of obtaining the riveted attention of a public to demands about which they otherwise would remain rationally ignorant.

The rational ignorance of the typical voter is an example of the general logic of collective action. Information about public affairs is for the typical citizen, no matter how well educated he or she may be, normally a public good; any benefits from the better information a typical citizen acquires about public affairs will normally be shared with the whole society, so the typical citizen will get a share of the benefits that is approximately given by the fraction of the country's national income he personally earns, yet he will bear the whole cost of whatever information he obtains about public affairs. Since the logic of collective action has been set out rigorously elsewhere and casually evoked earlier in this paper, no more will be said about it here.

The rational ignorance of the typical citizen that arises out of the logic of collective action suggests that simple ideologies and political slogans will play a gargantuan role in political life. As Anthony Downs has explained, ideologies are substitutes for detailed research and sustained reflection about public affairs.[3] If a citizen subscribes to one of the familiar ideologies, he or she will have some guidance on what to believe. If spending a lot of time doing research on public affairs is not rational for the typical citizen but a left-wing or right-wing ideology can be acquired at little or no cost, then understandably, many people would let ideology play a large role in determining what positions they take in political discussions and in how they will vote. The ideology will indicate, or at least appear to indicate, what general policy or what political party is best for people in one's own category or social class. Clearly most of the votes cast by ordinary citizens are greatly influenced by ideology (or party affiliation, which usually amounts to much the same thing).

To be sure, the rational ignorance of the typical citizen is not the only reason that ideology plays a large role in modern life. This qualification is obvious the moment one notes that some people who are social scientists, journalists, or politicians, and have strong professional incentives to be especially well informed about public affairs, are also highly ideological. Apparently some people have psychological attributes or political incentives that make them highly ideological even when well informed. Although these attributes and incentives will not be examined in this paper, I shall show that they interact with the rational ignorance of the typical citizen to give the familiar ideologies and slogans an extraordinarily large role in modern society.

The Ideologies in the Democracies don't explain Performance

As we all know, the centerpiece of ideological and political debate today is the dispute over the proper role of the government, particularly the extent to which it ought to aid those of slender means. From the right, and especially the classical liberal or *laissez-faire* right, the main argument is that the growth of government intervention impairs economic performance and individual freedom and that overgenerous welfare-state programs for low-income people have reduced the incentive to work and to save. From the left the most common argument is that modern society must not be fearful of using the resources and plans of democratic government to ensure that the society

3   Anthony Downs, *An Economic Theory of Democracy* (New York: Harper and Brothers, 1957).

develops in a desirable direction and particularly to ensure that there is compassionate provision for the needs of those for whom the market does not provide an adequate income.

In view of the preoccupation with the ideological debate, it is surprising how little study has been given to the question of how well each side in the debate succeeds or fails in explaining economic performance in different countries and historical periods. If the right or classical liberal side of the argument is correct, one ought systematically to find that those societies in which the role of the government is the smallest and the redistribution of income in the direction of low-income people is the least were growing the most rapidly and had the highest per capita incomes. Conversely, if the left or the democratic socialistic side of the argument is correct, one ought to find the most impressive economic performance and the highest standard of living, at least for the poor, in the societies in which the role of government is larger and the redistribution of income to the poor presumably more generous. One can also test the familiar ideologies by looking at changes across historical periods, because in different historical periods the role of government, and the extent of income redistribution by government, has differed.

One of the few people to look at the evidence on this central debate of modern democratic societies is David Smith.[4] In a 1975 article in the *National Westminster Bank Review*, he looked at the percentages of the national income or the gross domestic product (GDP) that were used or handled by government in different developed democracies and tested the relation between this variable and the rate of economic growth in the society. What Smith found, as I see it, was only a weak and questionable association. He emphasized that this association was a negative one; those societies with the larger role for the government had a somewhat slower rate of growth. The relation was so fragile, however, that, if one omitted Japan − a special country in many ways − from the statistical test, the relation disappeared. Japan has a smaller public sector and a faster rate of growth than the other major developed democracies, and it was largely responsible for any relation that there was between the role of government and growth.

Using somewhat more recent data, Erich Weede has also found a negative relation between the share of national output taken by government in taxes and the rate of growth of per capita income, but his results are also crucially dependent on Japan.[5] Weede also tests whether a Socialist party in the government or the governing coalition affects the rate of growth, but he finds no statistically significant relation.

In a valuable book, *Theories of Comparative Economic Growth*,[6] Kwang Choi explores whether there is any relationship between the spending and transfer

---

4 David Smith, "Public Consumption and Economic Performance," *National Westminster Bank Review*, 1975.

5 "Democracy, Creeping Socialism, and Ideological Socialism in Rent-Seeking Societies" *Public Choice*, 44: 349−66.

by government and variables such as the rate of economic growth and the level of investment. Choi found no strong relation between the role of government and the rate of economic growth.

One of the few other studies of this issue is an article by Samuel Brittan, the distinguished economic journalist for the *Financial Times*. In 1978 Brittan published an article on the "British disease"[7] in which he argued that one apparently *cannot* explain the surprisingly poor performance of the British economy in terms of the role of the state in Great Britain or the extent of income redistribution to low-income people. When one compares the United Kingdom with its European neighbors, Brittan pointed out, one finds it is not greatly different from the average of the European countries in the proportion of the nation's resources that are consumed by or transferred by government. The percentage of the national income consumed and transferred by government is in fact usually lower in Great Britain than in Holland, Sweden, Norway, and West Germany, but the latter countries have enjoyed a far better postwar economic performance than Great Britain has. This observation alone makes it unlikely that the role of government in Britain is the main explanation for its poor economic performance.

But Brittan brought forth even more persuasive evidence when he looked at the historical pattern in Great Britain. The British economy, he pointed out, began to fall behind the rates of growth of comparable European economies in the last two decades of the nineteenth century. At that time Great Britain and the British Empire had the closest thing to ideal *laissez-faire* government that the world has ever seen. The relatively slow British growth, I would add, continued through the interwar period and became all the more noticeable in the post-World War II period, when the United Kingdom was often under democratic socialistic governments and when the welfare state came into being. So Great Britain has grown relatively slowly under *laissez-faire* governments, moderate conservative governments, and labor or democratic socialistic governments alike.

To make the lack of any relation between the rate of economic growth, on the one hand, and the extent of government spending and transfers, on the other, visually clear, figure 1 has been prepared. In figure 1 the average annual rates of growth of per capita income from 1950 to 1979 are measured along the vertical axis and the average percentages of GDP used for government expenditures plus transfers in 1955, 1965, and 1975 are shown on the horizontal axis. Since the concern in this paper is only with developed democratic countries that are relevant to the debates in Great Britain, the countries included in the figure are those of the member nations of the Organization for Economic Cooperation and Development (OECD) for which the needed data

---

6   Kwang Choi, *Theories of Comparative Economic Growth* (Ames, Iowa: Iowa State University Press, 1983).
7   Samuel Brittan, "How British is the British Sickness?" *Journal of Law and Economics*, vol. 21 (October 1978), pp. 245–68.

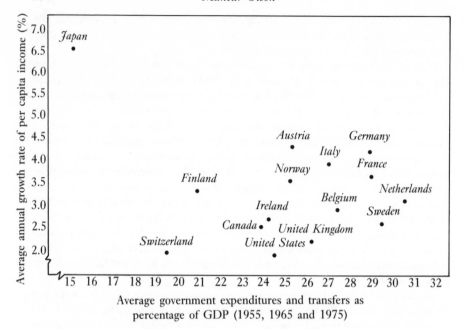

Figure 1   Economic growth and government spending and transfers, 1950–1979

Source: OECD National Accounts Statistics and OECD Economic Outlook, Historical
Statistics, 1988

are available. The figure makes it obvious that, except for Japan, there is no clear relation between the extent of government spending and transfers and the rate of growth. The level of government spending and transfers may, of course, have an effect on the rate of growth that has been obscured by other factors. I expect that the role of government does in fact have some effect on the rate of economic growth. Yet the evidence suggests any relation is not nearly so strong as one might expect from the overwhelming ideological preoccupation with the role of government and the welfare state.

I will now take a historical perspective, and ask in what historical periods economic growth has been most impressive, and then note what the role of the government and the extent of income redistribution has been in each of these historical periods.

   If one goes back to the nineteenth century, one finds that to a great extent in Great Britain, to some extent in the United States, and to a lesser extent in continental Europe, *laissez-faire* policies prevailed. Great Britain and its huge empire had not only *laissez faire* in domestic policy but also free trade. Apart from large subsidies to the railroads, the United States had something approaching *laissez faire* internally, though it certainly did not have free trade, and neither did several of the countries of continental Europe. Yet the world as a whole in the nineteenth century came closer to *laissez faire* and free trade than it has at any other time. The nineteenth century was also a period of impressive economic performance. So this piece of evidence, taken by itself, would argue on the side of the conservative or classical liberal argument that one should limit the role of the state and be wary of the adverse effect on the incentives to work and save of redistribution to those with lower incomes.

The interwar period was quite different. Though the period between World War I and World War II did not really see the establishment of the complete welfare state – in general, that occurred only after World War II – it was still distinguished from the period before World War I by an incomparably higher level of protectionism and economic nationalism. Protectionism and high tariffs were the most striking feature of the economic history of the interwar period; even the British Empire abandoned free trade. Now, as one knows, the interwar period was a time of poor economic performance and above all of the Great Depression.

Admittedly, different things happened in different countries, and I am perhaps being too aggregative and casual in talking about the interwar period in general. So let me switch for a moment to one country, the United States. Developments in that country were perhaps a little simpler and easier to describe than in other countries and at the same time instructive in this context.

In the United States in the 1920s the government, with the presidencies of Harding, Coolidge, and Hoover, was conservative and pro-business. Not only were these presidents conservative Republicans, but they also wanted to keep the role of the government and the transfers to the poor at a minimal level. At the same time, they supported extremely high levels of protection; the Fordney-Macomber tariffs were imposed and finally the colossally protective Smoot-Hawley tariff that passed just as the Great Depression set in. The American economy did fairly well under Harding and Coolidge and in the first months of Hoover's administration.

Then the deepest depression that the United States – indeed that the entire world – had ever seen, began. So a substantial period of conservative and pro-business (though protectionist) government ended in a catastrophic depression. This deepest of all depressions was not really cured, though it was somewhat ameliorated, under the New Deal administration of Franklin Roosevelt; only with World War II did the American economy fully recover.

Now I turn to the period from the end of World War II until about 1970. Two facts about this period of economic history stand out above all others. First, in all of the major developed democracies, the welfare state reached its full development, and the government came to handle a significant proportion of the national income. Second, all of the major developed democracies grew more rapidly than they had ever grown before. Some – like Germany, Japan,

and Italy − grew with incredible speed; but even the slowest-growing of these
countries, such as Great Britain and the United States, grew more rapidly
than ever before. So the welfare state, on the one hand, and unprecedentedly
rapid economic growth, on the other hand, came to the major developed
economies of the West at essentially the same time. The postwar period
showed the greatest increase in the peacetime role of the government, the
greatest level of income redistribution to the poor, and the most rapid
economic growth the world has known.

So, one must ask, was there a causal connection between large governments
and the welfare state and rapid economic growth? It would seem so, but this
observation does not fit with the experience of the nineteenth century; nor,
indeed, does it fit with the experience of the 1970s or the present, when the
welfare state in most developed democracies has become still larger and the
economic performance has usually turned sour. At first the welfare state and
big government were accompanied by rapid economic growth, but later in the
1970s and in the present they have been accompanied by poor economic
performance.

The reader may now say that the question I have raised is such a large one,
and the amount of relevant evidence so colossal, that one cannot draw any
conclusions without going into the matter in far, far more detail. I think,
nonetheless, that perhaps the detached reader will agree that no clear picture
emerges from a beginning study of the evidence about the role of the state on
the one hand and the rate of economic growth on the other. Given the almost
universal preoccupation with the role of the government and the extent of
income redistribution to low-income people, one would expect that, if either
side of the ideological debate had got the matter right, there ought to be really
clear and conspicuous evidence of an association one way or the other. Given
the widespread interest in the issue, one would expect that someone would
have shown a compelling association between the role of government and the
rate of growth, but (to the best of my knowledge) no one has. If the political
choices of most people are guided in large part by ideologies that focus on
what the role of government ought to be, one would suppose that those strong
convictions rested on clear and unambiguous findings about the role of the
state and economic performance. That clear and conspicuous evidence,
however, is not there.

There is the possibility that the size and ideology of governments have a
strong impact on the standards of living or low-income people, even if they
have no clear effect on the rate of economic growth or the level of per capita
income. Since there are generally fewer data on the standards of living of
relatively low-income people than on rates of economic growth, one must be
extremely cautious in drawing any conclusions about any connection between
the size or ideology of governments and the standard of living of relatively
low-income people. So far as one can tell from the available studies, however,
there is no strong evidence, if any at all, that the ideology or size of government is
related to the standard of living of relatively poor people.[8]

The Argument Thus Far

We started with Keynes's ringing affirmation of the overwhelming importance of ideas as compared with vested interests. Great Britain in the twentieth century has not, however, offered much support for Keynes's view: the country has been a leader, and for much of the century the indisputable leader, in economic thinking, yet over the course of the century fallen well behind comparable countries in its level of per capita income. An explanation of the British disease in terms of organized interests, on the other hand, fits the facts in Britain as in most other places quite well.

One reason for the failure of ideas to have more impact on outcomes is that the citizen (unless he is a professional student or practitioner of public affairs) does not have an incentive to incur significant costs to find out what economic policies and institutions would yield the best performance. The typical citizen in the developed democracies accordingly usually accepts one or the other of the familiar ideologies as an inexpensive guide about what to believe in and vote for. Neither of these ideologies has with any regularity produced policies that bring superior economic performance and there is no strong and stable association between the ideology of governments in the developed democracies and their economic performance.

Though advances in economic knowledge may on some occasions (such as Britain in the mid-nineteenth century) be translated into superior policies through popular ideology, there is no strong or regular tendency for this to happen. If the argument about collective action and institutional sclerosis evoked earlier in this paper is correct, the familiar ideologies even do considerable damage by encouraging people to focus excessively on the role of the state instead of on the collusion and cartelization that are often the most important obstacle to competitive markets and on the lobbying that is the main ultimate source of most mischievous governmental intervention.[9] Thus in the developed democracies the victory of one of the familiar ideologies over the other would not normally be sufficient by itself to eliminate institutional sclerosis.

---

8 Many of the relevant studies on the relation or lack of relation between the ideology of governments and the distribution of income are summarized in Erich Weede, "The Effects of Democracy and Socialist Strength on the Size and Distribution of Income," *International Journal of Comparative Sociology*, vol. 23, no. 3–4 (1982), pp. 151–65. See also Simon Kuznets, *Modern Economic Growth: Rate, Structure, and Spread* (New Haven, Conn.: Yale University Press, 1966); Malcolm Sawyer, "Income Distribution in the OECD Countries," OECD Occasional Studies (July 1976); Economic and Scientific Research Foundation, *Trends in Income Distribution: A Comparative Study* (New Delhi).

9 On this, see my "Ideology and Economic Growth" in *The Legacy of Reaganomics: Prospects for Long-Term Growth*, eds Charles R. Hulten and Isabelle V. Sawhill (Washington, D.C.: The Urban Institute: 1984, pp. 229–52).

We seem to be left, on both theoretical and empirical grounds, with the expectation that vested interests will normally prevail and that better ideas will have only a marginal impact on social outcomes. This expectation is not, however, in accord with the common-sense notion that ideas can sometimes make a big difference. It also is inconsistent with my claim, in *The Rise and Decline of Nations* and earlier in this paper, that the antidote for institutional sclerosis is a better understanding. Thus we must now search for openings through which better ideas can change the choices of societies.

The Conquered Domain, the Frontier, and the Stalemate

There is no doubt that the ideas of one great nineteenth-century economist, Karl Marx, have had a decisive influence on the pattern of institutions and policies in the Soviet Union and in other communist states. Here organized vested interests did *not* keep Marx's ideas, as developed by Lenin and Stalin, from having a decisive influence. This experience suggests one general route by which ideas triumph. There were vested interests, such as those of the Russian Tsars, nobility, army, and officialdom, that long resisted the advance of Marxism in Russia, but the superior German forces in World War I eliminated the power behind the Russian establishment (and gave Lenin a train passage through Germany to St Petersburg as well). The vested interests of Imperial Russia were so badly devastated that they could be done in by the not-very-well-organized forces of the liberal revolution of early 1917.

It was part of Lenin's genius that he realized this and (unlike the other Bolsheviks) sensed that the modern, democratic, and popular attributes of the liberal government did not much affect the prospects of an uprising by a minute minority, but that its not-yet-organized or unconsolidated character did. To the extent that one may summarize a complex historical event in a sentence, it was the prior destruction of organized interests and the paucity of well organized or established opposition that enabled Marxist-Leninist ideas to exert an overwhelming influence on social outcomes. (The ideas of Soviet reformers today about the advantages of decentralization and democracy confront, by contrast, a long-established opposition.) The general point is that, when devastation does in organized interests, any ideas the conqueror has about what is to be done can exert an overwhelming influence.

Another class of cases where ideas have surely had a decisive role is evident from a comparison of the countries that were once colonies of Spanish settlement with those springing from British settlement. The nations of Spanish-speaking America are systematically as well as drastically different from Australia, Canada, New Zealand, and the United States. Though Latin America was once prized much above any areas of British settlement, the Latin American countries now have per capita incomes that are only a fraction of those in the countries that were initially settled by the British. The extent and durability of democratic institutions has also been markedly less in the areas of Hispanic settlement. All sides agree that the prevalent ideas about political institutions and economic policies in most of these countries have all along been greatly different from those in the countries that were initially British colonial settlements. There is also general agreement that the great difference in civic cultures across the two sets of countries can be traced in part to the differences between England and Spain at the times the initial settlers colonized the countries in question.

I hypothesize that the fact that both sets of colonists moved to frontiers without vested interests or established organizations that could withstand or significantly influence the settlers was important in explaining the influence of the ideas or prejudices of the initial settlers. To be sure, many other factors were also very important, but there were so many separate British colonies (e.g., 13 in what became the United States) and so many countries that grew out of the old Spanish domain, and the marks of the preconceptions of those who initially migrated have been so conspicuous, that it is hard to resist the conclusion that there could not have been much organized resistance to the implementation of the beliefs of the original settlers about what institutions and policies should prevail.

The differences in popular beliefs in Britain and Spain in the centuries of colonization obviously need a separate explanation. I am not competent to compare the histories of Britain and Spain in the necessary detail and must defer to the relevant specialists. For the sake of theoretical closure, I shall nonetheless set out an uneducated and unoriginal hunch. In Spain, the unequivocal power that the accidents of history had given the Habsburgs and the conformity of their Catholicism with that of their Spanish subjects implied that civil order was readily obtained through uniformity and hierarchical control. In Britain, by contrast, especially in the seventeenth century, there was a great deal of religious (and other) diversity in the population. The monarchy, moreover, was not always perceived as entirely in keeping with even the protestantism that was the one common denominator to most of this diversity. The English initially were not at all tolerant or liberal about these differences and there was intense disagreement and even a civil war.

Without putting too fine a point on it, one might surmise that the diverse forces were not over the long run so greatly different in strength and that with the passage of time it became increasingly plausible that imposing religious uniformity or unqualified central monarchical control on the country would be, at best, very costly. Very loosely, there was a stalemate that made acceptance of some degree of pluralism, some grudging religious toleration, and some checks on royal absolutism the most practical solution for each of the powerful interests: the ideas of Locke rather than Hobbes were favored by the stalemate. Liberal or pluralist ideas were at least more nearly compatible with British than with Spanish realities. When there is no good alternative to living with diversity and pluralism, people get used to it, and ultimately perhaps a few see some gains from trade and other interaction among those with differences. There is then an inspiration or constituency for arguments of a Smithian kind as well.

So it appears that a balance of power or stalemate among the organized interests can leave an opening for new ideas. When the different organized powers or interests more or less offset one another, ideas may make a big difference, especially if they help the contending interests or powers get out of a tight spot.

Even when vested interests are not done in by force, and there is no unorganized frontier, and also no stalemate of offsetting interests, ideas can sometimes win. We turn now to an avenue by which better ideas can influence public policy even in sclerotic environments.

The Innocence of Masses and of Elites

In Great Britain and all of the other English-speaking countries the collusions and cartels that operate in the market and the lobbies that operate in the polity are uniformly small in relation to the whole society. In some cases an organization will have a membership in the hundreds of thousands or even of a million or more, but all such organizations are small in relationship to the whole society. Normally, organizations for collective action represent less than one percent of the population and also of the income-earning capacity of the society. When, as in Austria, Norway, Sweden, and (to some extent) in Germany, individual organizations for collective action encompass a large part of the income-earning capacity of the society, this will at least temporarily or episodically[10] make them mindful of the deadweight losses from their actions, since their membership will bear a large part of this loss. Thus the problem of societies losing their efficiency and dynamism through collusions and organizations for collective action is mainly a problem of *tiny* minorities exploiting the society at large. The minorities are tiny both in relationship to the population of the society and also in relation to its wealth. If a group, even if few in numbers, owned most of the tangible capital in a country, it would use any organized power it had in ways consistent with the prosperity of the society, since its own members would encompass enough of the society's income-earning capacity to give them an incentive to choose socially-efficient policies.

In any given case of market combination or of special-interest lobbying, then, the problem is that a tiny minority, both in terms of voting power and of wealth, rips off the rest of the society in ways that reduce the efficiency and dynamism of the society. The vast majority of losers have incomparably more muscle-power, voting-power, and wealth than those who are ripping them off. If the victims of distributional coalitions had even a faint idea what was really going on, they would easily put a stop to it. They lose only because of their rational ignorance and the shortcomings of the ideologies they accordingly rely on. They may have been persuaded by the propaganda of the organized

10 See Mancur Olson, "A Theory of the Incentives Facing Political Organizations: Neo-Corporatism and the Hegemonic State," *International Political Science Review*, vol. 7, no. 2, April 1986, pp. 165–89.

interests that only qualified solicitors should be allowed to convey real property, that only barristers should be allowed to try cases in court, that it hurts workers to allow the stores to be open any hour of the day or night, that strong unions help the unemployed, that farmers must be subsidized now to prevent starvation during wartime, and so on. But if they had not been propagandized they would have different views.

Since minute minorities are the source of the problem, it follows that they will be easily and quickly defeated if rational ignorance should be overcome. The minority that is the source of the problem in any given case is, moreover, so tiny that it will normally be outnumbered if even an elite of two or three percent — or often even less — of the population comes to understand the problem. Thus there is reason to hope that on occasion socially useful ideas can triumph simply because their opposition, though organized, is weak.

Of course, all the tiny minorities add up to a majority and then some. But this is not a serious problem: in any society with narrow distributional coalitions, the members of each distributional coalition lose from the redistributions in favor of each of the other distributional coalitions and the inefficiencies and obstacles to innovation that attend these redistributions. Though rational ignorance shows up here too, it is nonetheless easy to find examples of distributional coalitions that try to counter the deadweight losses from some other distributional coalitions. One example is provided by the American Medical Association, which has taken an official stand against cartelization and restriction of entry by medical technicians and nurses. The fact that the AMA's preference for free entry and competition was not impartially applied to physicians themselves not only adds charm to the example, but also illustrates both the problem of institutional sclerosis and the possibility of getting a cure.[11]

Since any distributional coalition that systematically generates large social losses on any single issue or in any single market represents only a minuscule minority, any large random sample of the society's population will be composed mainly or totally of people who are *not* a part of *this* distributional coalition, even though they will often belong to some other distributional coalition. In this, they will be rather like a typical jury or judge. When a jury or judge is chosen, the jurors and the judge are unlikely to be relatives or friends of either the defendant or the prosecutor. If they are, there is a social consensus (as well as laws) that no juror or judge should be a relative or friend of any party to the case in question. Thus societies have for a long time been able to provide reasonably detached and impartial judges and juries for most court cases.

---

11 Unfortunately, a situation where all groups are organized and the depredations and efficiency losses from each coalition are resisted by another never arises (Mancur Olson, *The Rise and Decline of Nations* (New Haven and London: Yale University Press, 1982), Implication 1, pp. 37–8), because some large groups have no access to selective incentives and can never organize.

With this legal parallel in mind, let us now look at the journalists, politicians, economists, sociologists, political scientists, civil servants, and others with an occupational interest in public affairs. The typical person in any of these lines of work is likely to be as self-interested (and probably as unsuccessful in taking a detached view of this self-interest in disputes and debates about public policy) as a businessman or factory worker. People in these lines of work may very well also be typical members of aggressive distributional coalitions; the journalist or the academic, for example, may well belong to a lobbying group or a union for journalists or for academics. In general, society will lose as much from the operation of these coalitions as from those for other groups in the population.

But those professionals who are rewarded professionally for being informed about one aspect or another of public affairs, and who are (at least in some specialized area of the society's interest) therefore *not* rationally ignorant, *will be relatively impartial about the claims and activities of most distributional coalitions other than their own, and about most public issues that do not relate in a singular way to their own occupation.* Since these individuals normally have no important personal stake on most issues, they are usually motivated in large part by some broad public interest; their situations are much the same as those of jurors or judges. It would be going much too far, of course, to claim that a professional interest in public affairs prevents ideological bias. But most such biases grow out of one or the other of the familiar ideologies; the partisans of one ideology are largely countervailed by the adherents of the other, and expert opinion in the aggregate is surely influenced by evidence and argument.

Thus there are substantial numbers of individuals that, on most important public issues, have some incentive to be informed and are also relatively public spirited, or at least partial only to some relatively innocuous encompassing interest. It is in large part through such individuals that better ideas about economics and public policy can, and sometimes do, influence public policy. Some of the journalists write editorials, for example.

Though a few of the voters that read these editorials may cast their votes to serve some narrow vested interest, the average election is not mainly about any one narrow coalition's special interest. Thus most voters most of the time, although rationally ignorant, are motivated mainly by public spirit, or by relatively harmless encompassing purposes like favoring their own class. The masses, like the elites, are mainly innocent.

Similarly, to the extent a country has a two-party system (as Britain has more or less had most of the time) and reasonably disciplined victory-seeking parties (as Britain usually has), the party leaders are also individuals who have an incentive to get good information and *an encompassing interest.* A political party leader in a country with a first-past-the-post-wins electoral system has an incentive to represent at least a plurality of the society and this plurality of voters is an encompassing interest. So encompassing political parties not only have relatively constructive incentives, but they also have (at least when they are running the country) an incentive to gather information on what will work, so that they can run for re-election on a you-never-had-it-so-good record. Thus the leaders of encompassing political parties (or, more probably, their advisors) are people through whom better ideas can influence social outcomes.

Evidence of the Impact of Ideas in Sclerotic Environments

Keynes's *General Theory* undoubtedly had a large impact in Britain, the United States, and some other relatively sclerotic countries within about a quarter century of its publication. The Kennedy tax cuts were beyond any doubt mainly a result of Keynes's ideas. When major ideas change important outcomes in a democratic society, it is by changing respectable opinion on both sides of the political spectrum. Thus Richard Nixon, when President, said "We are all Keynesians now." In the last couple of decades non-Keynesian thinking has partially supplanted Keynesian macroeconomics. Though it is popularly called anti-Keynesian, much of this thinking has been so profoundly affected by the technical advances in economics in the last half century that it would better have been described as "post-Keynesian" macroeconomics. This newer macroeconomic theory has also sometimes had an impact on policy, again with a considerable (though perhaps shortening) interval between the development of ideas and their influence on policy. Again the impact shows up across the political spectrum; a Democratic president might well say that "we have all outgrown 1960s Keynesianism now." It is pretty clear that the mechanism by which these macroeconomic theories affected public policy is very much like the one predicted by my argument here. Some other less well-known examples in which the same mechanism operated could be cited, but it is, alas, far easier to cite cases in which organized interests triumph.

It will be interesting to see how the opposing forces of narrow organized interests, on the one hand, and ideas about public policy motivated by encompassing or public-spirited interests, on the other, work out in the future. If the latter force does not sooner or later become more important than the former, the future is pretty bleak. If the process of sclerosis is not checked, which country will suffer most or succumb soonest? If the aggregate evidence of the twentieth century is any guide, Great Britain could easily be the first country to be borne by this sad wave of the future into catastrophic storms. The familiar ideologies have about as much influence in Britain as elsewhere, and probably this is a bad omen. Yet, given Britain's high achievements in economic and political thought, its encompassing political parties, and the longer time the country has had to observe distributional coalitions, it could also *easily* be the *first* country to solve this problem. The tides of technological advance would then, I believe, raise it above other countries in wealth and social performance. There is no telling what will happen, but the country will surely be an important one to watch.

6

Will the United States Decline as did Britain?

John A. Hall

Determining whether the United States is going to decline as did Britain has clearly become one of the questions of the age, with the presumption in the United States distinctively being that the answer is going to be positive. Thus Paul Kennedy's *The Rise and Fall of the Great Powers* lends itself to this interpretation, despite many cautionary words of the author.[1] Similarly, the first 1988 issue of the trade journal of American international political economists, *International Organisation*, has several articles whose analyses take for granted that American hegemonic decline has already occurred. If this is believed, it is likely to affect policy in a dramatic manner.

One broad thrust of this paper is sceptical of the claim that the United States will decline as did Britain. Two points are made against the Cassandras of decline. First, the extent of American decline tends to be exaggerated. A few others have seen this,[2] but it is noticeable that their arguments have failed to dent the self-confidence (no lesser word will do) of what the *New York Times* refers to as 'the school of decline'.[3] If evidence of American power is adduced, the characteristic reply tends to be that this does not really weigh much against what is considered to be a long-term secular trend: the United States may merely be at the stage of Britain in, say, 1880 rather than 1931 – what is held to matter is that worse is sure to come. My second point may help to resolve this stand-off in debate. Extremely forceful, if banal, considerations

---

1 P. Kennedy, *The Rise and Fall of the Great Powers* (New York: Random House, 1987).
2 B. Russett, 'The Mysterious Case of Vanishing Hegemony; or, Is Mark Twain Really Dead?', *International Organisation*, vol. 39 (1985); S. Strange, *Casino Capitalism* (Oxford: Basil Blackwell, 1986); S. Strange, 'The Persistent Myth of Lost Hegemony', *International Organisation*, vol. 41 (1987).
3 P. Schmeisser, 'Is America in Decline?', *New York Times*, 17 April 1988.

suggest that the world polity facing the United States now is nothing like that which faced Britain at the end of the nineteenth century. The differences, moreover, are systematically to the advantage of the United States; in consequence, it is extremely unlikely that it will lose pre-eminence so completely as did Britain. These points can be encapsulated by saying that the analogy, whether implicit or explicit, between the undoubted decline of Britain and the contemporary situation of the United States is of limited usefulness.

But there is another side to my general argument. To stress fundamental differences is not to dispute that there has been some decline in the position of the United States, nor would it be sensible to deny that it might go further. Different processes of decline are identified, with especial focus being given to the situation of 'hegemonic leaders'. More particular and detailed attention still is devoted to the ways in which adherence to certain aspects of liberalism accounts for decline. An implication of this last point deserves highlighting. It may well be that hegemonic leadership in capitalist society needs to adhere to the liberalism's insistence on the virtues of free trade, but there is no reason to believe that the Anglo-Saxon preference for well developed equity markets and for limiting state power should be seen as dictated by, or necessary to, hegemonic rule. In general, it will be maintained that the causes of the decline of the contemporary United States do resemble those recognizable from the British case. The processes identified are *not* those considered important by the most significant theory asserting 'hegemonic decline'; some credence is lent instead to the view that the particular nature of Anglo-Saxon liberalism is of importance in explaining decline.

Drawing up a balance sheet about the extent of American decline is a difficult task, but it is undertaken in the conclusion; this is a necessary preliminary to the final answer to the question posed. But first we must immediately consider different theories of decline, and certain implications which they raise; we can then analyse the British and American cases in turn.

Theories of Decline, Modern and Classical

We can start to gain some grasp of the nature of decline as an analytic category by noting and then commenting on three general causes of decline usefully identified by Mann.[4] First, economically powerful nation states which swim inside the sea of capitalist society are prone to suffer decline as the practices which account for their ascendancy diffuse throughout the larger society. Secondly, leading states tend to decline as the result of geopolitics, either because of over-extension or because of actual participation in war. Finally, societies tend to institutionalize the moments of their success, and thereby make it difficult to be as endlessly flexible as the demands of capitalist

4 J. M. Mann, *States, War and Capitalism* (Oxford: Basil Blackwell, 1988).

society necessitate; differently put, distributional coalitions are created which make social adaptation difficult.[5]

The most obvious comment needing to be made about these categories is that decline is seen as having two sources, either internal or external. The diffusion of practices throughout capitalist society is thus a more or less inevitable external cause of decline given that comparative advantage in general and the advantages of backwardness in particular have always allowed developing states faster growth paths than those of mature economies; in the same spirit, it must be said very clearly that some decline in the position of the United States in the last half century was made inevitable through the recovery of key economic competitors from a situation of considerable internal destruction – a recovery that the United States actively sought, largely for geopolitical reasons. Geopolitics can be as much a force affecting states from the outside, as when heavy expenditure for defence is made necessary by the presence of a ruthless, aggressive and powerful competitor; equally, however, it can be ascribed to internal factors, as when a rash elite foolishly and unnecessarily over-extends commitments. Social blockages, of course, are by definition to be considered entirely an internal matter. A more subtle point follows from this. Decline has two connotations which need to be clearly distinguished. On the one hand, decline is normal and inevitable, the result, as noted, of factors beyond the power of any single nation state. On the other hand, decline is seen as being linked to degeneracy and corruption; here the implication is of failure to do as well as one could. In consequence, we can say that the key question about recent British history is not relative decline *per se*, but the fact that this relative decline was so steep – becoming in fact absolute between 1979 and 1984.

All that has been said to this point refers to the decline of nation states in general. Let us now turn to an important recent theory – in order to advance an argument rather than to add, at least at this stage, to the history of ideas – that adds a further element to the picture. The theory in question has usefully been dubbed 'hegemonic stability theory', and it has gained general intellectual ascendancy in explaining the fateful careers of Britain and the United States.[6] The most obvious tenet of the theory is that the stability of capitalist society as a whole depends upon the presence of a leading power prepared to exercise hegemony – a term with rather different connotations, to be noted in due course – so that certain public goods can be assured. For Kindleberger the

5 Cf. M. Olson, *The Rise and Decline of Nations* (New Haven, Connecticut: Yale University Press, 1982).

6 R. Gilpin, 'Economic Interdependence and National Security in Historical Perspective', in K. Knorr and F. Trager, eds, *Economic Issues and National Security* (Lawrence, Kansas: Regents Press, 1977); R. Gilpin, *War and Change in World Politics* (New York: Cambridge University Press, 1981); R. Gilpin, *The Political Economy of International Relations* (Princeton, New Jersey: Princeton University Press, 1987).

most important such goods are a stable medium of exchange, the insistence on free trade, the export of capital for development and the ability to absorb world surplus capacity.[7] The cogency of this claim seems much reinforced by considering the other side of the coin. The absence of a single hegemon – before 1914 when Imperial Germany challenged Britain, and in the inter war vacuum when the latter was too weak and the United States unwilling to provide leadership – is held to have contributed to chaos, and then to war. All this is striking, if somewhat tautologous, and much of it has been accepted even by critics of hegemonic stability theory. Thus a liberal institutionalist such as Keohane,[8] whose somewhat implausible argument – derived, it should be noted, far more from theory than from evidence – is that co-operation between leading capitalist powers is possible in the absence of a hegemon, also fears the wars that can result from the way in which changes in relative national economic power affect the conduct of states; it is simply his prescription for world order that differs. In passing, however, it is worth noting that a genuinely radical critique, that of George Liska, is available.[9] He argues that war tends to result when a balance of power is disrupted by a single state, notably Britain in the nineteenth century, which gains too much power and thereby calls forth no-holds-barred rivalries. Interestingly, a follower of Liska, David Calleo,[10] has been led by the logic of this theory to resist frequent cries to prop up failing hegemonic power; it would instead be better to knock the hegemon off its perch as quickly as possible so that we can return to normal balance of power politics.

This paper is not centrally concerned with these key elements of hegemonic stability theory. Concentration is instead on the claim, not always spelt out clearly in the literature but distinctively a part of current political debate, that hegemonic power is necessarily self-liquidating, that leadership is such as to sap the strength of the power that provides it. Two key examples of this process are often given. First, hegemonic powers often allow industrializing states to protect their infant industries whilst continuing to offer access to their own rich and well-developed markets.[11] In the long run, this lack of genuine multilateralism undermines the hegemon's domestic industry, a claim made most strikingly by Representative Richard Gephardt in the US presidential campaign of 1988. A second service that the hegemon is seen as providing is that of defence against common enemies. Here too the hegemon is held to suffer as the result of carrying a disproportionate share of the

---

7 C. Kindleberger, *The World in Depression* (Berkeley, California: University of California Press, 1973).

8 R. Keohane, *After Hegemony* (Princeton, New Jersey: Princeton University Press, 1984).

9 G. Liska, 'Empire by Invitation?', *Journal of Peace Research*, vol. 23 (1968).

10 D. Calleo, *Beyond Hegemony* (New York: Basic Books, 1987).

11 S. Krasner, *Asymmetries in Japanese–American Trade* (Berkeley, California: Institute of International Studies, 1987).

burden; Olson and Zeckhauser[12] are typical here in using the language of collective goods theory in claiming that it is in the rational interest of smaller states to free ride on their leader. The economic consequences of this are held to be catastrophic. Thus, William Grieder[13] is a characteristic voice in claiming that the United States spends a much larger share of GNP on defence than its main trading partners, the presumption being that this plays a major part in explaining differential growth rates within capitalist society. The most discussed example here is NATO, perhaps curiously given that the situation of Japan makes the case much better. But in either case, the analysis results in calls for a renewed round of 'burden-sharing' negotiations.

All these theories consider that there are economic and geopolitical dimensions of both the rise to and decline from preeminence, as well as complex interrelations between them; I shall follow their lead. What is less obvious and so more in need of underlining is the implicit moral claim of the thesis that hegemonic power is necessarily self-liquidating. Jean-Paul Sartre famously declared that 'hell is other people'. Hegemonic stability theory implies that decline is 'other people'. The hegemon slaves away in the long-term general interest, but other states, selfishly thinking only of their own short-term goals, slowly undermine what is in fact the very source of their own prosperity. Thank goodness that virtue is its own reward! Sustained scepticism about this claim will return us to alternate theories of decline made forcefully aware of their very different moral flavour. Whilst it is very important indeed to recognize that key elite members as well as large sections of public opinion of hegemonic powers do sometimes see themselves in Durkheimian terms as providers of norms and services for the larger society, it is crucial to remember the view from below. Let us recall the comment of the British general Calgacus which Tacitus records in *The Agricola*: 'To plunder, steal, rape, these things they falsely call imperial rule; they make desolation and call it peace.'[14] Words quite as strong have been directed against the British and the American desire for open markets. Although openness is, according to liberal theory, designed to benefit all, the worm's eye view, especially as formulated by Alexander Hamilton and his German disciple Friedrich List, naturally leads to charges of hypocrisy – for some are more equal than others, and economically advanced nations in capitalist society naturally favour openness when they have the capacity to make the most of it.[15] This general point gains further

12 M. Olson and R. Zeckhauser, 'An Economic Theory of Alliances', *Review of Economics and Statistics*, vol. 46 (1968).
13 W. Grieder, 'Why Can't Our Allies Defend Themselves?', *Rolling Stone*, 16 June 1988.
14 My attention was drawn to this reference by my friend David Spiro.
15 W. M. Earle, 'Adam Smith, Alexander Hamilton, Friedrich List: The Economic Foundations of Military Power', in W. M. Earle, ed., *Masters of Modern Strategy: Military Thought from Machiavelli to Hitler* (Princeton, New Jersey: Princeton University Press, 1943).

salience once we remember the way in which leading powers tend to behave when they consider their power to be diminishing. Thus the United States has chosen to run a budget deficit nearly every year in the last quarter century – that is, it has broken the norms which its agency, the IMF, has so rigorously imposed on other states. This raises the analytic possibility that it is the hegemon which might choose to free ride on the system, that is, to use its undoubted muscle to extract systematic advantage from smaller and weaker powers. Still more important is the fact that those tasks judged to be common by the United States are often seen in an entirely different light by its allies, as evidenced by European members of NATO refusing to accept 'out of area' tasks, to the evident anger of the United States.

This sceptical note amounts to saying that a hegemon is not necessarily a neutral norm-giver akin to the Latin Christian church in the early European middle ages, as portrayed by Michael Mann.[16] On the contrary, a hegemon is a great power. Putting things like this makes it possible to contrast theories of decline which blame others with theories which blame the great powers themselves. We have seen that one such theory, present in the works of Polybius, Machiavelli, Gibbon and Montesquieu, concentrates on the way in which arrogance can lead to disastrous geopolitical over-extension. The rise of a great power is held to result from its having occupied a marcher position, a factor often linked to military prowess; decline results from over-extension which brings with it the costs of two-front wars and of the repression of nationalities.[17] Decline is the result of the great power mistakenly over-extending itself in a way that entails ruin, both geopolitically and economically. The other theory of this type, as noted, stresses the diffusion of practices throughout capitalist society. Adam Smith insisted against his friend David Hume that there was no inevitable reason why a rich country should not continue to stay rich; rather by moving up the technological ladder it would serve the general interest in allowing new states to take over old industries.[18] But this would only be possible, Smith asserted, as long as there were no 'errors of policy', that is, no governmental policies which allowed the institutional arrangements of one moment to gel and petrify. If Smith's theory had much to be said in its favour, it proved nonetheless to be a poor guide to practice. The very notion of society involves 'gelling' of expectations and institutions, as Polanyi famously stressed,[19] and no nation state within capitalist

16 J. M. Mann, *Sources of Social Power*, vol. I, *From the Beginning to 1760 AD* (New York: Cambridge University Press, 1986).

17 R. Collins, *Weberian Sociological Theory* (New York: Cambridge University Press, 1986).

18 I. Hont, 'The "rich country–poor country" debate in classical Scottish political economy', in I. Hont and M. Ignatieff, eds, *Wealth and Virtue* (Cambridge: Cambridge University Press, 1983).

19 K. Polanyi, *The Great Transformation* (Boston, Massachusetts: Beacon Press, 1944).

society has as yet been able to perpetuate the moments of its success. It is
worth noting how very difficult it is to imagine this happening. The rise to
power is often associated with the possession of a particular manufacture.
However, it is possible, as Gershenkron,[20] following Veblen, noted some time
ago, for an industrializing state either to copy the technology without accepting
various institutional limitations and social achievements, or to pioneer a new
technology that is closed off to the leading power because of that institutional
mix; both factors contribute to making the growth path of rapidly industrializing countries faster than that of the leading power. In addition, the leading
power tends, in its senescence, to export the capital its prior industrial success
had created; this necessitates export-led industrialization on the part of developing societies; however, such exports to repay loans are likely to undermine
the domestic industry of the leading power. All this can be summarized by
saying that hegemonic stability theory tends to assume that their place in the
world would have been assured except for the burdens that the hegemon was
forced to bear. I am suggesting that we should not accept this too easily. The
leading edge of capitalist society has never remained in the same place for
long, and there is no a priori reason to believe that it would have remained in
the United States for ever had that country *not* entered the world scene.

What has been said to this point can be summarized and highlighted. A
diminution in power of a leading state inside capitalist society might be
explicable in traditional terms, as the result of over-extension or internal social
rigidities, rather than as the result of the cost of services that it provides for
capitalism as a whole. We should in particular be suspicious of ideologists
claiming that hegemonic services are somehow neutral; differently put, we
should remember de Gaulle's complaint that the foreign policy of the United
States represented a traditional drive for ascendancy cloaked in idealism – a
complaint that was raised quite as much against Britain in the nineteenth
century. Nonetheless, it would be a mistake not to underline a key difference
between the traditional policy of great powers and that sought by Britain and
the United States. Where traditional rule often favoured conquest, Britain and
the United States preferred when possible to maintain an empire of free
trade; a contrast needs to be made, in other words, between formal and non-
territorial empire. The success or failure of ruling powers within capitalist
society is likely to depend upon the extent to which they can avoid formal
territorial possession.[21] If liberalism's aims here might in principle stave off
decline, the same may well not be true of adherence, as noted, to other
aspects of that protean doctrine.

20 A. Gershenkron, *Economic Backwardness in Historical Perspective* (Cambridge,
   Massachusetts: Harvard University Press, 1962).
21 R. Robinson and J. Gallagher, 'The Imperialism of Free Trade', *EcHR*, vol. 6
   (1953). Cf. B. Porter, *Britain, Europe and the World, 1850–1982* (London:
   George Allen and Unwin, 1983); M. Doyle, *Empires* (Ithaca, New York: Cornell
   University Press, 1986).

One final set of theoretical observations is necessary before turning to a comparison of the British and American cases. If real purchase is to be gained in this comparison, something needs to be said about the sources of state economic and geopolitical policy. Bluntly, to speak without question of 'the state' in the international arena is to prejudge key matters, to fail to examine whether state leaders act at the behest of societal forces. It is not at all easy to separate key social actors from each other. Was American post-war policy designed to secure a free world or a world open to a free economy? To what extent were such policies those of an elite genuinely autonomous from key capitalist actors? Occasionally such separation is analytically impossible: Cobden and Bright really believed that the progress of trade would serve the politics of peace. Nonetheless, it is *often* possible to locate moments of autonomy for particular social actors; it is worth while saying something about the particular actors that will have importance in the analysis given in this chapter.

The external actions of states tend to be seen in two ways. Realism in all its forms stresses that state leaders seek security for their society in an asocial world; in the modern world, this search has necessarily had to involve economics quite as much as traditional gepolitics. This is a rich theoretical tradition, but it is capable of being brutalized; Morgenthau did precisely this when he argued that the goal of every state was to enhance its power.[22] In fact, the goals of states can and do vary, with the desire for peace or glory being quite as real as the desire for power.[23] Another way of making this point is to insist that perceptions of security vary; such variations may result from national experience as a whole but they may, of course, reflect the perceptions of particular groups within a nation.

The force of realism in the contemporary world seems amply justified by the behaviour of states in Southeast Asia since the withdrawal of the United States. Great powers like to have weaker ones on their borders, and it is not at all surprising to discover China's hostility to Vietnam, particularly as seen in its adherence, in its support of Pol Pot, to the old geopolitical maxim that 'the enemy of my enemy is my friend'.[24] I mention this because the dominant version of the second way in which foreign policy has been conceptualized, namely that stressing its domestic roots, argues that the control of the state by capitalists causes war. This theory was first adumbrated by Hobson, and it is the way in which mainstream Marxism, which ought to be more troubled than it is by the sheer fact that capitalism is divided by states, has sought to explain state behaviour. As this approach is both powerful and well known, let me pay more attention to another domestic factor in the making of foreign policy, not least because its improperly understood implications are intellectually exciting and morally disturbing.

22 H. Morgenthau, *Politics Among Nations* (New York: Alfred Knopf, 1973).
23 R. Aron, *Peace and War* (London: Weidenfeld and Nicolson, 1966).
24 D. Smith, 'Domination and Containment', *Comparative Studies in Society and History*, vol. 19 (1977).

In so far as liberalism divorced itself from capitalist theory, it produced a distinctive theory arguing for popular control over state policy, a theory which reached an idiosyncratic apogee in the American founding fathers' desire to continue the spirit of their revolt against the state by controlling power completely by splitting responsibility between Congress and the Executive.[25] This tradition raises very complex issues, but two basic approaches can be distinguished, the more negative of which has tended to dominate debate. Tocqueville was amongst the first who stressed the negative side of the equation in the American case.[26] He argued that the people would be slow to anger, but remorseless in the execution of war. In either case, it would be difficult to conduct foreign policy according to realist principles: state leaders would be constrained from threatening when threats were needed, and incapable, because of popular passion, of calling a halt once war had ceased to fulfil its Clausewitzian role as a 'continuation of policy by other means'. This negative view, especially in connection with the United States, has been further stressed by George Kennan,[27] the author in the late 1930s of a manuscript seeking to curtail democracy, and by Henry Kissinger.[28] One reason for caution in accepting this view is the plentiful evidence of consensus between the people and foreign policy makers; Kissinger's habit of blaming foreign policy failures on the domestic political system occasionally masked his own misjudgements. Of course, this is to voice scepticism about the extent to which popular will constrains the makers of foreign policy. But there is a more positive view of the way in which popular will does constrain foreign policy elites. One element to this viewpoint received its most vigorous statement in Kant's *Perpetual Peace* (1795).[29] He argued that liberal states should establish a league, based on constitutionalism and economic interdependence, and that this would guarantee peace. In a brilliant article, Michael Doyle, in common with Margaret Thatcher, has pointed out that liberal states have a remarkable record of not going to war with each other — albeit he adds the cautionary note that the ideological nature of liberal states may make them particularly warlike to those they judge to be not just geopolitical but ideological rivals as well.[30] A second element to a positive appreciation of liberalism is that an appeal to the people may enable the foreign policy elite to escape from

25 J. A. Hall, *Liberalism* (London: Paladin, 1988).
26 A. de Tocqueville, *Democracy in America*, vol. 2 (New York: Vintage Books, 1945).
27 G. Kennan, *American Diplomacy* (Chicago, Illinois: Chicago University Press, 1951).
28 H. Kissinger, *White House Years* (Boston, Massachusetts: Little, Brown and Company, 1979); H. Kissinger, *Years of Upheaval* (Boston, Massachusetts: Little, Brown and Company, 1982).
29 I. Kant, 'Perpetual Peace' (1795), in C. J. Friedrich, ed., *The Philosophy of Kant* (New York: Modern Library, 1949).
30 M. Doyle, 'Kant, Liberal Legacies and Foreign Affairs', *Philosophy and Public Affairs*, vol. 12, nos 3 and 4 (1983).

sectoral pressure: the state may become *free from* particular groups if it can insist on a right to be *free to* represent a more general will. Nonetheless, the ultimate validation of liberalism remains the capacity of preventing state elites making chaotic mistakes.

As it happens, I believe that a liberal political system has opportunities and costs for the conduct of foreign policy. In order to see the ways in which this is so, and to cast light on the other issues raised, it is necessary, given that they cannot be resolved by fiat, to turn to the historical record. Let us first examine, in broad contours, the reasons for the decline and fall of Britain, and then turn to the more complex case of the United States in the modern world political economy.

Britain's Decline and Fall

Most British academics have their own theories about British decline,[31] and the version presented here amounts in large part to a gloss upon them. Before considering decline, however, it is as well to remember the nature of initial British pre-eminence and, still more important, for reasons which will become apparent, to recount the way in which this pre-eminence came to be challenged.

Britain entered the world stage at the end of the eighteenth century. John Brewer has recently demonstrated the sheer extent of the armed forces which made geopolitical triumph possible.[32] A crucial enabling factor in this connection was the financial revolution of the late seventeenth century, that is, the founding of the Bank of England and the related rise to pre-eminence of the City of London. This in turn is explicable only because of the absence of absolutism; as Tocqueville realized, the upper classes co-operated with the state, particularly in matters of taxation, precisely because it felt able to control it — itself a consequence both of the centralized nature of English feudalism and of limited state competition consequent on isolation from the European landmass. It is noticeable that this entry onto the world stage predates the industrial revolution; equally striking is the fact that it was the result of well-developed militaristic skills. However, after the industrial revolution, Britain not unnaturally adopted a rather full-blooded version of liberalism: commercial specialization and free trade were emphasized, even though this meant removing the protected status of home agricultural producers. Trading with the world was initially conducted without the benefit of much formal empire:

31 Cf. G. Ingham, *Capitalism Divided* (London: Macmillan, 1984); A. Gamble, *Britain in Decline*, 2nd edn (London: Macmillan, 1985); P. Anderson, 'The Figures of Descent', *New Left Review*, no. 161 (1987); Mann, *States, War and Capitalism*; K. Middlemas, *Politics in Industrial Society* (London: André Deutsch, 1979).

32 J. Brewer, *The Sinews of Power* (London: Hutchinson, 1989).

The middle class did not require diplomats to tout for trade for them, which would have been distasteful, or to go for war for trade, except in situations where such wars could be justified on higher and purer grounds. A young, vigorous, dynamic economy like theirs, without serious competitors in the world, could get along on its own, without help.[33]

This is to say that Victorian ideology, according to which the rule of the market had replaced the traditional conflict of states, was highly self-serving. Other states were well aware of this. They pointed out in particular that the supposed loss of geopolitical security consequent on the Repeal of the Corn Laws was in reality no such thing as long as Britain maintained a navy powerful enough to secure its sources of supply. Furthermore, Britain was perfectly capable of continuing to play at traditional balance of power politics when it proved necessary, as it did in the case of Egypt, even though middle class non-interventionist liberals might be unhappy with this.

It seemed for some considerable time as if the British liberal dream of peace through interdependence, of the spread of trade and eventually of the parliamentary system, might be realizable. Throughout the 1850s and 1860s tariff walls in Europe fell, and it could be claimed that this aided the general economic advance of the time. But there was always a worm in the bud of this liberal dream. States interfered with the market in the most obvious way. Each state desired to have a set of productive industries that would ensure strategic security. These military origins to industrialization led to the creation of surplus capacity in the world economy, something which became obvious in the recession of the 1870s.[34] At this moment, two possible strategies, neatly encapsulated in the title of Werner Sombart's *Handler and Helden*, came to the fore.[35] The trading policy was to adapt one's national society to the logic of the world market, to allow productive activities to die out as they became unprofitable; the heroic alternative was to maintain such activities, not least because they played a vital part in securing national security.[36]

The close similarity of the interests of capitalists and those of foreign policy makers in Britain meant that its trading strategy, albeit with the protection of the Royal Navy, was bound to be maintained. In contrast, Imperial Germany moved towards the alternative pole.[37] The state elite was responsible for this change. It drew upon its own militarist traditions, themselves based on

33 Porter, *Britain, Europe and the World*, p. 16.
34 G. Sen, *The Military Origins of Industrialisation and International Trade Rivalry* (London: Frances Pinter, 1984).
35 W. Sombart, *Handler und Helden* (Leipzig, Dunckler & Humblot, 1915).
36 Polanyi, *The Great Transformation*; P. Gourevitch, *Politics in Hard Times* (Ithaca, New York: Cornell University Press, 1986).
37 P. Kennedy, *The Rise of the Anglo-German Antagonism, 1860–1914* (London: George Allen and Unwin, 1980); H. U. Wehler, *The German Empire 1871–1918* (Leamington Spa: Berg, 1986).

Germany's insecure geopolitical position in central Europe, in insisting that to allow the entry of cheap grain would have made Germany dependent on the world market as long as access to that market was controlled by the British navy. Closely related to this was the fact that tariffs were an especially good source for raising revenue.[38] In the longer run, the Junkers, as traders of grain historically in favour of free trade, came to support this policy as it protected them against cheap grain from North America; their views were much magnified by the over-representation they gained in the Prussian Estates. Similarly, protectionism became attractive to heavy industrialists, albeit much less so to the traders of Hamburg. Nonetheless, the prime move towards protectionism was made by Bismarck, largely in order to be able to finance the army whose victories had cemented German unity.

The initial German move towards protectionism did not by itself lead to a visceral, no-holds-barred conflict between Britain and Germany. As long as Germany's expansionist aims were limited to mainland Europe, Britain would accede to them. In the last analysis Bismarck understood this. Perhaps too he understood the logic of the market. Germany's first bid for colonies was very clearly an exercise in geopolitics rather than in foreign economic policy, and Bismarck had no trouble at all in withdrawing from this first bid — not least perhaps because his banker Bleichroder had very quickly realized that the rates of return from colonial possessions were miserably low.[39] Nonetheless, German policy came to demand a place in the sun, even in the Congo, and a consequence of this was the 1897 decision to build a navy — the real origin of the Anglo–German antagonism. Such a policy was in the interest of particular capitalists. In addition, domestic reformist pressure, most notably that of the Social Democratic Party, supported an expansion of the navy rather than of the army, for fear that the latter could be used for internal repression. But the decision depended most of all on key state actors, most notably on Tirpitz whose brilliant propaganda campaign captured the ear of the Kaiser. In one sense perhaps, the decision needs no real explanation. It is normal for rising powers to exert their strength, and almost inevitable that challenges to Britain would be mounted once she had disrupted the balance of power by taking on a world role. Perhaps the fact that complex interpretations have been offered is the result of our knowledge that World War I was a catastrophe. Nonetheless, it is worth emphasizing that what matters about economics is often less economic reality *per se* than what is believed to be the facts of the matter: colonies might not have been immediately profitable but the rationale that they were necessary for long-term prosperity was widely accepted. It is noticeable in this context that capitalists tend not to produce their own geopolitical visions. In

---

38 J. Hobson, 'A Tariff History of Germany, 1818–1914' (unpublished paper).
39 F. Stern, *Gold and Iron* (New York: Vintage Books, 1986). Cf. L. Davis and R. Huttenback, *Mammon and the Pursuit of Empire* (Cambridge: Cambridge University Press, 1987).

Imperial Germany many capitalists who did not stand to benefit from empire nonetheless acceded to the geo-economic vision produced by others.

It would be unsatisfactory to leave matters at this point. Britain wished to appease Germany, and would have done so had that been possible. The problem was that no specific and negotiable demands were made by Imperial Germany, and this ruled out the sort of colonial settlements that had been achieved with France and Russia. The reason for this was simple. The German state was not truly modern; it was rather a court at which policy resulted from favouritism.[40] The absence of a bureaucratic and rational state meant that Germany ended up without a properly worked out grand strategy. For a short period under Caprivi a genuine attempt was made to embrace a trading strategy. However, concentration tended to be on *two* heroic strategies. *Weltpolitik* did not mean that the traditional drive to the East was abandoned — thus avoiding, through reconciliation with Russia, a war on two fronts. Instead no clear decision was made, with the result that a system of alliances against Imperial Germany was formed. Fears of encirclement, together with increasing middle class nationalist and militarist pressure,[41] meant that state leaders felt increasingly trapped; in the end they resorted to war in part from despair. The lack of a modern state apparatus was quite as much to blame for Germany's drift to war as was authoritarianism *per se*.

Some time has been spent understanding the German challenge because it is a key step in explaining British decline; later on, it will, by process of analogy, help us to understand American foreign policy. We can begin negatively by asking whether British decline resulted from the hegemonic services that it was providing for capitalist society as a whole. There is little truth to this. Britain was never a hegemon in the sense ascribed to that term by modern international relations theory. It had a short-lived primacy in the market, but scarcely ever enjoyed pre-eminence in state to state relations. Its decline cannot be ascribed to excessive defence expenditures for capitalist society as a whole since its main rivals had comparable costs by the beginning of the twentieth century.[42] In a similar vein, it is probably mistaken to see the pre-World-War-I monetary system as genuinely hegemonic. The Germans and the French had their own monetary blocs, and the latter were able to invest in Russia in francs rather than in sterling. The crucial evidence for a monetary hegemony comparable to that of the United States in the 1960s — when one power alone could increase money in circulation, thereby extracting seigniorage — would have been persistently large deficits of Britain with Paris,

40 I. Hull, *The Entourage of Kaiser Wilhelm II, 1888–1918* (New York: Cambridge University Press, 1982).

41 G. Eley, *Reshaping the German Right* (New Haven, Connecticut: Yale University Press, 1980).

42 John Hobson and I are presently collecting comparative information on state revenue and expenditure figures. Preliminary results lead me to disagree with Patrick O'Brien (Chapter 2 in this book).

Berlin and New York, that is, evidence to show that Britain financed its deficit by making others hold sterling. But most scholars believe this not to have been the case: 'Britain is said to have had sufficient income from trade, investment, and services, plus the Indian milk cow, to remain in balance with the other major centres', whilst such sterling balances as were held resulted from economic calculation rather than hegemonic coercion.[43] An assessment needing examination is that British industry was hurt by allowing continued access to its own markets whilst its own products were banned from much of the continent and from the United States – a claim which led Arthur Balfour to argue for what one theorist has termed 'specific reciprocity', that is, to force open protected markets by threatening to close off its own.[44] It is hard to know how to weight this factor; against it can be set, in a moment, a different economic model.

The more traditional, neutral factors of previous theories of decline seem to explain the British case with greater conviction. The single most important fact is simply that of exhaustion brought on by fighting Germany in two world wars. The financing of those wars led to the liquidation of most claims against the rest of the world. Much of this was, of course, hidden by the fact that Britain emerged on the winning side; nonetheless, fundamental weakness was absolutely apparent within months at the end of World War II.[45] Furthermore, Britain had become exhausted as the result of state competition more generally. It was the challenge from other states, and particularly the fear that imperial rule by other powers might close off markets, that led to the acquisition of formal empire towards the end of the nineteenth century. This was a sign of weakness rather than of strength. It was always likely that a territorial empire would cost more than it was worth, and modern economic historians have shown this to be the case;[46] the popularity of the empire and the need, given Britain's dependence on imported food, to protect trade routes nonetheless make the acquisition of territory comprehensible. As it was, resources and commitments were brought fairly closely into line before 1914, and it was this that enabled the first German challenge to be surmounted. In the inter-war years, however, the increasing strength of nationalism made it more difficult to concentrate attention on the challenges posed by Hitler.[47] Economic decline is

43 D. Calleo, 'The Historiography of the Interwar Period: Reconsiderations', in B. Rowland, ed., *Balance of Power or Hegemony: The Inter-War Monetary System* (New York: New York University Press, 1975), p. 241. Cf. P. Lindert, *Key Currencies and Gold, 1900–1913* (Princeton, New Jersey: Princeton University Press, 1969).

44 A. Friedberg, *The Weary Titan* (Princeton, New Jersey: Princeton University Press, 1988), chapter 2; R. Keohane, 'Reciprocity in International Relations', *International Organisation*, vol. 40 (1986).

45 R. Gardner, *Sterling–Dollar Diplomacy* (London: Macmillan, 1969).

46 Davis and Huttenback, *Mammon*; O'Brien, 'Costs and Benefits'.

47 Kennedy, *The Rise and Fall*, chapter 6.

probably best explained in similarly neutral terms. British industry had been based on a very limited set of key technologies, and these had conquered the world market without the benefit of having been sharpened by competitive rivals. It was scarcely surprising that an institutional package gelled on the basis of its historical success. Even when Imperial Germany was moving towards a second industrial revolution, based on technical education and on chemicals, it remained possible for Britain's older industries to remain in profit. Nonetheless, the British economy did not under-perform particularly badly before 1914, as its development of service and leisure industries clearly demonstrated.[48] Britain's initial economic decline was in largest part relative and inevitable.

If one reviews British policy as a whole, what is most striking is how normal is decline; it does not require, as would a miracle of rejuvenation, much commentary. The uneven nature of capitalist development was bound to lead to a loss of economic pre-eminence. When this was allied to geopolitical challenges and thereby to increasing imperial costs, British power was always going to be unsustainable. But if Britain had very poor cards to play, could it have managed better with them? The answer to this for the most part must be negative. The challenge from Germany was, as noted, real, and there were genuine limits to how far Britain could go in appeasement even though allowing the rising power a major role was the only route to safety. I am no longer even sure that the British decision to continue fighting in 1917 was so irrational, even given the destruction of war: if Germany had then held on to the territory that it had conquered, as it demanded, a further dose of *Weltpolitik* might have proved even more fatal. More importantly, it is extremely unlikely that the radical modernizing strategy of Chamberlain, much favoured by some later critics, would have reversed decline if it had been instituted. The fundamental weakness of the policy was less working class hatred of expensive food than the reluctance of Canada and Australia to be forced to remain primary producers; these states wanted genuine rather than dependent development.[49] Furthermore, imperial preference would certainly have intensified imperialist pressures elsewhere – pressures which were partly mollified historically by Britain allowing others to trade in her empire until the 1930s. All this can be summarized by saying that most British policy was determined by factors beyond national control, that placing foreign policy-making in different hands would have made very little difference.

Nonetheless, it would be grossly mistaken to argue that every avenue of change was closed over nearly a century. It became particularly clear after 1945, for example, that British decline was no longer simply the effect of

48 S. Pollard, *Britain's Prime and Britain's Decline* (London: Edward Arnold, 1989).
49 B. Semmel, *Imperialism and Social Reform* (London: Routledge and Kegan Paul, 1960).

other states catching up as the transfer of people from agriculture to industry enhanced their growth rates: that did help account for the strengthening of the position of both France and Germany, but it failed to account for the continued low rates of British economic growth. Whilst it is certainly true that British decline was exacerbated by the character of market forces created by British history, that is, trade tended to be in low technology goods with the Commonwealth, largely to repay wartime loans, rather in more competitive and dynamic European markets in the years immediately after 1945, the inability of the state to alter such structures and to modernize becomes ever more surprising.[50] It thus becomes necessary to establish which actors were responsible either for policies which exacerbated decline or for blocking others which might have led to renewal.

Some responsibility can be laid at the door of the people. In foreign policy, domestic pressure played some role in preventing Sir Edward Grey giving Imperial Germany the unambiguous warning that might have changed its perceptions.[51] In general, however, foreign policy makers were relatively insulated from popular pressure, and their successes and failure were largely their own. A much more celebrated argument concerning the way in which popular pressure caused economic decline is, of course, seen in the claim that a militant working class prevented economic restructuring. This view has dominated recent British politics and much academic debate. It is largely wrong. The British working class has only rarely been politically militant, and such economic views as it has had − whether original or in favour of keeping the status quo − were largely the result rather than the cause of economic decline. This point can be put differently by saying simply that the British elite had very considerable autonomy from working class pressures; the failure to create an economically dynamic economy is accordingly to be laid at its door. Some shading needs to be given to the boldness of this picture. Union power was from the beginning deeply entrenched in the Labour Party, and sustained attempts at economic renewal from that quarter might have met with resistance. Furthermore, the British working class was always likely to prove a poor corporatist partner because its long history prior to industrialization meant that it − in distinction, say, to its Swedish counterpart − lacked centralized institutions and a vital interest in national economic affairs. But it is doubtful how much of an obstacle this would have proved to a determined modernizing elite. No such elite was present in the crucial period until the 1960s − by which time union militancy had increased in such a way as to block plans for reform.

50 A. Milward, *The Reconstruction of Western Europe, 1945−51* (London: Methuen, 1984); P. Hall, *Governing the Economy* (New York: Oxford University Press, 1986).
51 C. Nicolson, 'Edwardian England and the Coming of the First World War', in A. O'Day, ed., *The Edwardian Age: Conflict and Stability, 1900−14* (London: Macmillan, 1979).

If attention is to be given to internal social blockages, to distributional coalitions standing in the way of societal flexibility, it makes much more sense, as many scholars now realize, to ask whether the policies of the British state were determined by the interests of the financial sector of capital.[52] There can be no doubt of the increasingly deleterious impact of the unholy trinity of City–Treasury–Bank of England upon British industry. First, the great sophistication of the equity market has meant that profits have been made through trading in money, rather than through investing in domestic industry. In consequence, British industry has suffered from low levels of capital formation, a factor which goes much further in explaining low rates of worker productivity than *de haut en bas* comments about the laziness of British workers; in addition, industrialists have constantly had to concern themselves with the provision of short-term profits so as to pay out dividends to share-holders – inattention to whose interests can easily lead to takeover bids. Secondly, the City has consistently argued in favour of high exchange rates. This lay behind the catastrophic return to gold in 1925, and the stop-go policies of the period from 1945–71; the growth of the Eurodollar market in London in more recent times has, if anything, enhanced the City's power. The judgement to be made about this is simple: the single biggest obstacle to British economic recovery has probably been the excessive strength of the pound and of the volatility of interest rates necessary to ensure that strength.[53] Thirdly, the triumvirate of City, Bank and Treasury has consistently argued against the adoption of industrial policies, a factor which reflects the idio-syncratic, 'budgetary' nature of British state capacity. Indeed, the best way in which the spirit of this whole package of policies can be summarized is that of adherence to economic liberalism in a very full-blooded manner; it is this complete trust in market forces that characterizes Anglo-Saxon liberalism as a whole. Such policies were a source of strength when Britain had a strong industrial lead, but they led to less than optimal industrial performance when other nation states developed strong banking–industrial links and to genuine catastrophe when, between 1925 and 1931 and since 1945, they caused Britain's exports to be priced out of the world market.

One way in which the importance of the financial sector can be appreciated is by reference to the work of Rubinstein.[54] His finding – that the very rich in Britain have been landowners and financiers rather than, at any time, indus-trialists – allows considerable scepticism to be cast on the thesis of British decline proposed by Martin Wiener in his influential *English Culture and the Decline of the Industrial Spirit*.[55] Wiener suggested that the aristocratic embrace

52 Ingham, *Capitalism Divided*; Anderson, 'Figures of Descent'; S. Newton and D. Porter, *Modernization Frustrated* (London: Unwin Hyman, 1988); Mann, *States, War and Capitalism*.

53 S. Strange, *Sterling and British Policy* (Oxford: Oxford University Press, 1971).

54 W. D. Rubinstein, *Men of Wealth* (London: Croom Helm, 1981).

55 M. Wiener, *English Culture and the Decline of the Industrial Spirit* (Cambridge: Cambridge University Press, 1981).

undermined bourgeois virtue, sending the sons of businessmen to semi-rural retreat in the spirit of William Morris and Laura Ashley. In fact, of course, the British elite had no aversion to money-making *per se*; to the contrary, it discovered the best avenue available. Nonetheless, we do need a theory which stresses the sleepiness of the British elite. There remains much to be said for the contention that the financial sector constrained rather than controlled the political elite.[56] That elite sought to restore sterling's international role for its own autonomous prestige reasons; thus we should not accept the view of Harold Wilson in the early sixties as a determined opponent brought to heel by finance capital — it makes no sense to say that he was defeated when he and his party had no real alternative strategy of their own. This conclusion can be generalized, and for the most banal of reasons. The reinvigoration of most advanced nation states within capitalist society since 1945 was the result of their elites being shocked by catastrophe, most notably that of defeat in war. Victory was taken as an imprimatur of the success of British institutions, something symbolized by the success of history and the scorn shown to sociology within that country. There was recognition that times had changed, but the strategy adopted was to continue things as close to normal as possible. This was particularly clearly expressed in Macmillan's words to Crossman whilst attached to Eisenhower's headquarters in Algiers in 1942:

> [We] are the Greeks in an American empire. You will find the Americans much as the Greeks found the Romans—great, big, vulgar, bustling people, more vigorous than we are, and also more idle, with more unspoiled virtues but also more corrupt. We must run this [HQ] as the Greek slaves ran the operations of the Emperor Claudius.[57]

Of course, this Polybian strategy of playing Greece to America's Rome was then generalized[58] — curiously given that the fate of the Greeks inside the Roman Empire was by no means entirely pleasant. This policy has proved to be disastrous. If continual loyalty to finance rather than to industry is one side of the coin, the other is continued adherence to the tradition of national militarism. A full 50 per cent of Britain's research and development funding now goes towards weapons, an absolute madness given the short production runs involved. In this connection, it is worth saying something about the 'Thatcherite Revolution'. There is no doubt about Margaret Thatcher's desire to

56 S. Blank, 'Britain: The Politics of Foreign Economic Policy, the Domestic Economy, and the Problem of Pluralistic Stagnation', in P. Katzenstein, ed., *Between Power and Plenty* (Madison, Wisconsin: University of Wisconsin Press, 1978).

57 A. Horne, *Harold Macmillan. Volume One: 1894–1956* (New York: Viking, 1988), p. 160.

58 H. B. Ryan, *The Vision of Anglo-America* (Cambridge: Cambridge University Press, 1987); C. Maier, *In Search of Stability* (Cambridge: Cambridge University Press, 1988).

treat economic decline as the moral equivalent to defeat in war, and there is no doubt but that she has fundamentally changed British political discourse by making generally obvious what has anyway been true for sometime – that Britain is a small state whose future depends on her ability to survive in the international market. But the desire for reform has not been met by any comparable overhaul of institutions or policy. If the key institutions that gave Britain initial success were those of the City and of the military, they have by no means been dismantled: to the contrary, what is most striking is the extraordinary degree of basic continuity. This is more generally true. Adherence to economic liberalism has not been limited to the recognition that Adam Smith still rules externally; rather, disastrous attempts have been made to impose his marketist views internally. This continued total loyalty to *laissez-faire* has meant that little attempt has been made to create comparative advantage through the creation of a skilled workforce and by means of industrial policy. Britain has survived the Thatcherite years by means of North Sea oil whose revenues have masked the huge increase in expenditures on unemployment that would otherwise probably have caused electoral revolt. But the failure of the 'Thatcherite Revolution', that is, the likelihood that Britain will continue to do far less well than it might, is a different story. All-in-all the best summary judgement on British decline in general remains that of A. J. P. Taylor: 'the English people of the twentieth century were a fine people and deserved better leaders than on the whole they got'.[59]

The United States: Down, but not Out

Two tasks confront us in considering the position of the United States in the contemporary world. On the one hand, the lack of appropriateness of the analogy with British decline can be demonstrated by showing first that American decline has not gone very far, and second that the structure of the world polity is likely to limit the extent of that decline. But, on the other hand, we need to see if the processes explaining such decline as there has been are similar to those that affected Britain. Is American decline, such as it has been, the result of traditional factors, or does it rather result from the provision of services for capitalist society as a whole?

One doubt is worth mentioning immediately. Theorists of decline occasionally give the impression that the United States once could do as it wished, but now is more or less impotent. This image of a golden age is much exaggerated. Difficulties with allies have plagued the United States throughout the post-war period, and it is not the case that American views always prevailed or that various allied contributions did not affect important outcomes. The United States sought, for example, to establish genuine multilateral liberal economic

59 A. J. P. Taylor, 'Accident Prone, or, What Happened Next', *Journal of Modern History*, vol. 49 (1977), p. 18.

norms and it hoped too to avoid a continental commitment to Europe: in fact it ended up with what Ruggie has felicitously called 'embedded liberalism' and with NATO, whilst its allies, from the start, refused to share its perceptions of the Soviet Union and thereby to place security above trade.[60] Nonetheless, the United States did and still does gain what it wants on crucial occasions, even if much sound and fury hides this basic fact. This is not to deny that there has been some change, most dramatically with the closure of the gold window in 1971. But we are coming to realize that what has changed is the manner in which power is exercised — now far less benign, indeed predatory on the part of the hegemon[61] — rather than any absolute loss of power. Let us consider in turn the military, economic and monetary bases of continuing American strength.

The military power of the United States is scarcely in question. It alone stands in rivalry to the Soviet Union, albeit its lead in nearly every key military technology makes it very much first amongst equals. But only these two states are genuine superpowers possessed of first- and second-strike nuclear capabilities. In itself, however, this does not convince the theorists of decline for the perfectly sensible reason that defence procurement in the end rests upon the capacity of an economy to support it. Can the American role be sustained now that the United States has moved from being $141 billion in credit to the rest of the world in 1980 to something like $500 billion in debt by 1988, with the clear likelihood that that debt will massively increase? It is necessary, however, to be rather sceptical of the various indices used to mark American decline. The figures of indebtedness to the rest of the world, for example, are exaggerated by the fact that the book value of American interests overseas is given at purchase price rather than current worth; such debt is, of course, much more the result of the policies of Ronald Reagan than of any long-term processes of secular decline. It should not be forgotten, in addition, that for much of the 1980s against the federal budget deficit should be set surpluses in key states such as California; once that has been done the total deficit stands at something like 2 per cent of GNP — not a strikingly high figure, and historically normal for this particular nation state. Further, one should not forget that debt is denominated in dollars; it is thus subject to diminution should the United States print money, and thereby inflate the dollar and the world's economy. Equal care should be taken when dealing with protectionism. Hegemonic stability theory suggests that a decline in economic strength will lead to a demand for protectionism, and the very considerable upsurge in

---

60 J. G. Ruggie, 'International Regimes, Transactions and Change: Embedded Liberalism in the Postwar Economic Order', *International Organisation*, vol. 36 (1982); Maier, *In Search of Stability*; M. Mastanduno, 'Trade as a Strategic Weapon: American and Alliance Export Control Policy in the Early Postwar Period', *International Organisation*, vol. 42 (1988); Gardner, *Sterling–Dollar Diplomacy*; A. Van Doermal, *Bretton Woods* (London: Macmillan, 1978).
61 Cf. J. Conybeare, *Trade Wars* (New York: Basic Books, 1987).

informal quotas of various sorts seems to suggest that this is true of the United States at this time. But protectionism is only half-hearted. It is important to note that the 1988 Trade Bill demanded, as have American negotiators over the last years, increasing *openness* in services, agriculture and shipping. It is equally important to be suspicious of what trade figures reveal given the huge increase in intra-firm trade — by now perhaps a third of all American trade. A more accurate index of American economic power is the share of world GNP controlled by American companies — and let it be remembered that much American investment has been of the multi-national rather than portfolio variety favoured by the British — and that this shows continued strength; more specifically, the loss of pre-eminence as debilitated economies recovered seems to have bottomed out in the early 1970s, with the United States holding more or less the same share over the last 15 years.[62] This index is itself open to question, and Robert Reich has suggested that American companies' share of world production means little if the international division of labour in such companies has the United States responsible only for invention and assembly, with profit-creating complex skills moving ever more towards East Asia.[63] This picture might seem to be supported by the discovery that an increasing number of patents for manufacturing purposes are taken out in Japan; but this in turn is questioned by those who argue that real industrial strength is best measured by software patents, vital for most advanced contemporary industrial products: these are still the preserve of the United States. It seems possible, moreover, that America is regaining a competitive edge in middle sized companies;[64] the most recent study suggests that the United States continues to dominate in the newest areas of high technology goods.[65] In general, there is little agreement as to the nature of economic power today; it is scarcely surprising, in consequence, that no index is accepted as its measure.

A similarly mixed story can be told about the position of the United States within the world monetary system. At first sight the seigniorial privilege of the dollar standard, that is, the unilateral right to expand the money supply, has been removed with the floating exchange rate 'system' inaugurated in 1973. But the dollar remains the world's key currency, and the United States seems to have retained enormous power within the world monetary system.[66] Under

62 Strange, 'The Persistent Myth'; R. Gilpin, *US Power and the Multinational Corporation* (New York: Basic Books, 1975).
63 R. Reich, *Tales of a New America* (New York: Vintage Books, 1988).
64 'A Portrait of America's New Competitiveness', *The Economist*, 4 June 1988.
65 R. McCulloch, *The Challenge to US Leadership in High Technology Industries (Can the US Maintain Its Lead? Should it Try?)* (Cambridge, Massachusetts: National Bureau of Economic Research, Working Paper 2513, 1988).
66 S. Strange, 'Still an Extraordinary Power: America's Role in a Global Monetary System', in E. E. Lombra and W. E. Witte, eds, *Political Economy of International and Domestic Monetary Relations* (Ames, Iowa: University of Iowa Press, 1982); Strange, *Casino Capitalism*.

the floating system, Germany ceased to be the key supporter of the dollar, but its place was taken first by Saudi Arabia and then by Japan. One of the services that a hegemonic power was supposed to provide, at least in Kindleberger's eyes, was that of exporting capital to the rest of the world. In fact, world capital has flown to the United States, largely as the result of Reaganomics. There is certainly no denying that it was the policy of the United States which created a strong dollar in the early 1980s, and it is the policy of the United States since the Plaza Accords which have made for a weaker dollar: in both cases, the largest player determined the rules of the game, and it has proved impossible for smaller players to design alternative rules without the co-operation of that player. The impact of these policies on Latin America is such that its export of capital to Western banks is now running at somewhere between 4 and 5 per cent. This is the brutal exercise of great power − so great, indeed, as to make the Third World's success in controlling its minerals and commodities pale into insignificance.[67] Hence this is an appropriate point at which to recall that a leading power can 'free ride' on the system, that is, strength can be used to extract advantage.

The present power of the United States can be summarized by saying that it stands at the top or close to the top on all 'power indicators'. But the question of decline is not likely to be resolved by noting this since what some see as a glass half full will seem half empty to others. Let us turn instead to those features of the world polity which make the position of the contemporary United States unlike that of Britain at the end of the nineteenth century. An initial point worth emphasizing is that the United States has not suffered a massive defeat in war. This is not to deny the importance of Vietnam. But the United States was able to pass on part of the costs of the war to its allies by sending its inflation throughout capitalist society. But perhaps this consideration will not much sway the school of decline: might not Vietnam be the Boer War of the United States with worse to come?

There are good reasons for believing this to be most unlikely. There is no equivalent to Imperial Germany facing the United States. Its geopolitical rival stands outside capitalist society, whilst its capitalist economic rivals are geopolitically dependent upon it. There is, in other words, none of that super-imposition of conflicts which tends to so increase the intensity of conflict.[68] Very importantly, both these sets of relations are essentially stable.

Recent evidence does give the clear impression that the difficulties that face the Soviet Union − above all, slowing growth at a time when the dynamism of capitalist society is ever more apparent − are far more serious than those which face the United States, a situation exactly opposite to that in which

67 S. Krasner, *Structural Conflict* (Berkeley, California: University of California Press, 1984).

68 R. Dahrendorf, *Class and Class Conflict in Industrial Society* (Stanford, California: Stanford University Press, 1959).

Britain found herself from the 1870s. The behaviour of socialist China since 1957 makes it now impossible to deny that *the* communist menace is a myth; the Soviet Union faces a war on two fronts, with a correspondingly enormous strengthening of the geopolitical position of the United States. The reform policies of both China and the Soviet Union seem set to make communism infinitely less threatening in any case. Moreover, there are well understood rules concerning spheres of influence between the United States and these major powers; the two superpowers, in particular, are ever more, to use Raymond Aron's expression, 'enemy partners', perhaps most obviously in wishing to prevent the proliferation of nuclear weapons.[69]

The situation that faces the United States within capitalist society is quite as stable, and it is so in a manner that is historically novel. Japan and Germany were reconstructed as the result of American geopolitical victory: both are secure democracies wedded to trading rather than heroic strategies. It is extremely unlikely that either Germany or Japan will mount a challenge to the American system. In addition to the particular character of these states, there are good general reasons for believing that the world economy will not return completely to a no-holds-barred conflict between trading blocs – albeit, there may well be some increase of this type (Gilpin, 1987).[70] The fundamental justification for this belief is simply that the speed of technological change makes it ever more catastrophic to withdraw from the world market, something realized by most state leaders and enshrined by them and their leading industries in the sudden spread of joint ventures of very varied sorts (Cf. Rosecrance, 1986).[71] In addition, there is now some awareness that traditional protectionist policies are no longer likely to work: how can one protect one's industries against, say, Japan, if that country chooses to assemble Thai and Taiwanese parts in South Korea and then to import them into the United States via Mexico? In the case of the United States, the impact of free trade institutions and mentalities, both internally and externally, is likely to make it particularly difficult to adopt any pure protectionist stance.[72] In addition, new political groupings demanding a retention of liberal multilateralism are springing up to counter others seeking protectionism.[73] Finally, it is very clear that the post-war settlement is popular amongst many states, and that they will go to considerable extents to preserve it: that settlement solved the

---

69 Aron, *Peace and War*, part 4.

70 Gilpin, *Political Economy of International Relations*.

71 Cf. R. Rosecrance, *The Rise of the Trading State* (New York: Basic Books, 1986).

72 J. Goldstein, 'Ideas, Institutions and Trade Policy', *International Organisation*, vol. 42 (1988).

73 I. M. Destler and J. Odell, *Anti Protection: Changing Forces in United States Politics* (Washington, D.C.: Institute for International Economics, 1987); H. Milner, 'Resisting the Protectionist Impulse: Industry and the Making of Trade Policy in France and the United States during the 1970s', *International Organisation*, vol. 41 (1987).

'German problem' and the 'Japanese problem', whilst there is widespread awareness that bipolarity in a a nuclear age has a great deal to recommend it.

This general situation gives the United States certain clear advantages. The weakness of its geopolitical rival and the absence of challenges from within capitalist society mean that it does not have to acquire formal territorial empires. Of course, Vietnam represented precisely such a formal commitment. But what may prove to be important about that debacle is that it will not be repeated; certainly the United States has an alternative available, as argued in detail below. But its situation as a whole is completely different: after all, the economic challenge of Germany and Japan is that of allied states. And there are additional reasons that make it probable that such states will not replace their trading strategy with a new autarchic and heroic alternative. Britain's move to territorial empire was made virtually inevitable by the extent to which it traded with the world, and it was scarcely surprising that this led other states to fear they might in the long run be excluded; in contrast, the United States trades far less, and therefore has less need to secure markets through territorial possession – something which may mean that the development of capitalist society is not again so dramatically interrupted by the logic of geopolitics. Crucially, however, the United States has very considerable leverage over its allied economic rivals, both because it provides their defence and because their economic success is partly dependent on the sheer size of the American market – which the United States could, unlike most other states, close given the huge resource base its continental status affords it. At times, seigniorage has been obvious, notably in the passing on of inflation under the Bretton Woods system; but it is as present today, from the necessity of supporting the dollar to Japan's enforced abandonment of its plans to build fighter planes, a geopolitical form of industrial subsidy.

The situation of the United States differs from that of Britain in a further, and absolutely fundamental way. Paul Kennedy is right to argue that Britain's decline had to be great since it had so massively overreached its natural power ranking, that is, the portfolio of demographic, geopolitical and natural re-sources.[74] Nonetheless, there certainly *has* been relative decline, and it is time to turn to assessing its causes. Let us begin by asking whether we should accept the claims of hegemonic stability theory in this case. Has the United States become exhausted because of the burden of defence it has provided for capitalist society as a whole and by its obeisance to liberal multilateralism in the face of formal and informal protectionisms elsewhere?

There is some truth to both these claims, but each has recently been subject to much exaggeration. Figures that indicate that the United States' economy is being undermined by high defence expenditure, both absolutely and in comparison to her allies, need to be treated with the utmost care.[75]

74 Kennedy, *The Rise and Fall*, chapter 8.
75 I shall address this question more fully on the completion of my collection of US state expenditure figures.

Most obviously, defence expenditure is not now particularly high by historical standards, and it is hard to credit it with causing economic decline given the economic success of South Korea and Sweden, both of which pay as large a share of GNP for defence as does the United States.[76] Equally, it should not too easily be believed that defence spending is bad for the American economy. The trade-off between defence spending and economic performance is extremely complex,[77] but it is clear that the United States, with long production runs and research at the frontiers of technology, has gained something; certainly the Japanese regard American defence spending – especially when overseen by the Defence Advanced Research Projects Agency – as more or less equivalent to an industrial policy.[78] Recent studies suggest that concentration on defence has not had deleterious affects on domestic industrial capital formation;[79] the National Research Council has added to this the discovery that there is sufficient engineering talent left after concentration on defence for the health of domestic productive industry.[80] Figures for allied defence expenditures tend to be highly distorted:[81] they do not include 'offset payments', nor do they allow for hidden allied costs such as those of conscription and the provision of physical assets.[82] A proper accounting would suggest that the major members of NATO – and France – pay nearly as large a share of GNP for defence as does the United States *for its worldwide interests*; Japan, of course, pays very significantly less. In the European case, some of the difference is explicable by the fact that Europeans prefer a defensive strategy which happens to be cheaper, in distinction to the expensive offensive strategy not unnaturally favoured by the United States. Importantly, all figures do not include the informal economic privileges that accrue, as argued, to the United States as military rent and as bribes to ensure that its markets remain open. It is this which leads the advanced states to prop up the dollar and, in Japan's case, to massively increase its aid budget rather than to establish its own

76 Cf. J. Nye, 'America's Decline: A Myth', *New York Times*, 10 April 1988.
77 S. Chan, 'The impact of Defense Spending on Economic Performance: A Survey of Evidence and Problems', *Orbis*, vol. 29 (1985).
78 Reich, *Tales of a New America.*
79 D. Greenwood, 'Note on the Impact of Military Expenditure on Economic Growth and Performance', in C. Schmidt, ed., *The Economics of Military Expenditures* (New York: St Martin's Press, 1987); K. Rasler and W. R. Thompson, 'Defense Burdens, Capital Formation and Economic Growth', *Journal of Conflict Resolution*, vol. 32 (1988).
80 National Research Council, *The Impact of Defense Spending on Nondefense Engineering Labor Markets* (Washington, DC: National Academy Press, 1986).
81 K. Knorr, 'Burden Sharing in NATO', *Orbis*, vol. 29 (1985); D. Wightman, 'United States Balance of Payments Policies in the 1960s: Financing American Forces in Germany and the Trilateral Negotiations of 1966–7' (unpublished paper); K. Dunn, 'NATO's Enduring Value', *Foreign Policy* 71 (1988).
82 G. Treverton, *The 'Dollar Drain' and US Forces in Germany* (Ohio: Ohio University Press, 1978); Knorr, 'Burden Sharing'.

aerospace industry; in these ways, the allies informally pay for the cost of defence. Equally sceptical points must be made about the claim that decline results from the protectionism of others. German economic success at the end of the nineteenth century may have been helped by tariff walls, but it was not fundamentally ascribable to that; the same seems true of Japan today. Bergsten and Cline argue that if Japan had no import barriers at all, America's 1985 near $50 billion trade deficit with Japan would only have been reduced by $5 to $8 billion, and that $5 billion would have been added to the deficit if the United States had removed its own considerable barriers to Japanese imports.[83]

Although they are hard to prove in any decisive manner, traditional theories of decline seem to offer a more plausible account of what is happening to the United States. Just as Britain insitutionalized its moment of economic success, so too America allowed a set of institutions to gel around those Fordist politics of productivity that came to the fore under Roosevelt.[84] Such industrial giantism seems less adapted to the flexible trading system of the contemporary world economy, partly because of the failure of the United States to provide the sort of social infrastructure that underlies it.[85] American failure to adapt partly reflects its sheer size; it has often chosen to use its power to change the rules of international norms rather than to make its society flexible enough to compete – an option which now seems to have ever diminishing returns. Equally important, however, may well be the importance of finance capital within American society; if this sector has not yet reached the historic importance it gained in British history, the ways in which finance is currently favoured over industry, as in the fact that 'junk bonds' are tax deductible, offer obvious resonances. The whole point at issue can be summarized by saying that one reason for distrusting the 'decline by service provision' thesis of hegemonic stability theory is that it fails to pay proper attention to the inventiveness, diligence and adaptability of modern trading states (Dore, 1986, 1987; Okimoto, 1988; Weiss, 1988; Piore and Sabel, 1984; Deyo, 1987).[86] Imitating such virtues would require lowering the extraordinarily high levels of GNP given to consumption by means of increased taxation, less perhaps for direct industrial policy and more for the creation of suitable social infrastructures. If such

83 F. Bergsten and W. Cline, *The United States–Japan Economic Problem* (Washington, DC: Institute for International Economics, 1987).

84 Maier, *In Search of Stability*.

85 M. Piore and C. Sabel, *The Second Industrial Divide* (New York: Basic Books, 1984); Hall, *Liberalism*, chapter 7; L. Weiss, *Creating Capitalism* (Oxford: Basil Blackwell, 1988).

86 R. Dore, *Flexible Rigidities* (London: Athlone Press, 1986); R. Dore, *Taking Japan Seriously* (London: Athlone Press, 1987); D. Okimoto, *Between MITI and the Market* (Stanford, California: Stanford University Press, 1988); Weiss, *Creating Capitalism*; Piore and Sabel, *The Second Industrial Divide*; C. C. Deyo, ed., *The Political Economy of the New Asian Industrialism* (Ithaca, New York: Cornell University Press, 1987).

policies are resisted because they are held to go against 'the American grain', this can only be ascribed to the particular character of Anglo-Saxon liberalism. As it happens, however, there are good reasons to believe that increased taxes, if mandated for educational or infrastructural renewal, might well be granted. Certainly individual states in America have been able to convince their citizenry of the need for greater taxation for industrial regeneration (Vogel, 1985, chapter 10).[87] There is, in other words, room for responsible national leadership to make a difference.

It is equally noticeable that the American economy has suffered from geopolitical over-extension, as seen most clearly in Vietnam. Involvement in Vietnam did not seem to have any immediate economic rationale to it, in terms of markets, investment or raw materials, and this has led Krasner (1978) to stress that this policy was the result of anti-communism – an *acte gratuite* whose extraordinary craziness will become more apparent in a moment.[88] There is certainly some truth to the claim that the 'best and the brightest', brought to Washington by Kennedy, suffered markedly from the arrogance of power, and should be held responsible for their actions. Nonetheless, Domhoff (1987) is surely right to argue that these advisers were but lesser men carrying out the implications of the grand strategy that America created between 1941 and 1950;[89] the responsibility of the advisers of the 1960s was – as had been the case with those who followed Bismarck – not to think their times for themselves. Still, it behoves us to try and understand the sources of postwar American grand strategy, not least so that the previous claim, that the United States has non-territorial possibilities closed to Britain, may be justified.

Discussion of the origins of American postwar strategy has been exceedingly lively for several years, and it is not possible here to give anything like a summary of recent research.[90] Nonetheless, it now does seem apparent that no account will be satisfactory unless it recognizes the autonomous impact of four factors. First, the revisionist historians and their followers are surely quite correct to stress that the American state, due to its liberal character and its historic lack of geopolitical involvement, was especially permeable – largely through the Council for Foreign Relations – to the wishes and demands of its domestic capitalists.[91] It was at this period, for example, that involvement in Vietnam became likely as Southeast Asia became defined as part of 'the national interest'. But the revisionist account is incomplete. In particular, secondly, we must note that many state leaders had, from the turn of the century, geopolitical visions of their own, a remarkable number of which were

87 E. Vogel, *Comeback* (New York: Touchstone, 1985), chapter 10.

88 S. Krasner, *Defending the National Interest* (Princeton, New Jersey: Princeton University Press, 1978).

89 W. Domhoff, 'Defining the National Interest, 1940–42: A Critique of Krasner's Theory of American State Autonomy' (unpublished paper, 1987).

90 J. L. Gaddis, 'The Emerging Post-Revisionist Synthesis', *Diplomatic History*, vol. 7 (1983); *The Long Peace* (New York: Oxford University Press, 1987).

formed in the surprisingly Kiplingesque surroundings of Groton.[92] This elite
enjoyed the power it discovered during the war, and embraced empire willingly.
Of course, there was a considerable overlap between the first and second sets
of actors; this was scarcely surprising since the latter saw multilateralism as a
means to ensure peace. Nonetheless, if the statements of the political elite,
public and private, are to be believed they were far more worried by questions
of security than by the needs of the American economy, whether seen from
their own point of view or as interpreted for them by capitalists and their
experts. It was traditional balance of power reasons that underlay the Truman
adminstration's decisions to allow the multilateral norms they preferred to be
diluted and to accept continental involvement in NATO. A third set of actors
were not American at all. The collapse of Britain joined with the vigorous if
defensively inclined security demands of Stalin meant that many Europeans,
most notably Bevin, actively sought an American presence.[93] This was an
'empire by invitation', and some part of its dynamic came from allied actions.[94]
Finally, the actual character of the grand strategy was markedly influenced by
the nature of American institutions and experience. The American people –
and in particular, voters with ethnic ancestries in Ireland and Germany – had
long been suspicious of foreign entanglements, and it did not prove easy to
gain support for a global policy.[95] The Truman administration in 1946 was
faced with an ebullient Republican Congress which was at once anti-communist
and keen to balance the budget. It proved possible to turn highly anti-
communist Republicans such as Vandenberg, who himself faced re-election
from mid-Western Polish–American voters, in an internationalist direction,
and to split them from that fiscally cautious mainstream headed by Taft which
remained suspicious of foreign involvement. There is as yet no agreement

91 G. Kolko, *The Politics of War* (New York: Random House, 1969); J. Frieden,
    'Sectoral Conflict and US Foreign Economic Policy, 1914–40', *International
    Organisation*, vol. 41 (1988); W. Domhoff, *The Powers That Be* (New York:
    Vintage Books, 1979); 'Defining the National Interest'; 'The Ruling Class
    Does Rule: State Autonomy Theory and the Origins of the International
    Monetary Fund' (unpublished paper, 1988).
92 H. K. Beale, *Theodore Roosevelt and the Rise of America to World Power* (New
    York: Collier Books, 1967); J. L. Gaddis, *The United States and the Origins of
    the Cold War, 1941–47* (New York: Columbia University Press, 1972); J. L.
    Gaddis, *Strategies of Containment* (New York: Oxford University Press, 1982);
    W. Widenor, *Henry Cabot Lodge and the Search for an American Foreign Policy*
    (Berkeley, California: University of California Press, 1980).
93 V. Mastny, *Russia's Road to the Cold War* (New York: Columbia University
    Press, 1979).
94 G. Lundestad, 'Empire by Invitation?', *Journal of Peace Research*, vol. 23
    (1986).
95 G. Gilbert, *To the Farewell Address: Ideas of Early American Foreign Policy*
    (Princeton, New Jersey: Princeton University Press, 1961); Gaddis, *Origins of
    the Cold War*.

amongst historians as to the exact input of public opinion on policy formation at this time, but there can be no doubt but that there was some. It would in principle have been possible to strike a simple 'spheres of influence' deal with the Soviet Union, as Kennan argued; that this did not happen was the result of the American people, and of many of their leaders, seeing foreign affairs in rather moralistic terms – involvement could be by crusade alone.[96] This all-or-nothing approach finally became cemented by the Korean War which seemed to justify the charges of the 'loss of China' made by McCarthy. The fear of electoral retribution, probably much exaggerated in point of fact, made politicians rather reluctant to see the world in other than bipolar terms. This led to over-extension – not in Europe, it should be noted, but in the Third World where bipolar vision prevents proper appreciation of local forces and where there are few strategic interests of any significance.[97]

The United States has an alternative grand strategy that it can adopt. One key element of such a strategy is that of learning, in contradistinction to American political experience, that states in the Third World need to be strengthened for developmental purposes, and that this does not represent an unadulterated attack on liberal principles, especially since the spread of national-ism is likely, as Kennan realized in the 1940s, to dilute the cohesion of the communist movement.[98] The second key element of an alternative American grand strategy is for the United States to realize the extent of its extraordinary power. It really does not matter if a state withdraws from the world market; this is likely to be temporary since the costs of such withdrawal, given the fact that it is capitalist and not socialist society which has abundant capital and significant markets, exact such an incredibly high price. One of the most interesting questions in world politics today is whether modifications to post-war grand strategy can be made which will recognize regional dynamics and 'take class out of geopolitics'. It seems likely that capitalists can be convinced, given the obvious increase in market power even with the loss of Vietnam; capitalists will not stand in the way of such a policy. Similarly, a determined political elite is likely to be able to achieve such a policy despite fear of electoral punishment. It is important to have international understanding so

96 F. Klingberg, 'Cyclical Trends in American Foreign Policy Moods and Their Policy Implications', in C. W. Kegley and P. McGowan, eds, *Challenges to America: United States Foreign Policy in the 1980s* (Beverly Hills, California: Sage, 1979); S. Hoffmann, *Gulliver's Troubles, or the Setting of American Foreign Policy* (New York: McGraw Hill, 1968).

97 S. Van Evera, 'American Strategic Interests: Why Europe Matters, Why the Third World Doesn't'. Testimony prepared for hearings before the Panel on Defense Burdensharing, Committee on Armed Services, US House of Representatives, 2 March 1988.

98 S. Hoffmann, *Duties Beyond Borders* (Syracuse, New York: Syracuse University Press, 1981); Gaddis, *Strategies of Containment*; Hall, *Liberalism*, chapter 7; Van Evera, 'American Strategic Interests'.

that no shocks will create such strong domestic pressure, as was the case at the end of President Carter's term of office when the Soviet Union invaded Afghanistan. However, domestic pressures can all too easily be exaggerated. Kennedy was able to 'lose' Laos, and Carter Zimbabwe, without such punishment, largely because the future of these states was not defined in advance as something that would adversely affect American prestige. The same could have happened in Vietnam, perhaps as late as 1965; that it did not necessitates blaming the political elite of the time rather than the American people. There is room, in other words, for responsible leadership.

Conclusion

The argument that has been made deserves summary. Suspicion has been shown to the claim of hegemonic stability that the decline of Britain and the United States results from their bearing the burden of services for capitalist society. In general, the decline of hegemons — of which the United States is in fact the only genuine representative — is best understood in traditional and neutral terms, that is, as the result of geopolitical over-extension and the inability to overcome social blockages. In particular, both Britain and the United States adhere to a full-blooded marketist ideology — seen most clearly in the freedom given to financial sectors and in the absence of industrial policies of varied types — that makes it hard to adapt within capitalist society. This more particular factor has been given separate analytic consideration because there is no reason in the abstract to believe that a hegemonic leader has to embrace every idea and institution beloved by Anglo-Saxon liberalism.

Two implications of the argument are worth highlighting. First, the theoretical presuppositions at work are largely realist ones, that is, it sees decline as the result of a hegemon's own mistakes. This argument is perfectly compatible with the other elements of hegemonic stability theory; indeed the most distinguished theorist of that school oscillates between the sorts of arguments I have made and the false self-liquidating theory of hegemonic rule.[99] Secondly, a distinctive policy implication follows from the argument. As the external burdens of hegemony are not the fundamental reasons for the relative decline of the United States, policy drives emphasizing burden-sharing are effectively a distraction of time and energy. Renewal is in the hands of the United States alone.

Final thoughts can now be offered as to whether the United States will decline further in a manner akin to that of Britain. A central tenet of the paper has been that the United States is in a much more advantageous position than was Britain. The uniqueness of its position as defender of capitalist society makes it likely that for some considerable and unspecifiable time the United States will be able to shore up its position by extracting seigniorage of various

99 Gilpin, *War and Change*; Gilpin, *Political Economy of International Relations*.

kinds from its allies. Nonetheless, some social processes reminiscent of Britain seem to be at work in the United States; this suggests that decline may yet go much further – albeit, given differential size, the United States is most unlikely to cease to be the key player in the modern world political economy. Despite the fact, for example, that American industrialists feature as heroes of a popular culture generally suspicious of Wall Street, the increasing importance of financial capital to the American economy is not in question; importantly, the sophistication of the equity market, not least when financed by junk bonds, places a disastrous premium on short-term returns only too familiar from a reading of British economic history. A shared Anglo-Saxon economic liberalism also seems present in the lack of industrial policy and of attempts to manufacture comparative advantage – although something like this may be happening at the state level in America today. If all this is similar, there is one place at which the United States seems almost worse off than Britain. American politics are not at present coping creatively with the problems discussed in this paper; it is proving especially difficult to contain or reverse decline by the means indicated – that is, by raising taxes to enhance competitiveness and by adopting the alternate geopolitical strategy. These policies have forceful logics to recommend them in the abstract; at present they do not seem politically feasible. Why is this?

Some authors suggest that changes in economic organization are responsible: as banks and industry become internationalized, they increasingly favour free trade at the expense of domestic renewal.[100] There may be some truth to this, as there is to the argument that the greater internationalization of business diminishes domestic manufacturing employment in a way that affects the American electoral system (Harrison and Bluestone, 1988).[101] But the argument is by no means completely convincing: it falsely suggests a degree of co-ordination between business interests and foreign geopolitical and geoeconomic policy for which there is, at least as yet, little evidence. Other authors have suggested that electoral pressures, particularly in a political system in which power is divided between the executive and legislative branches, make it hard to remain flexible, especially in foreign affairs. There may be some truth to this point as well, but it should not be accepted too easily. There are opportunity/costs to democracy in all areas: there *is* a danger of moralistic swings of mood replacing calculation but the possibility remains that democratic review may enhance the policy process. If I were to risk a judgement on the costs and benefits of democracy to the conduct of American foreign affairs, it would be to argue that the most serious mistakes of what has been all-in-all an amazingly successful post-war foreign policy are attributable to autonomous elite actions, some of which, notably those concerning the Reagan adminis-tration's actions towards Iran, would have benefited greatly from more open

100 Frieden, 'Sectoral Conflict'.
101 B. Harrison and B. Bluestone, *The Great U-Turn* (New York: Basic Books, 1988).

democratic scrutiny. Democracy is a resource quite as much as a stumbling block, at least for an intelligent and determined elite. This suggests a final factor whose impact is improperly understood but of undoubted importance. During the Second World War something like a political class was created in the United States. If this class was at times constrained by the popular passions it had itself in part aroused and by the institutional surroundings in which it had to work, its fundamental unity meant that it could, when it acted skilfully, have its way most of the time; a determined political elite could, I believe, still succeed in most of the tasks it set itself. But the unity of that class has been ruptured — by differential responses to the student movement and to Vietnam and as the result of divided loyalties over Israel. Much could be done in the United States with responsible leadership. The fragmentation of the political elite at present suggests, however, that American decline may not by any means as yet have bottomed out.

7

The US in the 1960s: Hegemon in Decline?

David P. Calleo

World Empire and National Decline

The decline of empires is a perennial topic among historians. Over the past generation, many scholars have been intrigued by the rise and fall of British global hegemony and its consequences for Britain's national economy. Today, a similar interest has begun to gather around the United States. As the American economy seems more and more plagued by internal and external deficits, high debt and low competitiveness, analysts wonder whether the postwar *Pax Americana* is not going the way of the old *Pax Britannica*. America's economy, apparently overstrained by the effort of maintaining a huge military establishment, is perhaps on a path similar to Britain's in the late nineteenth and earlier twentieth centuries. And as Paul Kennedy's magisterial survey, *The Rise and Fall of the Great Powers*, reminds American readers, variations on the same pattern can be found throughout the history of modern imperial powers.[1]

Theoretical arguments linking a global hegemonic role to national economic decline have been developed by a number of scholars over recent years, among them the economic historian Charles Kindleberger. Kindleberger's *The World in Depression* argues that a properly functioning liberal world economy requires a leading power with the military force to sustain global order and the economic strength and institutions to channel investment and trade in a generally beneficial fashion.[2] In particular, this leading power must act as the world banker of last resort and ultimate market stabilizer for commodity prices. A youthful hegemon in the mid-nineteenth century, Britain

---

1 Paul Kennedy, *The Rise and Fall of the Great Powers* (New York: Random House, 1987).
2 Charles P. Kindleberger, *The World in Depression, 1929–1939* (London: Allen Lane, 1973), Introduction, chapter 14.

took on these functions with relative ease and the liberal world order prospered accordingly.

In due course, Kindleberger observes, the hegemonic power begins to grow weaker relative to other major states and to the system as a whole. A liberal system naturally favors a diffusion of economic development, and thus a gradual diminution of the economic superiority of the leading power. At the same time, the hegemonic function – both military and economic – draws resources from the hegemon. Other states are "free-riders" on the "public goods" of order, growth and stability provided by the hegemon. As others grow stronger, they grow inclined to challenge the preeminence of the leading power. Keeping abreast of such challenges from several sides means a further burden on the hegemon's resources. The hegemon's decline can be not only relative but also absolute, if the strain begins to undermine the hegemon's economic vitality.

Eventually, this disproportionate drain means the hegemon can no longer fulfill its functions properly and affects the stability of the whole system. Challenges from rising powers bring on an interregnum. The liberal international order breaks down and the prosperity it has engendered disappears. The hegemon itself may enter a long period of national decline. Thus, broadly speaking, Kindleberger explains the decay of the *Pax Britannica* into World War I, the interwar Depression and World War II. Restoration of the liberal global economy awaited a new hegemonic power – the United States – after World War II.[3]

Some writers add a third stage to the hegemonic drama – the concept of a "hegemon in decay". After the youthful hegemon that creates the system, and the mature hegemon that is exploited by "free-riders", comes the enfeebled hegemon that tries to sustain its predominance by drawing resources from the system it has created. Various forms of imperial taxation, burden-sharing or monetary manipulation result. These may increase opposition to the hegemon, disrupt the system still further and hasten its breakup.[4] Thus, for example, the French economist Jacques Rueff explained the post-World War I "gold-exchange standard" as a device to rebuild Britain's ruined global financial position at the expense of international monetary stability. Rueff saw the consequent world monetary system as self-destructive and leading inevitably to the Great Depression. Rueff made, of course, the same predictions about

---

3 Ibid. Also, for the theme of the US taking over the role of the UK, Clarence Streit, *Union Now* (New York: Harper, 1939); E. V. Rostow, *Law, Power and the Pursuit of Peace* (Lincoln, Nebraska: University of Nebraska Press, 1968) and Dean Acheson, *Present at the Creation* (New York: Norton, 1969).

4 Barry Buzan, *Peoples, States, and Fear: The National Security Problem in International Relations* (Chapel Hill, North Carolina: University of North Carolina Press, 1983), pp. 136–50.

the gold-exchange standard laid out at Bretton Woods after World War II.[5]

As the concept of a hegemon in decay suggests, not all analysts regard a hegemonic system as an unmixed blessing. On the contrary, an ancient tradition favors a balance of power as the preferable organizing principle for an international system and sees the exercise and pretension to hegemony as the fundamental cause of war and instability.[6] Some historians, for example, ascribe heavy responsibility for World War I to Britain's unwillingness to accommodate Imperial Germany's ambitions for a global role.[7]

Abstract moral predispositions aside, whether a hegemonic or balance-of-power system is preferable would seem to depend greatly on whether the objective conditions favor one or the other. Where one power is overwhelmingly predominant, competent and well-intentioned, hegemony seems an ideal arrangement. Where that hegemon no longer has the relative strength to sustain its position without practices that seriously undermine the system it is supposedly trying to preserve, the time seems ripe for exploring the prospects for a more plural form of international governance. This should be true from the perspective of the hegemonic power as well as the others.[8] As Paul Kennedy points out, as a system grows more plural in its distribution of resources, the failure of the leading power to adjust – above all to limit its expenditures to its real resources – is itself a principal cause for the gloomy national decline that so often seems to afflict the world's quondam hegemons.[9]

An Interpretation for the Reagan Era?

That such theories should have a particular interest for Americans at the present time is not surprising. In the 1980s, the substantial annual federal fiscal deficits of the 1970s were multiplied three to four times in nominal

5 Jacques Rueff, *The Monetary Sin of the West* (New York: Macmillan Co., 1971). For a summary of Rueff's critique, see David P. Calleo, *The Imperious Economy* (Cambridge: Harvard University Press, 1982), pp. 48–51. For Rueff's views on the interwar system, see Judith L. Kooker, "French Financial Diplomacy: The Interwar Years," in *Balance of Power or Hegemony: The Interwar Monetary System*, ed. Benjamin M. Rowland (New York: New York University Press, 1976).
6 David P. Calleo, *Beyond American Hegemony* (New York: Basic Books, 1987), chapter 8.
7 See, for example, Sidney Bradshaw Fay, *The Origins of the World War* (New York: Macmillan, 1930); or David P. Calleo, *The German Problem Reconsidered* (New York: Cambridge University Press, 1978). For a classic diplomatic history that parcels out blame to all parties in World War I, see Luigi Albertini, *The Origins of the War of 1914* (London: Oxford University Press, 1952). For Germany's relations with England, see Raymond Sontag, *Germany and England: Background of Conflict, 1848–1894* (New York: Norton, 1969).
8 David P. Calleo, *Beyond American Hegemony* (New York: Basic Books, 1987), chapter 8.
9 Kennedy, *The Rise and Fall*, Introduction, pp. 438–47, 515.

Table 1 Revenues, outlays and deficits of the late 1970s and 1980s

Year	Revenues	Outlays (US$bn)	Deficit
1976	298.1	371.8	73.7
1977	355.6	409.2	53.6
1978	399.6	458.7	59.2
1979	463.3	503.5	40.2
1980	517.1	590.9	73.8
1981	599.3	678.2	78.9
1982	617.8	745.7	127.9
1983	600.6	808.3	207.8
1984	666.5	851.8	185.3
1985	734.1	946.3	212.3
1986	769.1	990.3	221.2
1987	854.1	1004.6	150.4
1988[a]	909.2	1055.9	146.7

[a] Estimates

Source: ERP 1988, p. 337.

terms (see table 1). These increases were sustained, moreover, during an unprecedented economic boom, i.e., at the top of a business cycle.

The same alarming deterioration has affected America's external balances. While the US did run significant trade and current account deficits during some years of 1970s, the corresponding deficits starting in 1983 have been at a nominal level three times higher than the worst deficits of the 1970s. Financing fiscal deficits has increased the national debt from $914.3 billion in 1980 to $2,355.3 billion in 1987.[10] Given America's notoriously low savings rate, much of the capital has had to come from abroad. As a result, the US has, in five years, been transformed from the world's largest international creditor to its largest debtor (see table 2).

Table 2 Net debt or credit position of major debtor countries

	USA[a]	Brazil[b]	Argentina[b]	Mexico[b]
		(US$bn)		
1975	93.6	−23.4	−4.9	−16.6
1980	106.3	−56.5	−15.9	−43.5
1986	−263.6	−90.0	−44.5	−88.0

[a] Net international investment position.   [b] Medium- and long-term debt.

Sources: Handbook of Economic Statistics, 1987 (CIA: Directorate of Intelligence, 1987), p. 61. ERP 1977, p. 303; ERP 1988, p. 369.

10   ERP 1988, p. 337.

That these deteriorating economic balances coincided with an administration that emphasized militant reaffirmation of America's traditional geopolitical hegemony, while conducting an exceptionally large and rapid peacetime military build-up, naturally suggests a relation between economic decline, foreign policy and military posture. In short, a "Reagan Syndrome" appears to illustrate clearly how hegemonic geopolitical, military, fiscal and general economic relationships can combine into a mechanism for national decline.

Among the most interesting historical questions raised by this Reagan Syndrome is whether the same deteriorating processes linked within it have been at work earlier in postwar American history. The most obvious parallel is with the 1960s, when there was also a military build-up accompanied by deteriorating fiscal and external balances.

Before delving into the 1960s, however, it seems appropriate to consider the essential elements of the Reagan Syndrome itself — in order to have them in mind while examining the earlier decade. President Reagan rode the crest of a wave of alarm and discontent over what seemed a dangerously low state of American military strength. Congress had been cutting defense spending throughout most of the 1970s (see table 3). Defense had stood at $225.6 billion (1982 dollars) in fiscal 1970 — 44.3 percent of federal outlays and 8.2 per cent of GNP. By 1978, spending had fallen to $155.0 billion (1982 dollars) — 23.8 percent of federal outlays and 4.8 percent of GNP. President Carter had begun to reverse the trend. Defense as a percentage of GNP was back to 5 percent by fiscal 1980. By fiscal 1982, Reagan's first full year in office, the percentage was up to 5.9 percent and was to be 6.4 percent by 1985.

Sharp fluctuations in defense spending are typical of American practice. Postwar American security policy, and its fiscal impact have been highly cyclical, so much so that it seems appropriate to speak of a series of "security cycles" in US defense and fiscal policy. The first major rearmament began in 1950, with the onset of the Korean War and the triumph of the security perspectives set forth in NSC 68 *Report to the National Security Council by the Executive Secretary on United States Objectives and Programs for National Security*, April 1950. After the election of President Eisenhower in 1952, military spending suffered a marked recession. The second cycle began with the Kennedy–Johnson rearmament and the Vietnam War of the 1960s, a build-up reversed by the cuts during the Nixon, Ford and Carter administrations of the 1970s. Carter had begun a new build-up, which Reagan greatly augmented. Their build-up was thus the third cycle and has already entered its recession-ary phase. While it lasted, however, the Reagan military build-up was America's biggest and most rapid in peacetime history. In constant 1982 dollars, defense outlays jumped from $171.4 billion in fiscal 1981 to $264.2 billion in fiscal 1987 — a real increase of 54 per cent.[11]

11   For NSC 68, see Calleo, *Beyond American Hegemony*, chapter 3, esp. p. 33ff. For defense spending in fiscal 1987, in 1982 dollars, *Survey of Current Business*, April 1988, p. 16.

Table 3 Federal budget and defense spending

	Outlays			As % GNP		
	Total (US$bn)[a]	Defense (US$bn)[a]	Defense as % of Outlays (%)	Outlays (%)	Defense (%)	Non-defense (%)
1950	42.6[b]	12.4[b]	29.1	15.9	5.1	10.8
1955	66.5[b]	39.9[b]	60.0	17.7	11.0	6.7
1960	340.4	192.1	56.4	18.2	9.5	8.7
1965	394.9	181.4	45.9	17.6	7.5	10.1
1970	509.4	225.6	44.3	19.8	8.2	11.6
1975	586.0	159.8	27.3	21.8	5.7	16.1
1976	609.8	153.6	25.2	21.9	5.3	16.6
1977	622.6	154.3	24.8	21.1	5.0	16.1
1978	652.2	155.0	23.8	21.1	4.8	16.3
1979	660.2	159.1	24.1	20.5	4.7	15.8
1980	699.1	164.0	23.5	22.2	5.0	17.2
1981	726.5	171.4	23.6	22.7	5.3	17.4
1982	745.7	185.3	24.8	23.7	5.9	17.8
1983	776.5	200.8	25.9	24.3	6.3	18.0
1984	788.8	210.4	26.7	23.1	6.2	16.9
1985	846.1	226.7	26.8	24.0	6.4	17.6
1986[c]	850.0	232.0	27.3	23.4	6.3	17.1

[a] 1982 dollars
[b] Current, rather than 1982 dollars
[c] Estimated
Sources: *Statistical Abstracts of the United States, 1975* and *1987* (Washington, DC: US Department of Commerce, 1975 and 1987), p. 314 (1975); tables 479, 481, 521; pp. 292, 295, 317 (1987).

Behind Reagan's increase was a strong national consensus to reassert America's position as the world's leading power. But, while the consensus was strong for spending the money, it did not encompass any corresponding will – either on the part of the Reagan Administration or the country as a whole – to provide the funds. Instead, the income side of fiscal policy was firmly in the hands of "supply side" tax cutters. The consequence was the tax cut of 1981. Reagan proposed to reconcile the new military spending and tax cuts with fiscal balance by heavy cuts in civilian spending. But since the President himself ruled out reducing most civilian "entitlements," the scope for significant cuts was extremely restricted, and his effort to achieve balance remained merely rhetorical. The result was a startling jump in the federal fiscal deficit.

152   *David P. Calleo*

Before Reagan assumed office, fiscal deficits in fiscal years 1980 and 1981 had already reached record levels of $73 and $74 billion (on-budget only) respectively, thanks in good part to a severe recession triggered by the Federal Reserve's heroic effort to halt the rampaging price inflation of the late Carter years.[12] By 1982, Reagan's first full fiscal year, the fiscal deficit was $120 billion. It jumped to $207.9 billion in 1983, rose to a high of $237 billion in 1986. By fiscal year 1987, it was still at $151.4 billion. By this time, the deficit could no longer be blamed on the recession. Since 1983, the US had enjoyed its longest postwar boom since the 1960s. In effect, as the authors of the *Economic Report of the President, 1984* had admitted, the US had acquired a "structural" fiscal deficit, i.e., a deficit at full-employment, whose size they reckoned at around $150 billion.[13]

Meanwhile, as fiscal policy began running these hitherto unimaginable deficits, the monetary side of macroeconomic policy was in the exceptionally resolute hands of Paul Volcker, Chairman of the Federal Reserve appointed by President Carter. Volcker, widely respected by the public, and with strong backing from the financial community, was determined to stamp out the high inflation that had grown endemic during the 1970s.

Macroeconomic conditions in the early Reagan Administration thus combined a highly exaggerated version of the traditional fiscal laxity – the product of a record military build-up and a record tax cut – together with Volcker's uncommonly tight and firm monetary policy. The effects followed logically enough. High fiscal deficits, combined with the habitually low US savings rates and the Fed's tight monetary policy, made for record real interest rates. These US interest rates were exceptionally attractive to foreign investors. Sharp increases in the net inflow of non-official (i.e. private) foreign capital began in 1981 and more than quadrupled by 1985 – to a total of $179 billion.[14]

With floating exchange rates, such an inflow prompted a sharp appreciation of the dollar. The German mark, which had stood at 55.1 cents to the dollar in 1980 fell to as low as 30.7 cents by the first quarter of 1985. The Japanese yen fell from 0.443 cents to 0.388 over the same period. The "multilateral trade-weighted value of the US dollar" – an index adjusted according to the significance of the various foreign currencies for US trade – rose from 84.8 in 1980 to 132 in 1985 (adjusted for changes in consumer prices). In other words, the currency changes in themselves meant that the real price of US products would have risen on average by some 56 percent against the foreign competition. Not surprisingly, the US merchandise trade balance, which had improved slightly in 1980 (thanks presumably to the recession spurred by

12 *ERP* 1988, p. 337. For an inside account of how the Reagan Administration brought on such deficits, see David Stockman, *The Triumph of Politics: How the Reagan Revolution Failed* (New York: Harper and Row, 1986).
13 *ERP* 1984, pp. 35–7.
14 *ERP* 1988, p. 365.

Volcker's tightening monetary policy) began deteriorating in 1981, accelerated downward in 1982, and reached astounding deficits of $144 billion by 1986, and $171 billion by 1987.[15]

The result, naturally enough, was a severe downturn for those sectors of the American economy producing internationally tradable goods. Hence, industries like automobiles, steel and capital goods formed a "rust belt" and US agriculture went into a severe slump. At the same time, the collapse of world oil prices depressed regions like Texas and Louisiana.

While cheap imports were disastrous for American producers, they were ideal for the American consumer. They also kept down price inflation, despite the stimulative effects of the fiscal deficit and the Fed's later shift to monetary ease.

It is worth noting how foreign and US macroeconomic conditions were opposite but complementary. Germany and Japan, for example, followed policies of relative fiscal tightness and only moderate monetary growth. Saving in both countries was heavy. Thus, the hungry US capital market with its high interest rates, found European and Japanese savings available. With the dollar high and foreign consumption low, foreign goods were also available for the booming US consumer market.

High US interest rates and the high dollar also greatly aggravated the financial plight of several of the world's major Third World debtors – notably Mexico, Argentina, and Brazil. The risk of their default hung like a sword over most major US banks, strained, in any event, by the widespread industrial, farm and oil-related bankruptcies in the US itself.

Faced with these conditions, and in particular with increasing evidence of the financial sector's instability, Volcker's Fed began to relent. The money stock began to grow more rapidly in late 1982. Conditions tightened again in 1984 but then accelerated very rapidly in 1985 and thereafter (see table 4).

The shift in monetary climate ushered in a second phase of the Reagan Syndrome. Despite the Gramm–Rudman Law, Congress's attempt to impose budgetary discipline on itself, a huge fiscal deficit remained. Changing the macroeconomic mix from tight to easy money had logical results. Domestically, as interest rates fell, the US began to enjoy a consumer and equities boom (see table 5).

Monetary conditions, however, grew less attractive to foreign capital. The dollar peaked in 1985 and began a fall as rapid and extreme as its previous rise (see table 6). As foreign investors grew conscious of the exchange risk, their enthusiasm for holding American investments grew qualified, despite the booming equities markets.

A falling dollar, it was hoped, would improve the trade balance. But, although the balance did improve in volume terms, it did not improve in balance-of-payments terms. This could be ascribed not only to the usual "J-Curve" effect, but to the still rampant US domestic consumer boom, combined

15 *Ibid.*, pp. 364, 371. Exchange rate figures are from *ERP* 1987, p. 365.

Table 4   Percentage growth of the money stock, 1981–1985

Year	1981	1982	1983	1984	1985	1986	1987[a]
M1	6.4	8.6	9.5	5.8	12.5	16.5	3.1
M2	9.9	8.8	11.8	8.4	8.5	9.0	3.3
M3	12.3	9.2	10.2	10.9	7.4	9.0	4.8

[a] Preliminary
Source: *ERP* 1988, p. 325.

Table 5   Interest rates and GNP growth, 1981–1987

Year	1981	1982	1983	1984	1985	1986	1987
Prime rate	18.9	14.9	10.8	12.0	9.9	8.3	8.2
GNP growth[a]	1.9	−2.5	3.6	6.8	3.0	2.9	2.9[b]

[a] Percentage expansion in constant 1982 dollars.
[b] Preliminary
Source: *ERP* 1988, pp. 251, 330.

with the still relatively restrained macroeconomic conditions in Europe and Japan.[16]

As the dollar continued its precipitous fall, foreign central banks grew more and more involved in its support. In effect, foreign central banks began to replace foreign private investors as the financiers of America's still undiminished external deficits. In 1987, foreign central banks spent roughly $140 billion supporting the dollar.[17]

The situation posed an extremely delicate situation for the Fed, now under a new Chairman, Alan Greenspan. Tight money that would raise interest rates and buoy up the dollar would also very likely provoke a crash in the over-extended US equities markets. A tightening of monetary policy did, in fact, provoke a severe stock market plunge in October, 1987. Further tightening would provoke and deepen the recession that was now widely feared. Given the fragility of Third World borrowers and big American banks, results like a

16 The trade deficit rose from $122 billion in 1985 to $144 billion in 1986. Then, despite the falling dollar, it widened to $171 billion in 1987. See *ERP* 1988, p. 364; *The Wall Street Journal*, March 17, 1988, p. 1.
17 David P. Calleo, Harold van Buren Cleveland and Leonard Silk, "The Dollar and the Defense of the West", *Foreign Affairs*, vol. 66, no. 4, Spring 1988, p. 850.

Table 6 Value of the dollar

Year	1980	1981	1982	1983	1984	1985	1986	1987
Yen/$	227	221	249	238	237	238	168	145
DM/$	1.8	2.3	2.4	2.5	2.8	2.9	2.2	1.8
Trade-weighted	84.8	100.8	111.7	117.3	128.5	132.0	103.3	90.6

[a] Multilateral trade-weighted value of the US dollar (March 1973 = 100)
Source: ERP 1988, p. 371.

further collapse of equities, higher interest rates and a recession could hardly be anticipated with equanimity. But under the same circumstances, easy money risked inflation, persisting giant external imbalances and a "hard landing" of the dollar, i.e. a panicked collapse.[18] In this predicament the Fed was reduced to alternate bouts of moderate easing and tightening – much like the old "stop-go" policy that plagued the British economy during its long postwar decline. Then, as now, such a policy seemed a recipe for slow growth, with bouts of recession alternating with bursts of inflation and monetary instability.

In summary, the Reagan Syndrome during its first phase combined monetary stringency with fiscal laxness – the latter caused by a military build-up and a tax cut not balanced by cuts in civilian spending. The results were an excessively high dollar, a huge trade deficit, mushrooming American debt to foreigners, a recession among American producers, rising protectionism and severe financial instability. The Reagan Syndrome in its second phase continued fiscal laxity but with a looser monetary policy. The consequences were a domestic consumer and speculative boom, a precipitous fall of the dollar, a continuing huge trade deficit, fears of inflation, replacement of foreign private capital by massive central bank support – suggesting further sharp drops in an already low dollar. The constant in both phases has been a huge fiscal deficit created by an unbalanced military build-up and tax cut. Considering its causes and probable long-term effects, the Reagan Syndrome seems a convincing enough case study of the mechanism of imperial decline at work.

Reagan and the 1960s

How do the elements of the Reagan Syndrome compare with the Kennedy–Johnson era of the 1960s? Needless to say, historical parallels on such a grand

18   See Stephen Marris, *Deficits and the Dollar: the World Economy at Risk* (Washington, DC: Institute for International Economics, 1985), and his update on the situation, *Deficits and the Dollar Revisited* (Washington DC: Institute for International Economics, August, 1987).

scale cannot be taken very literally. Kennedy, for example, was the nation's youngest president — a centrist liberal and self-conscious heir of the Roosevelt New Deal. Reagan has been the nation's oldest president, a rightwing conservative determined, in rhetoric at least, to roll back, or at least halt the forward inertia of the welfare state.

But while Presidents Kennedy and Johnson drew rhetorical inspiration from a very different segment of American domestic political culture, and certainly enlisted a different segment of American elites in the leadership of their administrations, there are nevertheless some striking parallels with Reagan's geopolitical, military and economic policies — and also their consequences. The Kennedy–Johnson era also began with a military build-up, saw domestic fiscal and monetary conditions deteriorate and developed seriously declining international monetary and trade balances. In so far as the parallel with the Reagan Syndrome is convincing, it is also significant for present policy. If the Reagan Syndrome can be seen as a regular or recurring postwar American phenomenon, it suggests that current American difficulties are less a question of eccentric mismanagement than of an abiding and fundamental mismatch between national ambitions and resources.

It is perhaps best to start the comparison by noting the most important difference for our purposes. This lies in the economic conditions inherited by Kennedy and Reagan. Kennedy came in after Eisenhower's eight years of determined fiscal retrenchment. Though Eisenhower had countenanced large counter-cyclical federal deficits during the recessions that marked the beginning and end of his tenure, he had refused the stimulatory neo-Keynesian tax cut pressed upon him by his Vice President, Richard Nixon, and his Chairman of the Council of Economic Advisers, Arthur Burns.[19] In Eisenhower's view, the ineluctable fiscal trend was toward higher spending to meet the growing demands of modern societies. The underlying danger was not unemployment, as in the 1930s, but inflation. Democracies being what they were, Eisenhower feared that taxes, once removed, would be difficult to restore, regardless of the changes in general conditions. And, given the underlying political and inflationary trends, anything that eroded the tax base was highly imprudent.

Although Eisenhower was unable to roll back government spending, he was at least able to arrest its growth. In 1952, government spending stood at 33.26 percent of National Income; by 1960, it had risen to only 34.49 percent. In 1961, by contrast, it was to jump to 36.54 percent and by 1968, it stood at 39.29 percent.[20]

Eisenhower was also concerned about the fiscal dangers of high military spending. His administration corresponded with the recessionary phase of the first security cycle. After a life in the army, Eisenhower was, if anything, more skeptical of military estimates and claims than many civilian presidents. He

19 See Herbert Stein, *The Fiscal Revolution in America* (Chicago: University of Chicago Press, 1969), chapter 14, esp. pp. 366–7.
20 G. Warren Nutter, *Growth of Government in the West* (Washington, DC: American Enterprise Institute, 1978), p. 73.

also had the good luck to be in office during a period when the US enjoyed a decisive lead in military technology. In 1952, the Soviets still lacked the means to deliver a massive nuclear attack on the US, whereas the US had a formidable bomber force and ringed the Soviet Union with Eurasian air bases. A strategy of "massive retaliation" therefore permitted the US to hold all sorts of commitments without the conventional forces that would otherwise have been needed. The most obvious case was the NATO commitment to Western Europe. In short, technology permitted the US to enjoy "hegemony on the cheap."

The advantage, however, was not fated to endure. By the later 1950s, American planners had to address the consequences of more formidable Soviet strategic capabilities. US strategy placed greater emphasis on tactical nuclear weapons, designed to halt superior conventional forces in their own theatre rather than through intercontinental escalation.[21]

Eisenhower's geopolitical position was not to renounce US commitments. He had been, after all, NATO's first supreme commander. Rather it was to hold those hegemonic commitments on the cheap — through the use of nuclear weapons rather than by sustaining a huge conventional mobilization to match the Soviets. Having negotiated an end to the Korean War, Eisenhower was careful not to fall into Third World commitments that would require large-scale US conventional forces, most notably in Indo-China and Suez. At the same time, it was during his administration that the Federal Republic of Germany was pressed to rearm — a necessary first step toward building an adequate European conventional balance.

All in all, Eisenhower's military strategy did allow him to maintain US commitments while substantially lowering military costs. Defense spending, which had stood at 13.4 percent of GNP in 1952 (during the Korean War), had dropped to 9.0 percent in 1960. This permitted, in turn, a substantial growth of federal spending for civilian purposes without regular fiscal deficits. In 1960, the budget was balanced and the economy relatively free from inflationary pressure. A reasonably steady monetary policy was thereby possible. The inflation rate in 1960 stood at an exemplary 1.6 percent (GNP deflator). At the same time, the rewards of fiscal virtue were apparent in US external balances. The US ran a substantial current-account surplus through most years of the 1950s, despite a large outflow for private capital investment and military and economic aid.[22] A bout of speculation against the dollar in the

21 For a general history of the evolving strategic balance and its consequences for US military doctrine and forces, see Lawrence Freedman, *The Evolution of Nuclear Strategy* (London: Macmillan/International Institute for Strategic Studies, 1981); John Lewis Gaddis, *Strategies of Containment* (New York: Oxford University Press, 1982); and Calleo, *Beyond American Hegemony.*

22 The figures on military expenditure as a percent of GNP, are calculated from *ERP* 1962, p. 207. For the GNP deflator and current account surpluses, the US investment position, etc. see *ERP* 1988, pp. 253, 364, 365. For more detail on these balances, see the *ERPs* from the 1950s.

London Gold Market in 1960, triggered in part by fears of Kennedy's election, had been successfully contained and, indeed, the new multilateral "Gold Pool" that resulted appeared to give the dollar new institutionalized stability.[23]

Kennedy's New Frontier

While historians may see Kennedy as fortunate to have been the heir of Eisenhower's fiscal conservatism, from Kennedy's perspective, Eisenhower's virtues were misplaced. Restraining defense spending had meant, Kennedy argued, a 'missile gap' that threatened the strategic superiority that sustained America's geopolitical commitments. Advancing Soviet nuclear and missile technology demanded a basic rethinking of America's strategic posture. Similarly, the rapid transformation of the Third World opened the door to a new form of communist imperialism. Effective techniques of guerrilla warfare gave revolutionary movements new prospects for success. Communist economic doctrines promised new nations rapid development along with economic self-determination. Combatting this growing threat in the Third World was thought to require generous and imaginative economic aid, linked to new techniques and forces for anti-guerrilla warfare.

At home, Kennedy believed the US had sunk into a dangerous complacency unjustified by its own comparative economic and social performance. Growth rates and productivity increases in the American economy were lagging seriously behind those of the Soviets and of America's West European allies (see table 7).

At the same time, American society, plagued by economic stagnation, was, Kennedy believed, accumulating greater and greater social tensions. In particular, insufficient progress had been made in bringing the Black minority into the mainstream of American economic life. Time was running out for avoiding explosive reactions. A complacent and stagnant America would, moreover, lose its intellectual and cultural primacy. It would grow less and less convincing as an ideal for liberal societies and forces everywhere.[24]

Kennedy, of course, had a rather extended view of America's special world responsibilities:

23 See David P. Calleo, *The Imperious Economy* (Cambridge, Massachusetts: Harvard University Press, 1982), pp. 17–20, 224; *1964 Annual Report of the Directors of the IMF*, pp. 131–2; and Robert Solomon, *The International Monetary System, 1945–1976: An Insider's View* (New York: Harper and Row, 1977), pp. 114–27.
24 For President Kennedy's views, see Theodore Sorensen, *Kennedy* (New York: Harper and Row, 1965); Arthur Schlesinger Jr., *A Thousand Days* (Boston: Houghton Mifflin, 1965); or Calleo, *The Imperious Economy*, chapter 1.

Table 7 Percentage increase of GNP and productivity in USA, West Germany, France and Japan in the 1960s

Years	USA		West Germany		France		Japan	
	GNP	Productivity	GNP	Productivity	GNP	Productivity	GNP	Productivity
60–78	4.5	2.6	4.2	4.3	5.4	4.9	10.5	8.9
68–73	3.3	1.2	4.9	4.1	5.9	4.8	8.8	7.7

Source: Historical Statistics, 1960–82 (Paris: OECD) 1984, pp. 44, 47.

Let every nation know, whether it wishes us well or ill, that we shall pay any price, bear any burden, meet any hardship, support any friend, oppose any foe to assure the survival and the success of liberty. This much we pledge — and more.[25]

Kennedy's vision represented a reversion to the high expectations of the earlier postwar period. In this respect, Eisenhower, who paid more attention to the limits and dangers of America's world responsibilities, was the more real innovator. But while Kennedy's rhetoric was exalted and radical, his actual behavior in office was more restrained. His narrow election victory, a skeptical Congress and the recurrently nervous foreign exchange and gold markets all promoted a certain prudence.

Kennedy began formulating and articulating his grand design immediately upon entering office. Strategically, he called for an urgent program for a new land-based intercontinental missile — the Minuteman. To sustain America's prestige and technological leadership, there followed, in 1961, the program to land a man on the moon. To cope with the implications for extended deterrence in Europe of the anticipated Soviet strategic advances, there was a new NATO strategy of "flexible response." This called for a broad menu of conventional and limited nuclear responses to contain any military confrontation in Europe at the lowest possible level. The strategy naturally required a wider range of new American and European forces. To keep on top of changes in the Third World, the Administration launched an ambitious initiative in Latin America, the Alliance for Progress, started the Peace Corps, increased economic and military aid generally and designed special military forces, like the Green Berets, to cope with the unorthodox challenges of guerrilla warfare.[26]

In parallel with these ambitious new programs to project American power into the world were a collection of programs to improve the vitality, quality and harmony of American domestic society.[27] Civilian expenditures had, in fact, grown rapidly throughout the Eisenhower Administration, despite official pressure for austerity. The US nevertheless was lagging noticeably behind the standards being set by the flourishing welfare democracies of Western Europe (see table 8).

Given Kennedy's basic perspectives and ambitions, it was not surprising that federal expenditures began to rise sharply (see table 9). It took time, of course, to gear up the programs. But once they got going, they developed an accelerating momentum of their own. The external programs that began with

---

25 *New York Times*, January 21, 1961.
26 See Freedman, *The Evolution*, pp. 227–56; Gaddis, *Strategies*, pp. 198–273; Calleo, *Beyond American Hegemony*, pp. 44–56.
27 Kennedy mostly expanded existing social programs, e.g. raising the minimum wage, expanding social security, extending unemployment benefits, and increasing funding for education. Schlesinger (*A Thousand Days*, p. 629), terms it, a "record of action on the domestic front unmatched in any single sitting since 1935."

Table 8   Domestic transfer payments as a percentage of national income in the USA, West Germany, France and UK in the 1960s

Year	USA	West Germany	France	UK
1950	5.77	16.02	14.79	6.45
1952	3.83	15.18	15.97	6.55
1954	4.67	15.16	16.95	6.48
1956	4.66	14.91	17.38	6.56
1958	6.34	17.59	17.68	7.53
1960	6.21	15.95	17.16	7.57
1962	6.59	16.23	19.27	9.21
1964	6.34	16.30	20.87	9.47
1966	6.32	17.08	21.60	10.50
1968	7.66	17.84	21.79	12.02
1970	9.17	16.42	22.98	12.32

Source: Nutter, G. Warren, *Growth of Government in the West* (Washington, DC: American Enterprise Institute, 1978) pp. 63, 65, 71, 73.

Table 9   Constant government spending (1960 dollars) during the Kennedy and Johnson years

Year	Total	Military	Space	Foreign[b]	Other (civilian)[c]
1960	92.2	45.9	0.4	3.1	42.8
1961	96.8	46.9	0.7	3.4	45.8
1962	103.5	49.5	1.3	4.4	48.3
1963	106.1	49.9	2.5	4.0	49.8
1964	111.3	50.4	3.9	3.9	53.2
1965	108.3	45.4	4.7	3.9	54.3
1966	118.9	50.1	5.2	4.0	59.7
1967	136.1	60.3	4.6	3.9	67.3
1968	146.5	66.0	3.9	3.8	72.9

[a] Excluding veterans' benefits.
[b] Officially entitled "International Affairs and Finance."
[c] Derived by subtracting military, space and foreign from the total. It includes veterans' benefits.
Source: Calculated on the basis of current dollar figures from *ERP* 1970, pp. 250–1, which were then adjusted using the GNP deflator figures from the *ERP* 1988, p. 255.

the Peace Corps and the Green Berets ended with the Vietnam War. The early welfare proposals encouraged a swelling social and bureaucratic political force of rising expectations that became embodied in Johnson's Great Society. All this momentum found its fiscal expression.

Kennedy–Johnson Macroeconomic Policy

Kennedy naturally was concerned with finding the additional resources needed
to finance the Administration's combined domestic and foreign ambitions. He
was particularly concerned not to set his various goals in fierce competition
with each other or with the private interest of the great majority of the middle-
class public. The way to avoid unmanageable conflict over income redistribution
to help the disadvantaged, or between external and domestic goals, lay in
creating sufficient economic growth to yield the needed new resources. In a
climate of burgeoning prosperity and opportunity, disproportionate improvements for the poor or defense would not automatically be considered a
deprivation of the middle class. In short, macroeconomic policy oriented
toward rapid growth was an integral part of the Kennedy Administration's
grand domestic and foreign policy.

The problem for Kennedy's economists was how to achieve such growth.
Understandably, they derived their inspiration from the prevailing neo-
Keynesian formula – based on aggressive demand management. Keynes'
original formula had been devised for the quite different economic conditions
of the 1930s. It was based on the assumption that the economy suffered from
a bias toward underconsumption that had to be cured by the government's
deficit-spending to ensure adequate demand. Supply, i.e. full production,
employment, productivity, investment and new capacity, would all follow from
the increased demand.[28]

Eisenhower's implicit assumptions had been the reverse. Eisenhower's fear
of inflation implied, in effect, that the prewar problem of underconsumption
had been replaced by a postwar problem of overconsumption. For a newly
imperial America in an age of welfare capitalism, the demands of domestic
improvement and world power could be expected to press heavily on the
available resources. In this perspective, fiscal policies to enhance demand
would only exacerbate the inflationary problem. Instead of savings and investment to achieve real growth, there would be overconsumption, inflation, low
investment and no real growth – because resources would be going into
consumption.

The Kennedy Administration embraced the neo-Keynesian formula only
gradually. Early fiscal measures to promote growth concentrated on direct
incentives to business investment including, for example, an investment tax
credit. Kennedy was disturbed by the prospect of deficits and originally
inclined to increase taxes to cover his increased military and civilian outlays.

---

28   For Kennedy's fiscal thought see Herbert Stein, *The Fiscal Revolution in America*
     (Chicago: University of Chicago Press, 1969), chapters 15–17; Seymour E.
     Harris, *Economics of the Kennedy Years* (New York: Harper and Row, 1964); James
     Tobin, *The New Economics One Decade Older* (Princeton, New Jersey: Princeton
     University Press, 1979), chapter 1; or Calleo, *The Imperious Economy*, chapter 1.

Only the vigorous arguments of his economic advisers dissuaded him. Kennedy, however, grew more and more dissatisfied with the country's economic performance. In 1961, Kennedy's first year, economic growth was at a low 2.6 percent. 1962 saw rapid growth (5.8 percent) which began to fall off as the year continued. 1963 saw an annual rate of 4.0 percent – respectable but judged insufficient for Kennedy's purposes.[29] By January 1963, Kennedy was ready to embrace the neo-Keynesian remedy pressed upon him by his economic advisers. The Administration called for a "full-employment" tax cut. It was finally passed in January 1964, one of the first great legislative victories of the new Johnson Administration.

The Kennedy–Johnson tax cut was hailed as the inaugural of a new era of fiscal "fine-tuning."[30] It marked the hegemony of neo-Keynesian perspectives over policy making. American politics had earlier accepted the notion that "counter-cyclical" deficits were acceptable during a recession, when government welfare expenses automatically rose and revenues decreased. Compensating surpluses should be earned later, it was widely believed, when the business cycle had turned upward. Eisenhower, himself, had run very large deficits during the two recessions of his tenure, but had insisted on surpluses once the economy began to turn upward.

Kennedy's tax cut was something novel. It came not in the middle of a recession, but after two years of rapidly rising GNP and with unemployment relatively low and falling (see table 10). In effect, the Kennedy–Johnson tax cut went beyond the old postwar consensus on using fiscal deficits to smooth out extremes in the business cycle. Instead, the new policy mandated a more or less permanently deficitary fiscal policy to force growth and maintain the economy close to full employment all the time.[31] Since 1964, the federal government has, in fact, run a fiscal deficit every year except 1969. As things now stand, the record will be unbroken at least well into the next decade, more probably into the next century.

For its advocates, the new policy was not profligacy, but a scientific effort to achieve high growth through constant fiscal stimulus. At "full employment," not only would the country be happily employed and growing rapidly, but the government's revenues would rise to provide the resources needed to cover its domestic and foreign aims.

Revenues did, in fact, rise sharply as the economy reached full employment. With falling unemployment, government finances improved. The federal fiscal deficit dropped from $5.9 billion in 1964 to $1.4 billion in 1965, owing mainly to nearly level overall expenditures reflecting a drop in transfer payments. By fiscal year 1966, however, as spending gathered momentum and rising inflation

29 *ERP* 1984, p. 223.
30 Stein, *Fiscal Revolution*, chapters 15–17; Arthur Okun, *The Political Economy of Prosperity* (Washington, DC: Brookings, 1970), chapter 2.
31 For the change in policy, see Stein, *Fiscal Revolution*; Okun, *Political Economy*, pp. 37–44.

Table 10   GNP, unemployment and inflation in the late 1950s and 1960s

Year	GNP[a]	Unemp[b]	Inflation[c]
1955	6.7	4.4	-0.4
1956	2.1	4.1	1.5
1957	1.8	4.3	3.6
1958	-0.4	6.8	2.7
1959	6.0	5.5	0.8
1960	2.2	5.5	1.6
1961	2.6	6.7	1.0
1962	5.8	5.5	1.1
1963	4.0	5.7	1.2
1964	5.3	5.2	1.3
1965	6.0	4.5	1.7
1966	6.0	3.8	2.9
1967	2.7	3.8	4.2
1968	4.6	3.6	5.4
1969	2.8	3.5	5.9
1970	-0.2	4.9	4.3

[a] Percentage change in 1972 dollars
[b] Percentage of workforce
[c] Consumer Price Index
Source: ERP 1981, pp. 235, 267, 293.

forced the Fed into tighter monetary policy, the fiscal deficit began to rise rapidly. By fiscal year 1968, the year when a reluctant Congress finally passed a tax increase, the federal deficit had grown to $25 billion (see table 11).

Inflation had risen as well. There is, of course, no necessary link between inflation and high fiscal deficits. Inflation results from an excessively rapid creation of money and credit in relation to the growth of the economy as a whole. As the first phase of the Reagan Syndrome indicates, a lax fiscal policy can be combined with a restrictive monetary policy, with the result that conditions in credit markets will grow tight, real interest rates will rise and attract foreign capital, but domestic prices will remain steady.

In the Keynesian perspective of the 1960s, however, monetary policy had nothing like its present intellectual legitimacy as an independent regulator of macroeconomic policy. Instead, it was seen in essentially negative terms. Too tight money could stifle growth, while easy money, in itself, was insufficient to stimulate it.[32]

When the Fed did restrict monetary growth in 1966, in response to the rapid rise in inflation, it was roundly attacked both by the Johnson Administration and in Congress. The Fed quickly relaxed as the inflation came down. In

32   See Stein, *Fiscal Revolution*, pp. 361–4, 378.

Table 11   Revenues, outlays and deficits of the 1960s

Year	Revenues (US$bn)	Outlays (US$bn)	Deficit (US$bn)	Inflation/GNP Deflator (%)
1960	92.5	92.2	0.3	1.6
1961	94.4	97.7	−3.3	1.0
1962	99.7	106.8	−7.1	2.2
1963	106.6	111.3	−4.8	1.6
1964	112.6	118.5	−5.9	1.5
1965	116.8	118.2	−1.4	2.7
1966	130.8	134.5	−3.7	3.6
1967	148.8	157.5	−8.6	2.6
1968	153.0	178.1	−25.2	5.0
1969	186.9	183.6	3.2	5.6
1970	192.8	195.6	−2.8	5.5
1971	187.1	210.2	−23.0	5.7
1972	207.3	230.7	−23.4	4.7
1973	230.8	245.7	−14.9	6.5
1974	263.2	269.4	−6.1	9.1
1975	279.1	332.3	−53.2	9.8

Source: ERP 1988, pp. 253, 337.

1967, as inflation again began to rise, the Fed felt inhibited from forcing up interest rates, not only by the usual domestic opposition but by international efforts to shore up the weakening British pound. It was feared, correctly as it turned out, that if the pound could not hold to its parity the dollar would itself soon face a major speculative attack. In short, sustained tight money was not feasible in the intellectual and political climate of the time.[33] A fiscal−monetary mix like that of the early Reagan Syndrome was not acceptable as a viable course for a policy oriented toward rapid growth. With the Fed unable to sustain tight monetary policy for any prolonged period, the fiscal deficits and high unemployment made price inflation inevitable. By 1968, the GNP deflator had reached an annual rate of 5.0 percent − roughly five times greater than in 1960.

When accelerating inflation finally compelled the Fed to tighten monetary conditions in 1968, an alarmed Congress was also ready for a sharp tax increase. Both monetary and fiscal policy thus contracted together and a severe recession followed. Even so, inflation continued at a high rate. Since inflation has a cumulative psychological character, the jump from 1 percent to 5 percent reflected an underlying inflationary momentum in the economy that

33   Okun, *Political Economy*, pp. 53−9 describes the accommodating monetary policy. See also Calleo, *The Imperious Economy*, chapter 2.

would not recede easily even when confronted with severely restricted monetary conditions. Not only did the inflation rate remain high despite the monetary tightening in 1968, but it was ready to resume its upward spiral as soon as Nixon began reflating the economy in 1970 through 1972. For a time, the wage and price controls installed in August 1971 held price inflation down. But when these controls were removed in 1973, the inflation rate exploded. It remained high in 1974 and 1975, despite the record postwar recession, and resumed its climb with the Ford–Carter boom of the later 1970s.

External Imbalances in the 1960s

Domestic US disequilibrium was paralled by external disequilibrium. As French critics like Rueff kept arguing, the US balance-of-payments deficit was, to some extent, a substitute for domestic price inflation.[34] Excess money created to accommodate expansionary fiscal policy, instead of pushing up prices at home, was being exported abroad. But the external deficits were more than a monetary phenomenon: they encompassed the real economy as well. Rising inflation was accompanied by a decline in the US trade balance (see table 12).

As with inflation, the balance-of-payments disequilibrium developed a certain momentum of its own. After the customary lags, the fiscal and monetary

Table 12   US trade and current account balances (in US $bn), 1960–1972

Year	Trade	Current account
1960	4.9	2.8
1961	5.6	3.8
1962	4.5	3.4
1963	5.2	4.4
1964	6.8	6.8
1965	5.0	5.4
1966	3.8	3.0
1967	3.8	2.6
1968	0.6	0.6
1969	0.6	0.4
1970	2.6	2.3
1971	−2.3	−1.4
1972	−6.4	−5.8

Source: *ERP* 1988, p. 364.

34   See Rueff, *Monetary Sin*, chapter 1. For an elaboration of his theory, see his *Balance of Payments* (New York: Macmillan, 1967).

austerity of 1968 and 1969 brought a brief rebound to the trade balance in 1970, while the reflation of 1970 brought an actual trade deficit in 1971 – the first since the nineteenth century. The trade deficit, in turn, fueled a powerful rise in protectionist sentiment – apparent in Nixon's mercantilist policies and rhetoric of 1971. Meanwhile, a number of expert studies, most notably the Peterson Report, began to stress America's industrial decline, as evidenced by its inability to compete in tradeable goods sectors.[35]

The decline in trade went hand in hand with a sharp falling-off in the current-account balance, which includes not only trade but also repatriated investment income from overseas. The current account declined with the rise of inflation after 1965, revived after the austerity of 1969 and fell into deficit in 1971.

As might have been expected, the weakening US external balances made sustaining the dollar's official exchange rate more and more difficult. The postwar monetary order, laid down in 1944 at Bretton Woods, was centered around the dollar as the system's "key currency." As the system was meant to work, the dollar was convertible into a fixed amount of gold; other currencies were convertible at a fixed parity against the dollar, an arrangement largely achieved by 1958. The dollar was also the world's principal "reserve currency." It was held by foreign central banks, along with gold, as a universal monetary asset. Most international businesses used dollars for their liquid reserves. The dollar was also the world's principal currency for international trade.

The US thus had a unique "hegemonic" responsibility for managing the world's money. Keynesian analysts tended to define this responsibility as the need to provide adequate "liquidity," i.e., monetary credit, to keep the international economy growing rapidly. Unreconstructed classic liberal economists, like Jacques Rueff, defined that responsibility as maintaining monetary stability, i.e., avoiding inflation. Others somewhere in between, like the Belgian–American monetary expert Robert Triffin, acknowledged the importance of an adequately increasing liquidity, but noted that providing it would inevitably weaken the national currency that was its source.[36]

The postwar dollar-based system, both Rueff and Triffin predicted, was doomed to self-destruction. Rueff prescribed a return to the classic gold standard, which would have deprived the dollar of its hegemonic place in the monetary system. Triffin, following Keynes, proposed a new international money issued by the International Monetary Fund according to the needs of a growing world economy. De Gaulle politicized the issue in 1965. In a famous press conference, he denounced the US for exporting inflation to the world

---

35   Peter G. Peterson, *The United States in the Changing World Economy* (Washington, DC: US Government Printing Office, 1971).

36   Robert Triffin, *Gold and the Dollar Crisis* (New Haven, Connecticut: Yale University Press, 1960). See also Robert Triffin, *The World Money Maze* (New Haven, Connecticut: Yale University Press, 1966).

and using its monetary hegemony to force other governments to finance both its wars and its corporate invasion of other economies.[37]

By the later 1960s, foreign governments were more and more having to finance America's balance-of-payments deficits. As the dollar outflow continued to accumulate in foreign hands, US gold reserves were increasingly insufficient to meet the obligation for gold conversion. Gold convertibility became a polite fiction, particularly as a beleaguered US began using direct political pressure on its principal creditors – Japan, the Federal Republic of Germany and Canada – not to request gold for their surplus dollars.[38]

In early 1968, a great run developed against the dollar in the gold market. The multilateral Gold Pool collapsed as other countries refused to use their gold to support the dollar and the US gave up any pretense of sustaining the official gold–dollar price in the private gold market. Henceforth, in the new "two-tier gold market," the US would honor the dollar's gold convertibility only in transactions among central banks – transactions, of course, that were subject to heavy political pressure.

Rueff always argued that the creation of the two-tier gold market in 1968 marked the real demise of the Bretton Woods monetary system. The system did, however, enjoy a remission as the US finally reversed its domestic fiscal and monetary policies in later 1968, while the Europeans developed serious problems of their own. But shortly after Nixon resumed an expansive macro-economic policy in 1970, the dollar's deterioration recommenced and led to the system's dramatic collapse in August of 1971.

False Analogies?

Even a quick sketch of policies and consequences suggests some rather obvious parallels between the Kennedy–Johnson and Reagan eras. To be sure, any one of the economic phenomena just described is subject to a variety of technical and political interpretations. To this day, noted economists will deny that the Kennedy fiscal policies or the tax cut of 1964 were inflationary, just as Reaganomics still has its ardent defenders among economists as well as

---

37 Charles de Gaulle, *Major Addresses, Statements and Press Conferences* (New York: French Embassy and Information Division, 1967), II, 179–81.

38 US balance-of-payments problems began before actual negative current-account and trade deficits. The basic balance (current account plus long term capital flows) had been in deficit since the 1950s. See David P. Calleo, *America and the World Political Economy* (Bloomington, Indiana: Indiana University Press, 1973), chapter 5; Calleo, *Imperious Economy*, Part 1; Robert Solomon, *The International Monetary System, 1945–76: An Insider's View* (New York: Harper and Row, 1977); and Susan Strange, "International Monetary Relations," in *International Economic Relations of the Western World, 1959–1971*, ed. Andrew Shonfield (London: Oxford University Press, 1976).

politicians.[39] In the longer view of history, however, their arguments are not likely to appear very convincing. Future historians are more likely to marvel that so much intelligence and ingenuity were devoted to denying the obvious. Perhaps they will find the short-term perspective of so many of the contemporary analysts a reflection of a deeper cultural and philosophical deficiency. Or perhaps it will be interpreted as a purblind will to hegemonic national power that would not be gainsaid even by the most obvious signs of excess and strain. If so, American behavior will not seem very different from that of earlier hegemonic powers at similar stages of decline.

Two alternative interpretations, however, do deserve to be taken more seriously. One is that which blames US fiscal over-extension not on US military spending but on US domestic self-indulgence. There is a prima-facie case for this view, based on the military's declining proportion of fiscal spending and GNP devoted to military as opposed to civilian purposes. (See table 3.)

Logically, fiscal over-extension results from the combination of military and civilian spending in relation to the government's income. Why blame the imbalance on one factor as opposed to another? Why not blame US insolvency on the excessive growth of civilian entitlements rather than on military spending? Or why not blame a self-indulgent society that refuses to tax itself sufficiently to cover its ambitions? Alternatively, why not, like Rueff, blame a monetary system that technically permits one nation to run perennial external deficits, and thus removes an essential barrier to national indiscipline? Finally, why not, like the neo-Keynesians of the time or the supply-siders of today, blame the fiscal deficit on the failure of economic policy to stimulate adequate growth?

These alternative arguments lose much of their force when American fiscal practice is compared with that of other comparably rich democracies (see table 13). Making such comparisons, of course, implies that there are certain norms typical of democratic societies at similar stages of economic development.

Comparing the US fiscal profile with that of countries like France or the Federal Republic of Germany does reveal certain major differences. While the US taxes itself less than the two European democracies, it also spends less. As a result, the American civilian welfare state seems grossly underdeveloped. That France and Germany have a greater constituency for high taxation than the US is therefore not surprising – particularly since much of the European social spending benefits the affluent and tax-paying middle class.

---

39 For the view that Kennedy's policies were not inflationary until the Vietnam War upset calculations of government spending, see Tobin, *New Economics*, or Otto Eckstein, *The Great Recession* (New York: North Holland Publishing Co., 1978). For a defense of Reagan's policies, see Herbert Stein, "A Reagan Economic Revolution?", the *New York Times*, April 16, 1985. For my contrary views see Calleo, *Imperious Economy*, chapters 2 and 9; *Beyond American Hegemony*, chapter 6.

Table 13   French, West German, and US Government sector spending patterns,
1983

	France	West Germany	USA
Defense spending			
as % GDP	3.2	2.9	6.1
as % total spending	7.4	9.3	23.7
Social sec. and welfare[a]			
as % GDP	22.3	21.1	10.6
as % total spending	44.0	50.0	34.0
Total spending			
as % GNP	43.9	31.1	25.7
Total revenues			
as % GNP	41.1	29.3	20.0

[a] Includes Social Security, welfare, housing, and community amenities.
Source: Government Finance Statistics Yearbook (Washington: IMF, 1987), pp. 52, 74, 78, 80, 99.

Not only does government in the US both spend and tax less, but a much greater proportion of its spending goes to the military – both in relative and absolute terms. It may be argued, of course, that the US, as the world's responsible hegemon, should expect to shoulder a much larger military burden than its rich but dependent allies. American citizens should accept higher taxes, and without the corresponding civilian benefits. But to expect such a view to prevail politically in the US assumes that Americans will remain forever willing to accept a sharply lower standard of civilian welfare than their affluent cousins in Europe. Perhaps they will. But they are more likely to prefer the view that rich allies should take on their own self-defense to the view that destiny compels Americans to be satisfied with markedly less domestic spending than these same allies.

These last considerations lead to a second alternative interpretation of US economic imbalances: Why not assume that America's combined domestic and international imbalances represent the system's way of compensating for America's outsized geopolitical role? Owing to its excessive military burdens, the US runs large fiscal and external imbalances. But the dollar's world role and the US government's capacity to manipulate the dollar allow America's imbalances to be financed to a great extent by its allies. This process constitutes, in effect, a form of involuntary burden-sharing. The monetary formula for imposing the burden-sharing changes – from Bretton Woods to floating rates, from loose money to tight money. Under Bretton Woods, allies were constrained to accumulate the dollar deficits in their reserves. Under Nixon's floating rates, the US could print money at will while the declining dollar improved American trade and depreciated American debts. Volcker's tight money induced foreigners to loan back the inflated money that the US had exported earlier. Each of these formulas has its inherent limits but policy can alternate between them indefinitely. The basic idea remains the same: the international monetary system is the mechanism for imperial taxation. It recompenses the hegemon for providing those public goods of security and leadership without which the global system would collapse.[40] Behind the monetary manipulations, of course, lies the American fiscal problem – itself the product of an unsatisfactory mix of military and civilian spending and inadequate revenues.

Broadly speaking, such an interpretation seems almost certainly correct. The imbalances seem the way that the present international organism channels the resources from the free-riders to the hegemon. Unfortunately, however, an organism that can only function in this fashion seems in poor health. A global liberal market economy seems incompatible, over time, with perpetual monetary instability. Where currencies fluctuate so widely, rational market calculations for long-range investment become more and more impossible. Capitalism geared to rational growth becomes transformed into "Casino Capitalism" geared to financial speculation.[41] Paradoxically, the rapid growth that postwar capitalism has brought to the world economy – the explosion of technological change and the spread of industry to the Third World – now poses challenges that current capitalism, stricken with monetary instability, seems less and less equipped to handle. Lenin once observed that the best way to destroy capitalism was to debauch its currency.[42] Unfortunately, this may prove one of his more reliable insights. In short, we may be approaching the point where the economic policies made necessary by America's hegemonic exertions are themselves a principal affliction for the international system the US is seeking to sustain.

Reflections of this kind suggest a gloomy future. Hence, the current preoccupation with the question of great power decline. Certainly, if there are great troubles in store, many analysts have long expected them. Meanwhile, those with constitutionally optimistic temperaments may put their faith in the fundamental vitality of liberal societies and the undoubted capacity of governments and other major actors to come up with successful expedients to keep an apparently unsound system going. To paraphrase Keynes' oft-cited dictum: In the long run we are all dead: meanwhile, most of us are doing quite well. There is always the possibility, moreover, that the United States can restore its own inner equilibrium, perhaps because it will find, with its principal allies, some more balanced and efficient form of "burden sharing" and management for the global system from which all have profited so handsomely.

40 For an extended view of this argument, see Calleo, *Beyond American Hegemony*, chapter 7.
41 The financial world's growing disarray is knowledgeably explored by Susan Strange in *Casino Capitalism* (New York: Oxford University Press, 1986).
42 Ascribed to Lenin by John Maynard Keynes, writing in 1919, "Inflation and Deflation," *Essays in Persuasion* (New York: W. W. Norton and Co. 1963), p. 77

8

The Rise of the State in China and Japan

Gilbert Rozman

The postwar experiences of China and Japan have challenged social scientists to rethink popular theories of social change, often with special attention to the role of the state in both historical and contemporary times. Out of the various images of the East Asian state that have gained a wide following have come some important correctives to Western-based theories as well as some idealized wishful thinking that proved deceptive. What is needed is not only to identify the general themes that appear to be of lasting significance for theories of the state, but also to summarize for each stage of historical development many of the striking features of Chinese and Japanese state formation and then to incorporate these findings directly into the comparative study of the state.

The histories of China and Japan can help us to avoid simplistic errors sometimes found in theories about the state. Even slight familiarity with the enormous impact on Japanese history of reorganizing the state (in the seventh and eighth centuries on a Chinese model, in the sixteenth and seventeenth centuries on an indigenous model, in the 1860s–1870s on an eclectic Western model, and in the second half of the 1940s on an American model) should cast suspicion on the Marxist (and especially Stalinist) deterministic theory of the state's insignificance as an independent force in social change. The failure of China's experiments after 1949 at massive recasting of the state (the Stalinist model, the Great Leap Forward, and the Cultural Revolution) should also alert us to the long-run futility of voluntaristic approaches that assume the state is highly malleable and can lead the society toward some leader's concept of Utopia. Moreover, the remarkable continuity of the Chinese state over 2,000 years and the continuous state-directed modernization of Japan over a century are but two of the striking features that should be examined in our search for regularities in state development.

Conventional definitions of the state and its functions run the risk of squeezing comparisons into an ill-fitting framework. Our emphasis is on

actual conditions, not on fine distinctions based on ideological or legal categories. To treat the Chinese Communist Party as separate from the Chinese
state after 1949 is to make unintelligible much of the close, centralized control
over the Chinese people. In real life, party authority overlapped with and
deeply penetrated state authority. After all, neither Deng Xiaoping nor Mikhail
Gorbachev exercised power on the basis of a state office before the latter
sought additional offices. In actual practice too, the long-time legal right of
the Chinese emperor to the land of his subjects did not normally interfere
with the prevalent land market based on private ownership. For Japanese
history in the Tokugawa era (1600–1868) we must be prepared to recognize
the simultaneous existence of more than 250 territorially distinct states, which
for some purposes can be usefully perceived as a single state and for others
as an interconnected network of states, each with its own personnel and
functions.[1] Focusing on the actual administration of the national territory is
necessary to appreciate the functions of the state in successive periods.

Looking back from the late twentieth century, we can discern at least three
powerful regional traditions with continued significance for the contemporary
world. The Western traditions placed the most limits on state authority, recognizing the vested rights of relatively autonomous interest groups; the
Northern traditions, primarily those of the Russian empire and its successor,
placed the fewest limits, relying on state ownership and controls such as those
over the state peasants and the embryonic heavy industries. Capitalism and
Marxist–Leninist socialism evolved from these traditions respectively. The
Eastern traditions of the Confucian sphere of influence were, in some sense,
intermediate between these extremes. To be more precise we should turn to
the histories of China and Japan for both premodern and modern times,
comparing the functions of the state within the region and beyond. As a
prelude to this, we may find it helpful to recall successive images of the East
Asian state which have gained popularity in recent decades.

Eight Postwar Images of the East Asian State

The state in China or Japan has been at the center of at least eight debates in
the postwar era. During the 1950s a debate still flared about how peculiarities
of the Japanese state in the Meiji era (1868–1911), perhaps rooted in the
preceding Tokugawa era (1600–1868), gave rise to Japanese militarism in the
first two decades of the Showa era (1926–88).[2] Meiji centralism, associated

1 Harold Bolitho, *Treasures Among Men: The Fudai Daimyo in Tokugawa Japan* (New
   Haven, Connecticut: Yale University Press, 1974), pp. 7–46.
2 Richard Smethurst, *A Social Basis for Prewar Japanese Militarism: the Army and the
   Rural Community* (Berkeley, California: University of California Press, 1974);
   James W. Morley, ed., *Dilemmas of Growth in Prewar Japan* (Princeton, New
   Jersey: Princeton University Press, 1971).

in Marxist writings with what was called an incomplete bourgeois revolution, somehow had managed to revitalize an ancient imperial institution and to keep alive aspects of the *samurai* heritage of devoted service. The result was symbolized by kamikaze pilots, mass civilian suicides on the island of Okinawa about to be occupied by the American armed forces, and other expressions of zealotry on behalf of the state. Such a dangerous tradition of state devotion needed to be expunged, the world and the newly critical Japanese agreed.

Simultaneously a debate was beginning about how peculiarities of the Chinese state had made that country ripe for communist revolution and the building of socialism. Mao Zedong was described as the heir to two millennia of Chinese emperors and to the expectations that a unified and strong state was essential to overcome greedy divisiveness and foreign incursions, of which warlordism, capitalism, and imperialism were the twentieth-century manifestations.[3] Whether revolution stemmed ultimately from the Asiatic Mode of Production, from peasant determination to restore the Mandate of Heaven, or from some continuity with the Qing dynasty's (1644–1911) Confucian claims to produce dedicated officials on behalf of a harmonious social order, communist demands for "thought reform" to achieve total commitment to the state's cause symbolized the new order.

From the second half of the 1960s the East Asian state acquired a new image; the most recent generalizations that postwar Japan was but a clone of American capitalism and that socialist China closely resembled its "big brother," the Soviet Union, were rapidly losing favor. The Tokugawa state (or states) impressed historians as the sponsor of commercial growth, urban development, and other preconditions of modern economic advancement, and the Meiji state found favor as the engine for modernization from above.[4] The concept of "Japan, Inc." suggested an intermediate path between capitalism or socialism or at least a form of capitalism in which the state enlisted the best minds as officials who worked together with the private sector in unwavering pursuit of international competitiveness. Observers discovered in the Japanese state, past and present, a powerful force for national advancement.

The Sino–Soviet split, soon followed by the Cultural Revolution, was at the same time fostering an image of the Chinese state uniquely oriented toward organizing grassroots participation in modern development. Through deprofessionalization and decentralization, as symbolized by the activist who

3 Chalmers A. Johnson, *Peasant Nationalism and Communist Power: The Emergence of Revolutionary China 1937–1945* (Stanford, California: Stanford University Press, 1962); Benjamin I. Schwartz, *Chinese Communism and the Rise of Mao* (New York: Harper & Row, 1951).
4 John W. Hall and Marius B. Jansen, eds, *Studies in the Institutional History of Early Modern Japan* (Princeton, New Jersey: Princeton University Press, 1968); Marius B. Jansen, *Changing Japanese Attitudes Toward Modernization* (Princeton, New Jersey: Princeton University Press, 1968).

was "both red and expert," the state could allegedly avoid bureaucratism.[5] Soviet "totalitarianism" and "revolution from above" had been rejected by Marxist populism, which claimed to "serve the masses." Already in just two or three decades four popular images of the East Asian state had appeared, each emphasizing its uniqueness within one country.

From the end of the 1970s the debate concerning the Chinese state turned abruptly. It now resembled the immediate postwar debate in Japan about undemocratic traditions. In both instances, the term "feudalism" depicted an intrusive state which disregarded citizens' rights and an unjust society divided by inequality not based on ability. In China the focus centered also on officials who basked in privileges at the expense of community interests. Within Chinese reform circles, the criticisms widened to reject the preceding models of socialism – treating Mao's Cultural Revolution as but a variation of Stalin's overcentralized model of state control.[6] Thirty years after the Chinese state had come to represent China's salvation and the Japanese state Japan's misfortune, the tide had been reversed as Japan, Inc. won world renown while China's state-led experiments to find a new path of development were renounced in favor of the conventional "four modernizations."

In the mid-1980s, a sixth image of the state was beginning to bridge Japan and China, premodern East Asian history, and the recent rise of the various countries with a common Confucian heritage. It was essentially an extension of the fourth image from Japan to China and the rest of the region. The ideological extremism of Maoist development had been replaced by pragmatic growth in which traditional entrepreneurship coexisted with a neo-authoritarian state that guides development. The positive role credited to the Japanese state two decades earlier was seen to be repeated everywhere in the region. Despite two more recent images, the popularity of this regional image remains high.

Late in the 1980s the tide of thinking about East Asian states turned again. Abruptly Taiwan and Korea shifted to more democratic practices, including tolerance for a genuine political opposition with real prospects for electoral victory. At about the same time Mikhail Gorbachev dramatized the urgency of political reform in socialist countries seeking to break away from the traditional model. External forces cast doubt on the impression that neo-authoritarianism could long endure, but it was primarily internal forces in Japan and China that provoked a further rethinking of the nature of the state in the two great powers of East Asia.

5 Franz Schurmann, *Ideology and Organization in Communist China* (Berkeley, California: University of California Press, 1966); Maurice Meisner, *Mao's China: A History of the People's Republic* (New York: The Free Press, 1977).
6 Stuart R. Schram, *Ideology and Politics in China Since the Third Plenum, 1978–1984* (London: Contemporary China Institute, School of Oriental and African Studies, Research Notes and Studies, No. 6, 1984); Gilbert Rozman, *The Chinese Debate About Soviet Socialism 1978–1985* (Princeton, New Jersey: Princeton University Press, 1987).

In the spring of 1989 the Recruit stock trading scandal brought down the Takeshita government, while posing a threat to the cozy relationship between the party "permanently" in power and the interests it best favors. The tone shifted from self-confidence to dismay as Japanese looked favorably on the need to place new checks on the state. They demanded further convergence with Western democratic ideals. The death of the emperor who had first led Japan's militarism and then after 1945 came to symbolize a quiet role for traditions in the midst of frenzied modernization also stirred debate for a time. Reexamination of the political process did not, however, imply rejection of the developmental state.

Simultaneously, student demonstrations following the death of former Party Secretary Hu Yaobang rallied the Chinese public against the continued un-representative rule of the communist leadership. Troubles with recent economic reforms and a high level of social discontent were traced largely to the nondemocratic character of the state; pressure within China mounted for reforms which, as in the USSR, would increase convergence with Western democracies. The seventieth anniversary in 1989 of the May Fourth Movement also spotlighted the recurrent struggle to establish a modern society based on science and democracy. After the brutal crackdown of June 4 the Chinese Communist Party refused to countenance further democratic changes which would threaten its own leading role in guiding not only economic policy but also the general contours of social change; yet the domestic and international image of what was needed was precisely that.

The most recent images follow from China's widely heralded "open door" and Japan's vaguely defined "internationalization." They do not deny the enduring regional heritage of the Confucian state, or the two separate histories of strong developmental nationalism, but they stress the prospect in the 1990s of continuing international integration and recognizing interest groups which make demands on the state typical of a modernized society. Critics now call on the state to catch up to the recent transformations of society.

While these eight images have been fleeting, persons interested in historical comparisons of East Asian states face some enduring questions. For a long-term perspective, we seek to know: 1) Has the gradual evolution of the state followed a different path in China or Japan from patterns found elsewhere? 2) Were the structures and functions of the eighteenth-century state, prior to the onset of modern development, distinctive? 3) Did the tradition of the state in each country play an important and unusual role in modernization? In each case, we seek to understand how Japan and China differed from predominant European patterns and from each other and why these differences arose. For the postwar era, it is appropriate to consider: 4) how did the state traditions of each country interact with the usually recognized patterns of socialism or capitalism? and 5) how are those traditions now responding to the challenge of internationalization? Even as we keep changing our short-term view of the East Asian state, we continue to reaffirm that East Asian states are significantly different and to recognize their growing importance for an understanding of world development.

The Directed Society

The history of China and Japan is the history of the rise of the directed society. State guidance normally has taken precedence over either outright administration or legal recognition of the vested rights of interest groups. Although there have been periods when old state forms were in decline, criticisms were largely directed against distortions in the principles of state government. Expectations continued to center on a paternalistic state capable of leading a harmonious society. Today, even at times of countervailing pressures against the nondemocratic aspects of the state, those expectations remain high. The resurgent societies of the East Asian region are led in international competition by strong states.

The two principal alternatives to the directed society were largely discredited in Chinese and Japanese history. On the one hand, the administered society had fallen into ill repute following the Warring States era in each country as incapable of winning the hearts of the people. In China the "legalist" state of the Qin dynasty (220–206 BC) was well-remembered as the foil of the much revered Confucian state – too reliant on laws which failed to take individual motives and personal relationships into account, too harsh in its application of laws and procedures, and too little concerned with governing by virtuous example and moral suasion.[7] Recently the Maoist form of socialism has been associated with this negative image of the obtrusive state. In Japan sixteenth-century lords who, in a time of internecine warfare, had acted in haste through commands to gather together the resources of their domains were recalled as self-destructive for their failure to nurture the long-term development of the areas that provided for their well-being.[8] Severe measures might be justified, but only if based on accurate surveys of ability to bear the burden and on collective community responsibility. Concepts such as harmony, moderation, and service to the people all drew attention to the need to limit the state's direct intrusion into the daily lives and orderly affairs of the people. The heavy-handed Japanese state in the 1930s and the first half of the 1940s is also remembered as stifling diversity to the detriment of the national welfare.

On the other hand, a society of vested rights and powerful interest groups – religious organizations, guilds, autonomous localities, etc. – had become associated in each country with periods of widespread disorder or anarchy when elementary security was difficult to provide. Recurrent reminders in Chinese history of the price of civil disorder or warlordism and the freshness of the Warring States destructiveness for Tokugawa Japan left a strong bias against a weakened state. There was fear of ideological confusion and fractious clashes among schools of thought, associated with armed movements and a

7   Frederick W. Mote, *Intellectual Foundations of China* (New York: Alfred A. Knopf, 1971).
8   Peter Duus, *Feudalism in Japan* (New York: Alfred A. Knopf, 1969).

new outburst of violence and disorder. Not a balance of power among contending social groups, but a monopoly of power exercised with restraint provided by moral instruction and internal administrative checks was deemed by many to be the proper form of government. The self-serving Chinese Communist Party and Japanese Liberal Democratic Party each held up the specter of civil disarray (linked to the breakdown of family stability in the West or to recent domestic memories such as the Cultural Revolution and Japan's student protests in 1960 or 1969).

Conscious of the two extremes they wished to avoid, Chinese and Japanese were attracted to a third approach to the state rooted in the thought of Confucius. Confucius and his leading followers were theorists of the state and of the social setting in which it operated. They envisioned a state that had to be bolstered against aristocratic fiefdoms and to be secured through both impressive symbols of legitimacy and outstanding professional service.[9] Confucius proposed a social agenda, which he equated with civilization and which could only be achieved from the top down, beginning with a ruler who acted virtuously under the advice of scholars who were "superior men." The state would be judged according to how well it served the welfare of its citizens, who, in turn, were to be educated in the proper behavior toward their superiors. From these teachings came the image of the state directly linked to its citizens and ruling through moral suasion and careful arrangement of social institutions as well as through dedicated civil servants.

Functions of the Premodern State

Guided by the Confucian political culture, Chinese leaders responded to the advance of the "forces of production" to build a state on an unprecedented scale but with modest ambitions. In some ways, it was remarkably modern in its organization. The search for the most able officials, based on ability rather than ascription, led one thousand years ago to an exam system legally open to almost all males and administered in accessible, district capitals (and, for those who qualified for higher exams, more central locations) throughout a vast land. Rather high premodern levels of urbanization, commercialized agriculture, and fluidity among social classes were utilized as a base for more bureaucratic government. Yet, the political culture originally designed to thwart hereditary privilege was not adjusted to favor the interest of new forces based on commercial wealth.

The Chinese state did not seek to build a different order on the basis of the commercial revolution which gathered force about 1,000 years ago. Extensive means already existed for the massive inflow of tax revenues through countless rivulets originating from a population rising into the hundreds of millions.

9   Kung-chuan Hsiao, *A History of Chinese Political Thought*, vol. 1, tr. F. W. Mote (Princeton, New Jersey: Princeton University Press, 1979).

External challenges before the nineteenth century were insufficient to arouse interest in a reorganization of the state. The Chinese state jealously guarded its prerogatives without innovating for new purposes.[10] Potential rival sources of power were carefully divided or coopted; when rebellion did succeed, it was not led by the commercial elite but by those for whom the old image of the state order was too compelling to discard.

The premodern Japanese state (or states) proved more variable, as it was massively reorganized from the top down on two occasions and from the bottom up at other times. Two factors operated with greater force than in China: conscious planning in response to changing conditions and trial-and-error in a highly competitive environment. Yet, in the seventeenth century when government reached its final and most stable premodern form, Japanese leaders reaffirmed the Confucian principles.[11] They gave precedence to the ideological functions of the state and established an environment in which state demands became predictable. Japan's blend of Confucian traditions and *samurai* way of life, updated to reflect the organizational capacities of an already relatively urbanized and commercialized society by premodern standards, led to many differences with the Chinese state; although both were Confucian in their self-image and functional orientation.

Historians have long contrasted the state systems of Qing China and Tokugawa Japan. They have labeled the former autocratic and centralized; a powerful emperor ruled through a single national bureaucracy. In contrast, Japan has been called feudal for its division into more than 250 separately administered domains. Its emperor remained weak, and in seclusion in Kyoto, while the *shōgun* in Edo directly administered barely one-fifth of the country. The *shōgun* as well as the *daimyō* who administered the domains relied on personal vassals grouped together into hereditary *samurai* bands. Conscious of this diversity between the two great East Asian countries, historians have found it easy to overlook the commonalities.

If we examine four functions of the state, we can gain a general impression of the Chinese state's evolution and its performance in the Qing era. First is the ideological power of the state. This includes education, censorship, guardianship of the traditional philosophy and worldview, religious supervision, and paternalistic concern for social life. The Chinese state regarded these tasks as central to a well-functioning society. Emperors prepared commentaries on Confucian classics and launched massive projects to organize knowledge. They sought to win over scholars, initially those who were holdovers from the previous dynasty. Their strategy was to control the people through virtuous

10 Gilbert Rozman, ed., *The Modernization of China* (New York: The Free Press, 1981).
11 Herman Ooms, *Tokugawa Ideology* (Princeton, New Jersey: Princeton University Press, 1985); Peter Nosco, ed., *Confucianism and Tokugawa Culture* (Princeton, New Jersey: Princeton University Press, 1984).

examples, especially using the many scholars who were awarded examination degrees. A literate population well-informed about the Confucian principles of behavior was deemed most suitable for ideological control.

Chinese leaders sought moral influence through graduated methods targeted for different levels of education. Tightly controlled examinations defined the path to prestige for the most ambitious. Morally infused basic education reached much larger numbers. For others there were also lectures read in villages throughout the land. Undoubtedly the lectures became ritualized, and crude suppression of heterodox ideas often took precedence over moral suasion.[12] Yet the amount of attention and the percentage of state resources devoted to ideological objectives are testimony to the unusual development of ideological functions for a premodern state.

A second function of the Chinese state was revenue gathering. Large sums were involved, but on a per capita basis they did not amount to much.[13] Moreover, in the Qing period tax quotas were long frozen despite a vast upsurge in the economy and the population. The state's uses for money and revenue in kind were clearly specified, centering on supplying the official community in Beijing, supporting a standing army in scattered garrisons, and redistributing relief to areas beset by famine. The costs were normally modest in comparison to resources available to a population climbing to 300 million in the eighteenth century and 400 million by the middle of the nineteenth. While corruption diverted increasing local surcharges away from state coffers, these were irregular sums. The state did not continuously enlarge its appetite.

The third function to consider is the state's role in managing the Chinese economy and reorganizing the society. There was a tradition of state monopolies that persisted, especially through the large salt monopoly of the Qing era. Yet, the state did not sponsor new types of production or export. It was little concerned with promoting economic change.[14] Powers of licensing and regulation of merchant guilds and transport organizations were in part customary, allowing existing units to obtain protection from ex-officials who wielded continued influence at a higher administrative level, and in part arbitrary, permitting the magistrate who temporarily exercised state power to act for personal ends. The state yielded or it stifled, but it did not mobilize.

Finally the premodern Chinese state was obsessed with maintaining an orderly and harmonious society through reenforcement of family and lineage organizations and suppression of intermediate and heterodox organizations with any potential for turning into a mass movement or a center of power. The Chinese concept of order posited a self-limited state serving the interests

---

12   Kung-chuan Hsiao, *Rural China: Imperial Control in the Nineteenth Century* (Seattle, Washington: University of Washington Press, 1960).
13   Yeh-chien Wang, *Land Taxation in Imperial China, 1750–1911* (Cambridge, Massachusetts: Harvard University Press, 1973).
14   Rozman, *Modernization of China*.

of the ordinary people through a meritorious elite it selected and rewarded without the interference of interest groups.

The usual forces thought to transform the premodern state played a less conspicuous role in China. Powerful landowners in certain regions showed that they could defend class interests, but on the whole social classes could not solidify against the bureaucratic Chinese state. Moreover, other states were of little consequence prior to the 1840s. The emperor of China wielded great power in opposing any individual or locality; yet, as a rule, his power was bound by a bureaucracy steeped in custom. The major check on the state was from within – based on universalistic criteria of hiring and idealistic contents of training. Often insufficient in preventing misconduct, these checks made systemic change difficult. The Chinese state was also relatively unresponsive to the development of technology; its worldview, organization, and bureaucratic size changed slowly. This was a state with extraordinary power to renew itself, but little impetus to transform itself.

Tokugawa Japan appears to contrast sharply with Qing China in its state mechanism. In place of a single centralized state bureaucracy under an all-powerful emperor, Japan supported numerous separate bureaucracies each under its own lord. The lords owed allegiance to the *shōgun* in Edo on condition that he respect their autonomy on most matters and not seek to alter the territorial balance of power. Hereditary *samurai* warriors served as state servants in place of China's scholars who had personally passed a series of grueling exams to become mandarins.

The ideological commitment of Japan's many states derived from the same Confucian writings followed in China. There was no examination system to induce years of intense memorization and less state concern with Confucian lectures and ritual on a mass scale; yet Japan in the Tokugawa era became much more Confucianized than it had been. Moral commitment to the state for the *samurai* fused feudal and Zen loyalties. Organizational attachments made ideology a more active force in a competitive setting of personalized bands of retainers. With the rapid spread of mass literacy, the ideological function in Japan approached the level already reached in China and, for an elite group, became even more intense and immediate.[15]. The state's function was to instruct its citizens and to command their devoted service in the name of a common cause.

Unlike China, Japanese states mobilized vast resources directly from the production of each farming household. The domains taxed heavily in order to pay the stipends of their many *samurai* and the heavy expenses of travel to Edo and maintenance of large estates there. They were under pressure to expand revenue, but normally did not further increase taxes. Instead, they sought to stimulate exports. Thus the Japanese states surpassed China in creating monopolies (but within a nationwide competitive environment) and promoting

---

15 Ronald Dore, *Education in Tokugawa Japan* (Berkeley, California: University of California Press, 1965).

182 *Gilbert Rozman*

commerce. Having removed *samurai* from direct involvement in the local
economy, the states established formal and relatively impersonal controls,
which enabled long-term planning.[16] In both revenue gathering and economic
management, the Japanese experience contrasts to that of China because of
the depth and regularity of the state's role.

Japanese states also organized society in the interests of harmony and public
order. They adopted new principles of social organization as part of social
engineering without precedent in China. Japan took advantage of centuries of
economic development to reorganize cities. New types of merchant groupings
rose successively in the Tokugawa era. The degree of public order for over
two centuries was extraordinary, but society accommodated new forces.

There can be no doubt about the considerable autonomy of the Chinese
and Japanese states in the Qing and Tokugawa periods. The elite classes were
state-created and heavily dependent. The Japanese states paid stipends to the
samurai and, in times of financial need, borrowed from them. Despite an
increasing perception of poverty on the part of lower *samurai* and alarm about
other classes gaining in income, the *samurai* were in no position to protest.[17]
They owed complete obedience to their lord and lived by a code of honor that
made suicide more acceptable than rebellion. Chinese scholar-officials gained
their elite status through state recognition and then depended on the state for
appointed office or informal influence. They too were steeped in an ideology
of service and public calling. Through these legions of hundreds of thousands
of loyal and carefully groomed officials or officials-in-waiting, the state reached
down to the population below.

Autonomy rested on tight military controls (though these tended to break
down across the vast expanses of China and neighboring Central Asia), on
purposeful social organization to deny challenges to state power, and on
ideological controls. For the elite, at least, the last of these was expected to
take precedence.

While the Confucian state in each instance is autonomous and emphasizes
ideological controls, Japan and China also present a contrast in state development. The Tokugawa state, drawing on advances in infrastructure, became
more mobilizational. By the early seventeenth century in the cities and the
early eighteenth century in the countryside, it became a potent engine for
change (even though there was still no perception of the need for modernization). The state's power had grown in Japan, in part, because in a period of
civil wars and intense competition strong states outperformed their rivals –
they measured farm areas precisely and taxed to extract the maximum burden
affordable, they consolidated territories by locating a new city at the most

16 Susan Hanley and Kozo Yamamura, *Economic and Demographic Change in Preindustrial Japan, 1600–1868* (Princeton, New Jersey: Princeton University Press,
1977).
17 Kozo Yamamura, *A Study of Samurai Income and Entrepreneurship* (Cambridge:
Harvard University Press, 1974).

accessible point and developing transport to it, and they gathered merchants and artisans to support the newly consolidated *samurai* bands. Japanese also learned the lesson that a strong state can cut the losses to despotism by curtailing the use of force against its own people and by establishing a predictable environment in which those of the same status are treated equitably.

The Transition from Premodern to Modern

In most obvious respects the premodern states of China and Japan were unprepared for the confrontation with the states of the West. The old governments were doomed. As in other regions of the world, the struggle began to establish new states capable of developing the domestic economy, meeting the external military challenge, and maintaining internal order.

In a matter of several decades, the Japanese state achieved all of the goals common to the late developers. It took little time for its numerous premodern governments to become joined into one centralized modern state. This transition is known as Meiji centralization.[18] Comparisons with China, which spent about one century in the transition to a modern state able to exercise nationwide authority, help us to appreciate how Japan's rapid transition occurred. Our purpose here is not to restate these comparisons, but to identify what was distinctive about each of the two East Asian states in transition.

Infrastructural power greatly depends on the international level of industrial development; even when a country remains little modernized it can acquire the advanced technology from outside that permits its government to penetrate the rest of society to a degree previously unrealizable. Japan built the new infrastructural power more rapidly, in part because its premodern infrastructure (of cities, urban bureaucracies, tax revenues, transportation networks, etc.) was greater. Also the new Japanese state adopted premodern functions that were more easily converted to centralization. Yet, these same functions served the needs of state building in China too.

One key to Japan's success was the ability of its leaders to convert the ideological function to modern purposes. Domain loyalty in the competitive Tokugawa environment reappeared as Japanese nationalism in the world system of states. This switchover was facilitated by the symbolism of the emperor, who after centuries of obscurity became the central ruler, and by the rapid spread of mass elementary schooling with an emphasis on moral upbringing.[19] Chinese ideological expectations lacked a close association with nationalism, a new symbol, and a modern mechanism for dissemination.

---

18 Marius B. Jansen and Gilbert Rozman, eds, *Japan in Transition: From Tokugawa to Meiji* (Princeton, New Jersey: Princeton University Press, 1986).

19 W. G. Beasley, *The Meiji Restoration* (Stanford, California: Stanford University Press, 1972); Richard Rubinger, *Private Academies of Tokugawa Japan* (Princeton, New Jersey: Princeton University Press, 1981).

Eventually communist ideology began to fill the vacuum for many Chinese, who found a replacement for Confucianism in its universalistic claims and promises of social harmony associated with moral superiority. As Chalmers Johnson noted, China's war against the invading Japanese forged a strong bond between growing nationalism and communism.[20] Under Mao Zedong, the communists squandered their opportunity by turning against each other and failing to understand the requirements of modernization.

The ideological factor gained more and more prominence in Japan's prewar development. The state was proclaimed to be the highest level in a unique hierarchy including community and family that enabled Japanese to act in unison with little social disorder. As justification for its aggressive pursuit of an 'East Asian Co-prosperity Sphere,' Japanese claimed to be transferring these superior forms of social solidarity to other countries which shared the Confucian heritage.[21] Tight censorship and police controls over academic deviance were consistent with Tokugawa insistence on ideological conformity,[22] while the use of state Shintoism to reinforce state authority represented a further step in bolstering the state's moral authority. Despite the prominence of the Japanese military in foreign policy decisions and leadership clashes, Japan did not become a tightly administered society (apart from the exigencies of the peak war years). Socialization took precedence over coercion.[23]

The Contemporary Chinese and Japanese States

Japan's state development over the past four centuries can be divided into three stages. The late sixteenth-century unification of the country after a century of Warring States culminated in the development of the Tokugawa state system. The reform era of the 1860s and 1870s brought Meiji centralization and the prewar and wartime state. Finally the reforms of the allied occupation produced the contemporary state.

The postwar state in Japan started with a push away from authoritarianism and especially militarism, and a pull toward democracy. The result has been a combination of Japan's East Asian traditions and Western democratic institutions. In many fields we can see a "reverse course," pulling Japan away from the letter of the occupational reforms. In education, despite continuous resist-

20 Chalmers Johnson, *MITI and the Japanese Miracle: The Growth of Industrial Policy, 1925–1975* (Stanford, California: Stanford University Press, 1982).
21 Ramon H. Myers and Mark R. Peattie, *The Japanese Colonial Empire, 1895–1945* (Princeton, New Jersey: Princeton University Press, 1984).
22 Richard H. Mitchell, *Censorship in Imperial Japan* (Princeton, New Jersey: Princeton University Press, 1983).
23 Kazuko Tsurumi, *Social Change and the Individual: Japan Before and After Defeat in World War II* (Princeton, New Jersey: Princeton University Press, 1970).

ance from left-oriented teachers' unions, Japan has centralized the curriculum and reinserted moral education.[24] In industrial policy, after the *zaibatsu* were split up, Japan has reinforced the prewar reliance on administrative guidance.[25] Ezra F. Vogel describes meritocratic guidance by the state without loss of private initiative. The central bureaucracy is powerful, leading bureaucrats have attended the best universities and enjoy great respect, state planning plays a major role. Vogel is not alone in attributing much of Japan's postwar success to 'central direction' which does not stifle local initiative.[26]

The Japanese state is not in decline. Although its military expenses remain low relative to the GNP and its direct intrusion into many spheres is still limited by the shadow left from memories of World War II, the state has been credited by the Japanese people with stunning postwar success. Predictions for Japan's future take for granted the further enlargement of the state's role in a context of expanded internationalism. Yet, there is also a spreading image of the state as the handmaiden of special business interests and of the general standard of living as too low for an economic superpower. State reform is likely to mean more checks on political corruption if not a reduced role for the state.

In the case of China the state is currently the subject of much controversy. The combination of the Confucian tradition and the Stalinist model, produced a state that combined administrative guidance through moral appeal with direct state control, through a command economy and planning of virtually all facets of life. China's current communist leaders vigorously criticize this older socialist state, yet until 1989 insisted that only modest structural reforms are necessary. Reformers demand a sweeping critique of past errors, insisting on political reforms commensurate with economic ones and capable of breathing new life into economic incentives. The reformers are increasingly in the ascendancy among the urban population, especially the intelligentsia.

The old model is now seen as a failure. It was unstable, leading to frequent shifts in direction. It was contradictory, claiming to operate according to principles it directly violated on a large scale. The Chinese state has become less intrusive since the reforms of Deng Xiaoping began in 1978, but much more is demanded in an environment where clientalism and dependency remain widespread, especially in places of employment.[27].

Battles over the future of the Chinese state have erupted periodically over the past decade. One of the most open clashes of views occurred in late 1986 before the clampdown of early 1987 that followed student demonstrations. In

24 William K. Cummings, *Education and Equality in Japan* (Princeton, New Jersey: Princeton University Press, 1980).
25 Johnson, *MITI and the Japanese Miracle.*
26 Ezra F. Vogel, *Japan as No. 1* (Cambridge: Harvard University Press, 1979) pp. 53–96.
27 A. G. Walder, *Communist Neo-Traditionalism: Work and Authority in Chinese Industry* (Berkeley, California: University of California Press, 1986).

the spring of 1989 the students again took to the streets, with more stunning effect. Beijing lags behind Moscow under Gorbachev in acknowledging the shortcomings of its political system and recognizing the need for political reforms. Criticisms of Stalinism in the Soviet Union are harsher than those of Stalinism or Maoism in China. Democratic initiatives such as those adopted by the 19th Party Conference in Moscow, or those initiated in Taiwan at roughly the same time, exceed those acceptable to Chinese communist leaders. Yet, the pressure from below and from Gorbachev's example have created a powerful force for reform that cannot be ignored for long.

The Chinese state continues to insist on an ideological function greater than that found in Japan. Although a crisis of ideology occurred at the end of the 1970s when the Cultural Revolution was repudiated, campaigns against "spiritual pollution" recur with some regularity. The situation is precarious because the ideology of the 1980s deviates sharply from the reality of the formerly successful economic policies and of the currently inconsistent policies of retrenchment. The most creative Marxist intellectuals who have sought to place ideology on a new, more accurate, historical footing have found themselves the targets of orthodox ideological campaigns. Just as Mao insisted on mass ideological purity that Stalin had made little effort to foster, current Chinese leaders feel a need to supplement economic programs with ideological ones. It is less the Confucian heritage than the besieged communist ideology which keeps this preoccupation alive in Beijing.

China's "Open Door" policies bring foreign influences into the country on an increasing scale. The long-term tendency, temporarily interrupted by the military repression from June 1989, is for the Chinese state to continue to adapt to the needs of world ties, while relaxing its direct controls in response to effects of modernizing reforms at home and foreign intellectual currents reaching a new generation of leaders. Resistance by party and state officials whose power is at stake has delayed reforms in the state system. China's transition to a directed society with moderate administrative interference and a rising voice for middle class and capitalist interest groups remains especially uncertain. Yet, the combination of pragmatic policies, the needs of modernization, international influences, and Confucian traditions will all lead in that direction. The added force of intense popular pressure is difficult to resist.

Functions of East Asian States in the Near Future

Japan is now one of the three superpowers, while China's military aspirations and recent economic growth rates together with its vast population may soon justify the recently popular claim that it too is a superpower. Both countries are moving cautiously into the role of global power in an era both describe as a time of decline for the two preexisting superpowers. Japan defines its international role largely in economic terms, although its growing rivalry with the Soviet Union is propelling increased involvement in matters affecting the global strategic balance. China is seeking regional influence as a great power and is also reaching out to other parts of the Third World.

Analysts in both countries claim to have found a lesson from the decline of the United States and the Soviet Union.[28] They see an excessive military orientation — efforts to do too much at too high a cost. They also see spiritual decline, deteriorating values as people have lost a sense of purpose. Chinese and Japanese leaders and analysts expect to fill some of the gap left by the two receding superpowers, but also focus attention on how they can learn from the mistakes that have been made.

Mainstream thinking in two countries agrees that moral education is vital to national success. They must avoid a sharp deterioration in the moral climate, leading to high crime rates, drug use, juvenile dissatisfaction, and family instability. The state is charged with regulating the moral climate — keeping the attentions of youth fixed on education in Japan and limiting the infiltration of spiritual pollution in China. Also essential is the avoidance of overoptimism or overconfidence. The state sets the tone by making modest claims. As the world becomes more interdependent, it is increasingly necessary to look elsewhere for solutions to problems, to be outward-looking. At the same time, the search for spiritual strength to prevail focuses on the state's encouragement of traditional values.

Chinese reformers and Japanese pragmatists reject ideological rigidity. In place of "continuous revolution," the Chinese now favor "continuous reform." The state must guide in the discarding of outmoded institutions. Responses must be based on accurate information about the outside world. As in earlier Confucian thinking, the quality of the society is seen to depend on the quality of the thinking of the officials who lead it. Of course, Chinese reformers realize that their own country is still far from following the ideals that they advocate and Japanese pragmatists appreciate the need to adjust their own country's practices in order to work together with other societies in an increasingly highly interdependent world. Intensified internal struggles to change their own states are likely to continue in the 1990s even if there is no reason to doubt the persistence of the East Asian model of state guidance over the economy and over the society in general.

---

28 These comments on the Chinese and Japanese views of the Soviet Union and the United States are derived from two recent research projects (Rozman, *The Chinese Debate* and "Japan's Soviet-Watchers in the First Years of the Gorbachev Era: The Search for a Worldview for the Japanese Superpower", *The Pacific Review*, vol. 1, No. 4, 1988, pp. 412–28). The internal (neibu) Chinese journal *Shijie jingji yu zhengzhi neican* (Internal Consultation on World Economies and Politics) and various Japanese journals often discuss the topic of declining superpowers.

9

Birth and Death of Nation States: Speculations about Germany and India

Meghnad Desai

My aim in this paper is to exploit the distance between the notions of nation and nation state, in order to say something about the life cycle of nation states. Nations have no precise chronology of birth and death, no life cycle. Indeed one feature of nationhood is the need for the champions of a nation to argue that the nation in question has very early origins and also that all assertions of its death are exaggerated – the nation will rise again, etc. States by contrast can and do have a finite life cycle – upstart, dissident states which end up at the losing end of civil wars – the Confederacy, Katanga, Biafra are examples of finitely lived states. But I am more concerned in particular with states which claim to be nation states but where the nationhood of the state is at issue and in turn determines the shape of its life cycle.

This happens in my view when the nation and the state which purports to embody the nation don't coincide. Although nations are said to be timeless entities nationalists have taken the view that statehood is necessary for continued life of the nation. But when statehood arrives – when the nation state is born – it often incorporates either a fraction of the nation or it contains more than one nation. Given the ambiguity of nationhood, statehood and nation statehood, it is often the case that both these alternatives – multi-nationality and partinationality – can be used to characterize the state. When this happens, the life cycle of the state is affected if not foreshortened.

My examples to illustrate this contention are Germany and India. In each case I shall argue that the process of constituting a nation state involved a choice among several alternatives, some more inclusive than others. A variety of historical, ideological and personality forces conspired in each case for the

The author would like to thank Gary Llewellyn of the London School of Economics Geography Department Drawing Office for drawing the maps which appear in this chapter.

nation state to be constituted around the exclusive rather than the inclusive option. In the case of Germany, the Reich embodied a particular variant of the alternatives available: the *Kleindeutsch* solution. The Reich had a finite life of 75 years. The Indian case is parallel. In constituting an independent nation state, there was a partition with two states — India and Pakistan. In the 41 years since Independence, Pakistan has again fragmented into two: Pakistan and Bangladesh. India has had to deal severely with subnational movements, most recent of which, Khalistan, has been quite bloody. There are noises of Baluch or Sind nationalism within Pakistan.

Argument by analogy is a procedure which raises many problems. Obviously there are many ways in which Germany and India differ. In comparing two cases across centuries and continents, one expects this. I shall later dwell on the differences which are crucial to my argument. But well before we get into problems posed by analogy, there is a prior problem. The case of Germany is an *ex post* one. Here the nation is already dead. But even then it is difficult to establish a causal link between the choices made at the moment of the formation of nation state and its eventual death. Other hypotheses concerning the death of the Reich have been advanced. There is a lively and still unsettled debate between those who see a continuity in German history from Bismarck (if not before) to Hitler, and those who argue that the Third Reich represents a structural break. I have no hope of being able to add to that debate but in as much as this paper relates to it, the argument here locates a structural break in the 1860s *prior* to the formation of the Reich but does not necessarily take a view on the continuity/structural break post-1871.

It is at this stage, granting that I am able to establish a causal connection, that the argument by analogy faces its real obstacle. While for Germany we are talking of birth and death of the nation state as facts of the past, for India we are talking about a prospective, possible event. This is of course liable to invite the most hostile reaction especially in India where the talk of break-up of India is attributed to be a bloodsport practised by the imperialists. In partial mitigation of this, I wish to point out that India not only split in 1947 but that one of the two constituent states, Pakistan, split again in 1971. Pakistan thus represents an analogy closer to the ground of the German case since the nation state of Pakistan as of 1947 had a life of 23½ years. Pakistan is also closer to India culturally and historically hence, although the German analogy may not be directly transferable to India, mediated through the experience of Pakistan, the argument becomes slightly stronger. But that having been said, the bulk of my discussion about India will also rely on events which took place before 1947, i.e. which are facts although their interpretation still raises many differences.

Ambiguities

To begin with, even the names Germany and India are ambiguous. As a cultural notion, Germany comprised a larger area than what we now call

Germany. In 1801, 1848 or even up to 1865, the word Germany comprised Austria, Prussia and what came to be called The Third Germany: the many smaller states and principalities which were vassals of the Holy Roman Empire and got reconstituted in the course of the Napoleonic War and especially by the Congress of Vienna. The Confederation, as it was called, with its diet in Frankfurt was the most comprehensive territorial expression of Germany but it was not a nation state. But in the 1860s Germany meant the Confederation. It was only after 1871 that it meant Germany as we understand it today.

India is a similarly ambiguous word. Like Germany we come across India as cultural expression in ancient times. But the Government of India (GOI) Act of 1935, one of the longest pieces of legislation debated by the British Parliament to date was meant to apply to British India and the 660 native states. The *goi* Act 1935 was a result of seven years of discussion following the Simon Commission Report, three Round Table conferences in London, parliamentary debates, and the visit of a joint party delegation from Westminster to India. Throughout this debate the discussion concerned the self governance of India as defined in these larger terms. This continued to be the case up to April 1947 although by then proposals for two separate states had been put forward. When independence came in August 1947, two nation states were set up. Calling the larger of the two successor states India meant a lot to the Congress Party and to Nehru, its leader. This meant that India continued from British India and Pakistan was a breakaway state. For Jinnah, this was a distortion of facts. He thought of India as comprising Pakistan and Hindustan, a Muslim and a Hindu nation each embodied in a nation state. In its constitution, the country is called 'India that is Bharat', thus coming half-way between India and Hindustan. When Pakistan split in 1971, the larger successor state called itself Pakistan and the dissident state called itself Bangladesh. Thus India of 1935 was different from India of 1956, and Pakistan of 1950 differed from Pakistan of 1975. Germany of 1850 was not Germany of 1875.

There is a higher order ambiguity about nationality which, though somewhat obscure, merits attention. Although nationalism arose in the nineteenth century as a reaction to the French Revolution and in the periphery as a reaction to the experience of imperial domination, the territorial limits of nations have been as much a product of the external—imperial domination as anything else. Napoleon had more to do with giving a German nation territorial extent than anyone else, by his dismantling of the Holy Roman Empire. It was this defeat in the first wave of Napoleonic wars that began the crystallization process of German nationalism. If Napoleon had won at Waterloo, it is a moot question whether European nationalism would have taken the shape it did.

In case of India, there is a similar ambiguity. Between AD 1500 and 1800, various European maritime countries competed with each other in the Arabian Sea and the Indian Ocean for a monopoly of trade. What they faced was a multiplicity of kingdoms. The Indo Gangetic plain − Hindustan narrowly defined − had been ruled by one or other dynasty ruling from Delhi, first Afghan, followed by the Moghuls in the mid-sixteenth century. Southern

India was often beyond the reach of the Delhi Sultanate and was an open, seafaring economy in contrast to the landlocked subcontinental economy of Northern India. If there was a unifying notion combining these various areas, it was that of a Hindu society. Hinduism, however, was not a unifying creed, certainly not in its sixteenth-century form before it reformed in reaction to the Western challenge. The notion, therefore, that foreigners ruled over India, or that the British conquered India, is a nineteenth-century reconstruction of a much more chaotic process. The Portuguese, the Dutch, the Danes, the French and the English at various times between 1500 and 1800 occupied bits of territory of what we now call India. If they had all stayed, the geography of India could have been very much like that of Africa today with several constituent 'nations'. The English marginalized the Portuguese and the French. With the Dutch and the Danes having quit earlier on, by the middle of the nineteenth-century, the English had succeeded the Moghuls and even extended into the South much more than any previous kingdom. This allowed the Indian nationalists to reconstruct their national past in territorial rather than religious terms alone. It was therefore only then that one could speak of the 'Aryan invasion of India' or of the Battle of Plassey in 1757 marking the beginning of the British conquest of India when both these were regional events, one in the Punjab and the other in Bengal.

Thus it is impossible to avoid some ambiguity in using national labels. It is the essence of nationalism to repudiate the notion advanced above that the nation did not exist prior to its conquest. But if we can avoid teleology, we have to admit that as of, say, 1750, alternative counterfactual scenarios were plausible which could have given us different territorial and political arrangements than those which became Germany and India by 1900.

In order, therefore, to keep ambiguity to the minimum and even at the risk of seeming pretentious, I shall call Germany before 1871 Germania, and India before 1947 Indica.

Two Tentative Propositions and a Corollary

The ambiguity in the terminology of nation states is not an accident but constitutes the essence of the problem. Nations can be defined vaguely. The sense of 'an imagined community' is constituted by some common cultural bond – language, religion, a common historical experience – but need not involve a precisely defined territory. A nation state on the other hand has to have defined boundaries. It is a legal not a sentimental entity. But nations are often much larger than the state which purports to embody them: the Jewish nation is not coextensive with Israel as a nation state. The Palestinian nation, when it acquires a nation state, may well be in a similar situation. In the case of both Germania and Indica, two interrelated propositions can be advanced as true:

1   The process of forming a state to embody the nation was subjected to

compulsions which argued for a powerful (in military-economic sense) nation state even at the cost of leaving some of the nation outside its boundaries; i.e. a fragmented nation state was formed.

2   The fragmented nation state having been formed, it sought to reconstitute nationhood in terms of its boundaries; i.e. the nation was redefined in the narrower territorial terms, with the excluded portion of the erstwhile nation being redefined as non-national in the new, narrower sense of nationhood.

I shall advance evidence for these two propositions in the subsequent sections. But before I do that, let me advance a corollary of the two above propositions which is not a question of fact but of an arguable speculative nature.

3   That the attempt to reconstitute nationhood as under (2) above becomes problematical precisely because the basis on which the ur- nation was defined is no longer appropriate. The new fragmented nation state ends up giving territory a much more prominent place in defining nationhood than previously, and assigns uncertain status to cultural factors such as language or religion. Territorial integrity and its defence become nationalist ideology.

Germania to Germany

The Holy Roman Empire was dissolved as a result of Napoleonic wars in 1806. Prussia's defeat goaded it into a series of reforms to make it a model of rational bureaucratic absolutism. In 1815 at the Congress of Vienna, the German Confederation was set up with Austria as the senior member and Prussia as the junior member and 36 (much fewer than in 1806) smaller states comprising Third Germany. The Confederation, with its Federal Diet in Frankfurt, was a loose association of independent princely states, its *raison d'être* being the preservation of the balance of power in Central Europe.

Starting in late eighteenth century but intensified by the French Revolution as well as the Wars of Liberation from French rule, German nationalism grew among the conscious middle classes. *Kulturstaat* as an ideal was a popular, liberal if not entirely democratic nation. It saw the 'unity (of Germany) via common spirit founded upon the equality of all human beings and growing out of the development of human liberty'.[1] But the liberal Kulturstaat movement had no clout. It operated in a monarchical and imperial context within the Confederation and internationally in the context of a balance of power. Without the acquiescence of the larger and smaller princes, a German nation state could not be realized.

The Confederation was not a nation state but a conclave of princedoms, many small, some medium sized such as Bavaria and Prussia and of course Austria. It was supposed to be guided by Austria as the major power but Prussia, especially after 1848, wanted a bigger say in running it. The Federal

1   Darmstaedter, *Bismarck* (London: Methuen, 1948), p. 330.

Diet was an assembly of ambassadors from the princely states meeting in Frankfurt. The Confederation could not however act as a unit; it could not for example sign international treaties. As such, liberal nationalism saw the Confederation as the machinery of reform to obtain a strong German nation state.

But the liberals operated not in a parliamentary constitutional climate but in monarchical absolutism of various degrees. A constitutional monarchy represented the limit of their radical imagination. Thus when the princely order was temporarily undermined in 1848, the Federal Assembly (elected on a limited franchise but elected nonetheless) could only invite the Prussian King to take the crown of all Germany, i.e. the Confederation. The Habsburg empire had been eclipsed by the uprising in Vienna, and Prussia was always more to the liberals' liking than reactionary Austria. But the liberals realized their limitation when Frederick William IV of Prussia rejected their offer. In his view, such an assembly had no authority to cancel the crowns of princes and choose one among them. 'If the thousand year crown of the German nation, which for forty two years has been in abeyance is to be awarded once again, it is *I* and those such as I who will award it.'[2] He also rejected the offer of the crown of Germany without Austria when it was offered by the same Assembly in April 1849.

The 1848–9 episode established several things. A liberal democratic movement did not have the power to bring about a German nation state. It needed the willing support of at least one major monarch. But the monarchs together were jealous of their legitimacy and suspicious of the revolution, i.e. anything which might overthrow legitimate rulers. Thus for someone like Frederick William IV, a voluntary agreement of the princes was the only way to bring about a German Kingdom.

But the Assembly also articulated the two alternatives for a German state – *Grossdeutsch*, i.e. the Confederation, or *Kleindeutsch*, the Confederation minus Austria. It is around these two alternatives that subsequent debate centred. The *Kleindeutsch* alternative had a firm basis in reality in as much as the *Zollverein* – the customs union of the kingdoms in the Confederation excluding Austria – already existed. Austria tried under its new chancellor Schwarzenberg in the early 1850s to bully its way into the *Zollverein*. Austria wanted a tariff agreement for the whole of Central Europe, i.e. the Confederation as a prelude to a *Grossdeutsch* run by Austria. But Prussia prevented this and the *Zollverein* stayed within *Kleindeutsch*. On Schwarzenberg's death, the issue fell by the wayside.

In the late 1850s liberals formed the *Nationalverein*, a lobby for the *Kleindeutsch* program. They were in office in Prussia between 1859 and 1862. For the liberals, a programme of nationalism was also a programme for parliamentarism. They asked Prussia to take the lead in encouraging the growth of a constitutional monarchy at home and pushing the electoral principle

2   L. Gall, *Bismarck the White Revolutionary*, vol. 1, *1815–1871* (London: Allen & Unwin, 1986), p. 63.

in the Federal Diet. They also pushed the *Zollverein* as the mechanism for integration. But the Prussian Regent who later succeeded to his brother's throne was reluctant to toe the parliamentary line. By September 1862, he had appointed Bismarck as his Minister President and the liberals, while in parliamentary majority, were out of office. It looked like the death of the *Kleindeutsch* idea.

Austria on the other hand was dead against the *Kleindeutsch*. It sponsored the *Reformverein* which would promote the *Grossdeutsch* alternatives but Austria's commitment to the electoral principle was suspect. It preferred an indirectly elected assembly for the federal parliament. In 1862, Austria put such a proposal forward in Frankfurt. A federal parliament was to be made up of delegates from the parliaments of individual states. The new federation was to be administered jointly by a committee of five princes of which Austria, Prussia and Bavaria would be permanent members. This was discussed at a Congress of Princes of the Confederation in August 1863. The King of Prussia refused to attend and on the urging of Bismarck proceeded to scuttle this plan for a stronger version of the Confederation. As a diversionary card, Prussia proposed a directly elected federal parliament. There was however a problem. Not only were many suspicious of Bismarck's parliamentarist credentials but there was a regional divide as well. In the South, there was a greater preference for the *Grossdeutsch* solution. There was a religious affinity in catholic Bavaria and Austria while Prussia was a protestant stronghold.

Thus, as of 1863 several possibilities were open for Germania:

1   A gradual strengthening of the Confederation run jointly by a conservative alliance between Austria and Prussia. Prussia however wanted parity with Austria and did not wish decisions regarding defence and foreign policy to be subject to majority vote in the Confederation.

2   A Confederation dominated and run by Austria. This was the Schwarzenberg plan tried in 1849–50 and revised in a milder form by Austria in 1862. This was the principle of majority decision in the Confederation but by a chamber of princes. Such a confederation would have evolved towards a stronger state if the *Zollverein* could have been extended to Austria. This would have created a Central European Free Trade Area covering all of Germania.

Bismarck was against both these alternatives as he feared the weakening of Prussia within such a Confederation. His alternative plans were

3   A Prussian led Germany comprising Germania excluding Austria. This was the liberal *Nationalverein* formulation but the liberals wanted it through a move towards parliamentarism among all the princely states. Bismarck preferred Prussia to absorb *Kleindeutsch* under its domination.

4   A minimal plan proposed by Bismarck to the Austrians was of Prussia dominating a protestant North German Confederation, restricting the *Zollverein* to this region, thus excluding the catholic states of South Germany and especially Bavaria. This could have led to a division of Germania into North and South along protestant/catholic lines, with Austria leading the South and Prussia the North. [See Map 1 for the various alternatives mentioned.]

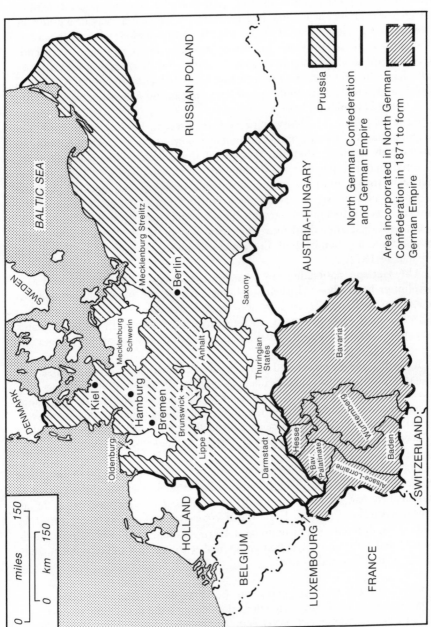

Map 1   Germany before and after the Reich

Source: Agatha Ramm, *Germany 1789–1919* (London: Methuen, 1967)

Legend

Prussia

North German Confederation and German Empire

Area incorporated in North German Confederation in 1871 to form German Empire

Map labels

BALTIC SEA

SWEDEN

DENMARK

RUSSIAN POLAND

Mecklenburg Strelitz

Mecklenburg Schwerin

Berlin

Saxony

Anhalt

Thuringian States

AUSTRIA-HUNGARY

Kiel

Hamburg

Bremen

Brunswick

Lippe

Oldenburg

Darmstadt

Hesse

Bav. Palatinate

Alsace-Lorraine

Bavaria

Württemberg

Baden

HOLLAND

BELGIUM

LUXEMBOURG

FRANCE

SWITZERLAND

0   miles   150

0   km   150

Of these four alternatives only 1 and 2 preserved Germania intact. They were both *Grossdeutsch* solutions. But apart from the Schwarzenberg variant of 2 which was no longer feasible in 1862, they both meant a weak or a gradually strengthening nation state. For the liberals both solutions also denied or at least restricted the principle of nationalism, i.e. democracy, and were conservative monarchical condominium arrangements. Bismarck wrecked 2 by advancing the principle of adult franchise for the election to federal parliament which he knew Austria would not accept. He proposed 1 as his maximal plan and 4 as his minimal plan.

As it happened the *Zollverein* proved too strong a binding force for South German states of Bavaria and Wurttemburg to break off and form a *Kerndeutsch* union with Austria. After the renewal of the *Zollverein* treaty in 1865, the German national question was decided by war in two phases. In 1866, the war between Austria and Prussia (a civil war in a sense) quickly decided the issue in favour of Prussia. Bismarck got a North German Confederation with a directly elected federal parliament. This was the pattern of the Reich which was established after the Franco-Prussian War of 1870–1. By this time, the South German members of the *Zollverein* joined as well. The Reich was created in 1871.

The German nationalist movement got its *Kleindeutsch*, but it came as a revolution from above. Instead of being created out of a popular unity as a *Kulturstaat* it was created by war as a *Kriegstaat*. It was not so much a *Kleindeutsch* (Lesser Germany) as *Grosspreussisch* (Greater Prussia). Bismarck was quite conscious that it was the national idea by itself that was integrative:

> Its cachet and its power had come to consist much more in the fact that it had a unifying effect that spanned all political division and all decisions of class and interest and that even spanned denominational barriers ... The national idea together with all the hopes and expectations that depended on it, changed after 1866 from being a distinctly oppositional ideology, as it had been up until 1848–9, to being an integrative ideology.[3]

But in achieving national integration of a fragment of Germania, and especially doing it in a revolutionary abrupt way via two wars, the nature of nationalism had to be changed. It was no longer a cultural union of all German-speaking people. Even the *Kleindeutsch* union had not evolved by sinking its differences and defining a German identity. The Reich was militaristic and illiberal; its creation compelled it to create a national ideology in terms of territory and power.

Given that the *Reich* had come into being as the product of military and power related manoeuverings, rather than through the democratic process, it had from the very outset, never been sufficiently integrated politically. This

3   Gall, *Bismarck*, p. 331.

particular type of deficit created a perpetual search for some kind of com-
pensation. . . (F) or fear of a relapse into weakness and impotence, categories
such as 'unity, solidarity and adaptability' were valued more highly than
others such as 'freedom, tolerance and a plurality of opinion'.[4]

I am aware that there is an arguable link here. A *Grossdeutsch* solution along
the lines proposed by Austria in 1862–3 with a Central European Free Trade
Area and initially indirectly elected but ultimately directly elected is not just a
counterfactual hypothesis. It was one of the three or four real alternatives. It
had the cultural logic and the history of a Holy Roman Empire on its side.
Such a state would not have been a federation with a centralizing logic but
could have integrated as a result of economic forces (as the European
Community seems to be doing). *Ex post* it has been argued by many that the
logic of economic growth favoured the *Zollverein* and integrating Austria
would have been economically damaging. I cannot at the present evaluate this
argument since it would require a close examination of the economic structures
of the regions at that time. It has also been argued that in some sense history
was not on Austria's side but on Prussia's side but that need not prejudge the
outcome as of 1865. As August Bebel speculated:

> If Austria had won (i.e. in 1866), its government would in all probability have
> attempted to rule Germany by reaction. In so doing, it would have aroused
> the hostility of not only the entire Prussian population, but also the majority
> of Germans and a good number of Austrians. If ever a revolution had fair
> prospects of success, it was against Austria and at that particular time. The
> result would have been the democratic union of the *Reich*, something which
> Prussia's victory made impossible.[5]

Thus Prussia's victory in 1866 led to the less inclusive alternative of *Kleindeutsch*
being chosen. The desire for a strong state had a lot to do with the connivance
of the liberals in this. Liberals were convinced, Bismarck's biographer tells us,
that the chief reason for their failure in 1848 'had in fact been neglect of the
power question. . . To the detriment of its own cause it had pursued more
"ideal politik" and not, . . . "real politik".'[6] The power question for the nationalists had to do with military strength of the nation state. As Bismarck articulated it for them 'the upsurge in national feeling, part of the whole trend of
the time, is pushing us, as is the demand *for protection against attacks from
abroad*, towards the objective of closer German unification, at least in the
fields of defence and material interests'.[7] But once such a feeling is articulated,

4   R. Von Thadden, *Prussia: The History of a Lost State* (Cambridge: Cambridge
     University Press, 1987), p. 62.
5   Quoted in Von Thadden, *Prussia*, p. 63.
6   Gall, *Bismarck*, p. 204.
7   Ibid., p. 117 (my emphasis).

the wish can become father to the thought. Thus the only 'attack from abroad' that led the Confederation to a national integration was from Austria. To justify the strong but fragmented nation state, a part of the erstwhile nation had to become the enemy. Later when it had served its purpose, the threat could shift and come from others – catholics at home (*kulturkampf*), the social democrats.

When the Imperial Reich ended, the habit of searching for the enemy, for 'attacks from abroad' did not cease. The Weimar Republic was haunted by the 'stab in the back' idea. A nation state built on war and militarism had lost a war and thus a new logic had to be defined for the nationhood. A defeat in war could not be a unifying theme but betrayal at home and the humiliation of the Versailles Treaty did become surrogate unifying themes. In the Anschluss, the Confederation was realized as a nation state in a perverse, degenerate way.

As Rathenau once put it 'compare the Holy Roman Empire and the German Reich: what do you have left? Prussia. Remove Prussia from Germany and what do you have left? The Confederation of the Rhine. An extended version of Austria. A clerical republic.'[8] After the Second World War we are back to this. A Prussia without Poland and its borders as of before 1815, a confederation of the Rhine and Austria. Maybe the counterfactuals in German history have yet time to realize themselves.

From Indica to South Asia

Indian nationalism grew up in an imperial context and in some ways, like German nationalism, it was not up to people alone to achieve a nation state. A major part of the answer lay in Westminster and its Viceregal agent in Delhi. The certainty that Indica would be part of the British Empire as a self-governing dominion for the next 30 or 40 years was accepted as late as 1930s by various Indian leaders including Nehru and Jinnah. There had been promises of increasing but strictly supervised self-government in 1909 (Morley-Minto) and 1919 (Montagu-Chelmsford). Under Gandhi, the Indian National Congress had abandoned the moderate constitutional path and launched a non-co-operation movement in 1921. Gandhi had deep religious convictions and used the religious idiom to mobilize a much larger movement than the Congress had been able to hitherto. He harnessed Muslims by championing the Caliphate's survival against threat of its abolition by the Allied Powers after 1918. Thus was born the Hindu–Muslim unity under the banner of the Congress strategy for independence. Gandhi had envisaged independence within the year of launching non-co-operation. Despite the tremendous mass response, he abruptly called off the movement when a police station was burned down in Chaurichaura. The movement collapsed among bitter recriminations.

8   Rathenau, *Der Neue Staat* (Berlin: 1919), p. 24.

This was the high point of a mass disobedience movement as a way of winning power. Gandhi had succeeded by shrewdly combining religious symbolism in an ecumenical way in launching an all-Indica movement. The odds against doing so were formidable. Indica was then administratively divided into British India (five-sixths of the population) and 660 'native' princely states (one-sixth). Never before in its long history, had a single 'ruler' controlled directly as much as five-sixths of the population and had 'paramountcy' over the rest. The alien power was a formidable one not just in being militarily well equipped to control the population but also ideologically in offering in its domestic politics much that was admired by the nationalists. In addition to the administrative divisions, there were other divisions. A very small number of 'Europeans' and a slightly larger but still small number of Anglo-Indians claimed privileged status of belonging to the ruling caste. Beyond this were the Indians, the majority (over 75 per cent) Hindus, the largest minority Muslims plus Christians, Parsees, Jains, Sikhs etc. There were several languages, although English was the lingua franca of politics. The population in 1921 was around 300 million, the overwhelming majority of whom were illiterate, rural and poor.

The Indian National Congress had begun in 1886 but until the turn of the century had been a loyal organization of urban, Westernized professionals. It took a popular turn in the agitation against the partition of Bengal into West and East roughly along the lines of Hindu and Muslim majority areas. In East Bengal, Muslims were the bulk of the peasantry and Hindus were sub-infeudating rent collectors and absentee landlords. In the event the agitation was successful and the partition of Bengal was undone after five years. The First World War had further radicalized the situation. In return for Indica's war contribution, a further instalment of self-government was promised whereby at provincial level there would be some ministers chosen from the elected element. There were legislatures elected on a limited franchise in British Indian provinces and at the Centre but no popular element in the Viceroy's Council at the Centre.

In disrupting the path of a slow growth of constitutional rule, Gandhi articulated a radical demand for self-government (*swaraj*). In mobilizing a large mass to disobey the established order, he profoundly altered political consciousness but in failing to deliver the promised independence, he exposed the limits of the popular path. From here on, Indian nationalists had to deploy the mass movement in combination with negotiation in committee rooms.

The major parties to the negotiations were:

1 The British government operating within its own party and parliamentary context
2 The Indian government although formally subordinate, still a powerful voice being close to the ground
3 The Indian native states
4 Indian political parties – constitutional ones such as The Liberal Party

and popular ones such as Indian National Congress and All India Muslim
League

The Muslim League was not a mass party as the Congress was. It was as the
Congress used to be in the first 20 years of its life, a loyalist organization
which purported to represent Muslim interests. Muslims were not only the
largest religious minority; they also had special problems of economic and
social deprivation. The last rulers in North India had been Muslims before
the British came and they had spawned a landed aristocracy of Muslims in
North India. There were also professional Muslims who served as func-
tionaries as did Hindus. With the introduction of Western liberal education,
Hindus adapted much quicker than Muslims to the new opportunities. By the
end of nineteenth century in professional, commercial and industrial spheres,
Hindus were predominant. Muslims did not take to the new opportunities
until special efforts were made by their leaders such as Syed Ahmad Khan.
Muslim society had feudal lords and poor peasants and artisans; the middle
was sorely lacking. A small articulate Muslim middle class began to grow only
during the twentieth century. The leadership of the Muslim League was
shared between the feudal elements and the middle class. But middle-class
Muslims also belonged to the Congress as well as the Muslim League till the
late 1930s.

A major plank of the Muslim League's programme was protection of its
minority population and what we would today call positive discrimination in
favour of Muslims − reservation of jobs etc. The League also demanded
separate electorates for Muslims. This demand was known to be potentially
divisive in the nationalist movement. At various stages, there were 'pacts'
emphasizing the need for Hindu−Muslim unity and safeguards were promised. Jinnah, who was later to be credited with the creation of Pakistan, was in
the early decades called an ambassador of Hindu Muslim unity, being a
member both of the Congress and the Muslim League.

The difficult problem was one of combining electoral politics with protection
of minority interests. Congress was committed to a demand for total independence with a popularly elected constituent assembly to frame the constitution
of the independent state. The British Government was offering limited autonomy with a quasi-popular element in administration elected on a limited
franchise and with differentiated representation for minorities. For Congress
there was at stake the principle of equality of all citizens. The Congress
wanted universal adult franchise with minority rights to be discussed by the
Constituent Assembly. The British Government took the view, partly as a way
of delaying radical change, that it could not hand over power without certain
guarantees. A small but noisy minority of the Conservative Party in Parliament
led by Churchill was against any concessions.

With universal adult franchise and first-past-the-post elections, Muslims
feared that they would be swamped by Hindus who were better educated and
more likely to grab the economic perks which the state was now handing out.

They wanted special seats reserved for Muslims. In most provinces of British India, Muslims were in minority ranging from as small as 8 per cent in Madras to 33 per cent in Assam and Delhi. In the heartland of Indica, United Provinces (now Uttar Pradesh) – Indica's Prussia so to speak – out of a population of 55 million in 1941, 15 per cent were Muslim. In two states, Bengal and Punjab, the Muslims had a bare majority of 55 per cent and 51 per cent respectively. In the states of Sind and North West Frontier Province they had an overwhelming majority of 72 per cent and 91 per cent. (These areas are marked in Map 2, which is taken from a pre-partition publication.) A major stage was reached in the negotiations when, after the appointment of a Commission (1928), and three Round Table Conferences (1930, 1931, 1932), a bill was passed in the British Parliament. This was the Government

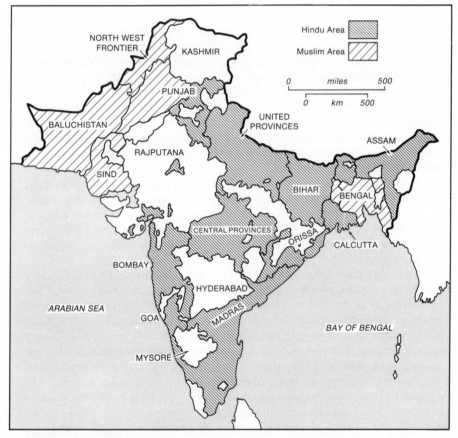

Map 2   Pre-partition India
Source: Rajendra Parsad, *India Divided* (Bombay: Hind Kitabs, 1946)

of India Act 1935. It provided for popularly elected ministries at the provincial level in British India, for reserved seats for Muslims (as well as some other minorities) and for some elements of popular ministry at the Centre. It also proposed an eventual Federation for India if a sufficient number of native states acceeded. There was to be a Council of States (Upper Chamber) and a Federal Assembly (Lower Chamber). In these, the native states had respectively 40 per cent and 33⅓ per cent of the seats despite a much smaller proportion of the population. The Federation was to come into effect if the number of states acceding was sufficient to occupy half of the seats on the Council of States and represent half the total population of the native states.

The Constitution was heavily weighted against the popular nationalist element. The Federation would be compromised by the large weight for the native states and the fact that in the provincial assemblies only 657 seats out of 1,585 were open, the remainder being reserved for some minority or other. Muslims had 482 seats out of 1,585, about 30 per cent as compared to their population of 25 per cent.

Not enough native states joined in (or were cajoled to join in) by the time war broke out in September 1939 when the context changed. But while the Federal part never became a reality, the British India part did. Despite severe misgivings, the nationalists decided to try the scheme by taking part in the election. Elections were held in 1937. These were the first elections to be held in Indica with the promise of office for the winning party although the franchise was limited. The seats reserved for Muslims were a major matter of contention. Although Congress purported to represent all sections of the population, it contested very few Muslim seats. Overall it emerged as the largest single party contesting 1,161 (out of 1,585) seats and winning 716 (26 Muslim seats). It had outright majority in six provinces; United Provinces, Bihar, Orissa, Central Provinces, Madras and Bombay. In Punjab and Bengal a local coalition party won a majority by combining the various religious communities, although in both the Chief Minister was a Muslim. The Muslim League won 109 out of 482 seats reserved for Muslims. However, it claimed to have contested only 226 seats.

At this time the League was not yet a mass party. It had been moribund for many years. Jinnah, who had left Indian politics to resume practice at the Bar in London, was recalled in 1935 to revive it. He tried to make an electoral machine out of the League and appealed to various Muslim groups at regional level to fight under the League's umbrella, but ultimately he achieved only limited success. The composition of its leadership was such that the League could not be seen as a democratic party. It was shocked to find that seats reserved for Muslims did not guarantee office for the Muslim League. The League had no majority in any province in 1937, not even in Muslim majority provinces. The League's strength was in those provinces where Muslims were in a minority − Uttar Pradesh (27 out of 64 Muslim seats) and Bombay (20 out of 29) − but also where there was a professional Muslim middle class. The numerical majority of the Muslim population however lay elsewhere. The

League was also shocked that Congress refused to form coalition cabinets with the League. The Congress did not need to; it also refused to countenance the League as anything but a collection of British Government toadies.

Just as the German national question was transformed between 1863 and 1871, the Indian situation was also completely transformed in the ten years between 1937 and 1947. Here again it was a war that caused it, though the war was not started by one of the parties as an instrument to solve the question. On the declaration of war in Europe, the Viceroy in India also announced India's adherence on the British side. Since he did this without consulting any of the elected representatives at the Centre or in the provinces, the Congress Ministries resigned in protest. The Congress took the view that while it was keen to fight for democracy on the Allied side, it was a mockery to do so without popular participation in the war effort. Retrospectively many have argued that this was a tactical blunder. The Congress lost power and initiative in the subsequent developments. The Muslim League was able to form government in some provinces and collaborate with the government in the hour of its need. The Congress launched a popular Quit India agitation in August 1942 but this was put down and its leadership jailed for the remainder of the war.

By the time the war ended many things had changed. Britain had been weakened despite winning the war and the hegemonic position had passed to the USA. The latter had been goading its ally through the early 1940s to make a gesture towards Indian opinion. With the end of the war and the election of a Labour government, events were speeding up. The Labour Party had long maintained fraternal relations with the Indian National Congress and so the latter was confident of winning the argument.

But if in 1935 only weak Federation was on the cards, now the argument had shifted. For one thing the Congress demand for a Constituent Assembly elected with universal adult franchise was the starting point. But on the other hand, the Muslim League had grown in the mean time. Jinnah had been able to transform it into a mass nation-wide party. It had some experience of office. It had also articulated a two-nation theory and formulated a demand for Pakistan.

Of all the various issues in Indian history, the late emergence and very quick crystallization of the demand for Pakistan came as a complete surprise at the time and led to a continuing controversy for ever afterwards.[9] It was a demand originally thought up by some Muslim students studying in Britain meeting in the Waldorf Hotel on the Aldwych. The Joint Parliamentary Committee on the Government of India Bill asked two leading Muslim politicians their view of this recently articulated demand for Pakistan. One of them, A. Yusuf Ali, said Pakistan was 'a student's scheme which no responsible

9   C.H. Phillips and M.D. Wainwright, eds, *The Partition of India: Policies and Perspectives, 1935–1947* (London: Allen & Unwin, 1970).

people had put forward'. Another, Sir Mohammed Zafrullah Khan, later to be Pakistan's Foreign Minister said, 'we consider it chimerical and impracticable.'[10]

This was said in 1934. In 1940, at its Lahore Congress, the Muslim League adopted the Pakistan resolution. The idea was that the Muslim majority provinces in the North West, i.e. Sind, North West Frontier Province and Punjab, and those in North East Bengal plus, for good measure, Assam (34 per cent Muslim), would form independent states. But as yet there was only the vaguest notion of what such independence would entail. In 1940 and even till 1945, all discussions had proceeded on the assumption that the subjects of defence and foreign affairs would be co-ordinated with Westminster even after dominion status had been granted to Indica, as was the case with Australia, New Zealand and Canada. So the Centre was to have these portfolios. Were these clusters of states to be independent nation states, to be subfederations or what?

The theory now put forward was that there were two nations in India – a Hindu nation, Hindustan, and a Muslim nation, Pakistan. But of course the Muslim 'nation' was scattered all over Indica, and not only in the two clusters. At this stage it was not envisaged that there would be any population transfers. Indeed, it was said that the Hindu minority in Muslim majority provinces would act as hostage to ensure the safety of the Muslim minority in Hindu majority provinces. Thus there were two nations and two states, but each nation (i.e. population professing a religion) would be split in the two states.

Although in 1940 the Muslim League had articulated the demand for Pakistan, it was not a negotiating plank when negotiations resumed after the War. The League wanted to be acknowledged as the sole representative of all Muslims, with the right to nominate Muslims for reserved cabinet seats if there were to be any. It wanted some safeguard for Muslims and a large degree of autonomy for Muslim majority areas.

The Congress at first refused to recognize the League as the sole representative of the Muslims, or to contemplate partition. But a lot of things had happened since 1937 and particularly since the imprisonment of its leaders in 1942. Step by step they began to come to terms with the demand for Pakistan, which by 1944 could not be evaded. First was a proposal by Rajagopalachari for a plebiscite in the Muslim majority areas on the issue of partition. In case of partition there would still be a common purposes agreement on defence, communication and commerce. Having got Congress to talk of Pakistan Jinnah raised the ante by rejecting this proposal as one for a 'moth-eaten Pakistan'.

Jinnah's view was that Muslims were a nation with the right to self-determination, and hence in any plebiscite only Muslims should be allowed to vote on the issue of partition. Of course the Congress did not counter by saying that in that case all Muslims, of majority as well as minority provinces should be allowed to vote. Jinnah wanted the plebiscite before Indica was free

10　Quoted by B. Shiva Rao in Phillips and Wainwright, *The Partition of India*, p. 416.

and not after as was being proposed. He also rejected the idea of a common agreement on joint subjects.

Congress continued to insist that while Congress and the League could have parity in any interim government, Congress could not be confined to choosing only Hindus. After all a Muslim, Maulann Azad, was Congress President. The Muslim League may exclusively represent Muslims but Congress would represent everyone. Here was a clash of two different views.

In July 1945 Labour came to power in Britain and the Indian situation began to change dramatically. In the 1946 elections, the changed position of the League became clear. In the Central Legislature Congress had a majority 57 out of 162 but the League won all 30 Muslim seats. In the provinces the League also won handsomely in Bengal and Sind but not a majority in Punjab or in NWFP. It did however win 439 out of 494 Muslim seats in the provinces. In the nine years since 1937, the League had moved up to fulfil its boast of being the sole representative of the Muslims. The question still was..did that imply the separate sovereign nation states cutting the two nations in two ways?

There was here a fundamental clash about the concept of nationhood. Congress saw nationality as an attribute of all 'native born' Indians by virtue of their being in Indica and also implicitly by being ruled by a foreign country. Only independence would bequeath full nationality on Indians by giving them a nation state to embody nationality. Congress defined national as meaning not communal, i.e. neither Hindu nor Muslim but Indian. There were other communal parties representing Hindus, Sikhs and others, but the main contention was with the League. The League took the view that religion defined nationality.

In June 1946, a Cabinet Mission which had been negotiating for three months with the various Indian groups proposed a confederate solution. This would have made the provinces primary units free to write their own constitution. A second tier was provinces to form groups to see if they wished to have a regional, subfederal grouping. Two such groups were the one in North West and the other in the North East. There was to be some freedom for individual provinces to leave a group if they saw fit but only after the Constitution had been written. There was to be a Central legislature with reserved seats. The Centre was to have only a few subjects – defence, foreign affairs, communications. There was to be an interim cabinet at the centre with representatives of the major groups. Between June 1946 when the proposal was made and about nine months later the plan was abandoned. The precise details as to which party accepted and which didn't, the qualifications made, the mistake of angry statements and violent retaliation, are too complicated to dwell on here. Many however have felt then and since that such a Confederation was the best way to keep the country together. It was the '*Grossindische*' solution.

The reasons why it broke down included a clash of views concerning the nature of the nation state. When the Congress accepted the plan it did so with many reservations and caveats. The League accepted *in toto* to begin with but reserved its right to move towards Pakistan. The Congress view was that the Constituent Assembly which was to determine the Constitution must be sovereign and could not be made to submit to restriction; in short the view was independence first, discuss concessions later. The League view was independence only if the two nation principle was conceded. The Congress had also over years formed the view that independent India would need a strong central authority to tackle the economic problems it faced. Thus one major reservation the Congress had concerned the list of subjects the Centre would control. It wanted planning, foreign trade, currency and finance to be Central responsibility. The League was reluctant to grant taxation as a central subject.

When the final parting came it was not until May–June 1947. By then the Congress had worked in an interim government with the League and found its hands severely tied. It had always sought undisputed power for effective economic and social action. It agreed to a partition of Indica with two sovereign states only when it seemed the only way to have a strong state. The Constitution of India as framed by the Constituent Assembly made a strong quasi-federal arrangement with the Centre paramount. The provinces and their boundaries were changeable at the Centre's behest. This was as the 1935 Act would have it. By 1947, the native states did not obstruct the arrangement. They were persuaded by the outgoing British to accede and most did so willingly. Only in the case of Kashmir did it lead to an armed conflict of a protracted nature.

Thus between 1935 and 1947, Indian discussions centred on federal or quasi-federal arrangements to keep together the various communities and the native states. The 1935 Act was one such gross solution but the native states imposed an indirectness in the elective element. For their small proportions of the population, these states were treated indulgently by those elements in Britain which hoped to bolster reaction. At that time much was made of the difficulty of getting the states to agree. The then Viceroy could not get half of them to agree within four years. In 1947 it took less than four months. The 1935 Act is rather like Austria's proposal of 1863 for reform of the Confederation. But the nationalists were committed to parliamentarism in Indica as in Germania.

The 1946 solution (leaving aside many which were advanced in between the two dates) foundered not on the native states question but on the issue of the nature of the nation state. If the nation state was to be independent and autonomous as well as strong, it had to be free to make its own internal arrangements about minority rights. If the nation state was to embody a nation defined on religious lines, then the internal arrangements would be made prior to the independence.

Despite the acceptance of Confederation, albeit temporarily and with reservations, the conduct of the two sovereign states subsequently makes clear that they wanted strong centralized states. Pakistan went through the problem again in 1970 when the strong centre fell foul of the desire for regional autonomy on the part of the Bengali Muslims. Having assumed that being Muslim was the only criterion of Pakistani nationhood, no care had been taken to accommodate other dimensions. Thus the federation broke again in 1971. It broke on the incompatibility of the electoral principle with the theory of nationality when East Pakistanis had numerical majority in the Parliament, the hitherto majority West Pakistan decided to retain power by armed action. It took a civil war to settle that issue.

So in the end three nation states emerged out of Indica – India, Pakistan and Bangladesh. The inclusive solutions which would have kept a loose confederation were rejected in favour of an exclusive but powerful solution. Even before the break-up of Pakistan in 1971, it was quite clear that both sovereign states had a problem of constructing a nationalism. Unlike Germania, Indica lacked a common language. A history that could have been common to a single nation became contentious as soon as two nations were discerned side by side. Since the nation state did not embody the entire nation, Pakistan had the additional problem of having to piece together its history. When did Pakistan's history as a nation begin? In 1947? surely not. Did it begin with the founding of the Muslim League or did it begin with the first arrival of Muslims in India? Since the history of Muslim Kingdoms from the tenth to the eighteenth century centres around Delhi and the Indo-Gangetic plain, was that history Pakistan's history?

But India's task has been no easier. History writing and teaching has not been treated as an academic matter anywhere but certainly not in India. History is one way of creating, and especially re-creating, the consciousness of nationhood but if the nature of nationhood is itself disputed so will be the content of the history. If one accepts the theory of the Muslim League that there were two nations in Indica – a Muslim nation and a Hindu nation and that Pakistan represents a crystallization of the Muslim nation within Indica as a nation state, then the partition left behind India (that is Bharat) as a Hindu nation. The history of such a nation must treat the entire period since the arrival of Afghan Kings in the eighth century as a long period of foreign rule against which various Hindu kings struggled. But the Congress while accepting partition denied the two-nation theory – Muslims are still a substantial minority in India because Pakistan did not embody the Muslim nation within Indica if such there ever was. Pakistan was only the accidental creation of contiguous Muslim majority provinces in the North West and the North East of Indica. Muslims were scattered all over Indica and were 24 per cent of its population in 1941. Even after the Partition, enough remained behind for India to be one of the three or four largest Muslim population states in the world. Thus the Muslim nation if there was a separate identifiable one within Indica was split into Pakistan, its fragmented national state and those remaining behind. India maintains that it is a secular democratic republic and as such religion has no official status in its constitution. In practice, the official version of Indian history emphasizes Hindu-Muslim tolerance, praises kings in the past who enjoined tolerance and is mildly embarrassed about fanatical Hindu leaders who fought Muslims as the enemy. Needless to say, the official version of Indian history is only one version and it is contested from a Hindu India angle, among other rival interpretations.

In suppressing religion as a dimension along which Indian nationhood could be defined, the Congress ideologues (Nehru in particular) left open the question as to what does define Indian nationhood. A common history is a dubious resting place for an effort to define nationhood. As I said briefly above, history at the Indica level is a disputed terrain. There are also many regional differences, with the heroes of one region being villains of another. Much of Maratha history, which Hindu nationalists want to claim as a glorious last fight against Muslim domination, becomes an episode best forgotten in the regions that received Maratha Army depredations. The south of the country resents northern domination in the culture of history writing as well as in other dimensions and so on.

Denied history and religion as uniting forces, the construction of Indian nationhood has become a problem. The official ecumenical—secular version of India's past and present is contested. There is no common language — as a basic element in any grid defining nationhood. The split of East from West Pakistan hinged on language as well as other issues. The Bengali speaking Muslims have shown by their struggle that it is the language—religion combination that most satisfactorily defines nationhood on the subcontinent if not elsewhere. Thus as India's leading sociologist, T. N. Madan, has observed the Bengali Muslims behaved as Muslims in 1947 in joining Pakistan and as Bengalis in 1971 in liberating themselves from Pakistan. They did not however join their West Bengal brethren in founding an independent Bengal nation. It is precisely the combination of language and religion that constitutes nationhood in Bangladesh.

But if that is so, India is either a fragment nation state of the one ecumenical—secular nation that was embedded in Indica and for which the nationalist movement fought. Or it is a conglomerate of many nations defined on language or language—religion grounds. It is in this latter sense a multinational entity with national consciousnesses defined along a matrix of the main religions of Hinduism, Islam, Sikhism, (plus Christianity, Zoroastrianism, Buddhism) and the 16 languages officially listed in the Constitution. This is not fanciful. The demand for Khalistan at the present is an attempt of a part of the Punjabi-speaking state to distinguish itself from the rest. Punjabi-speaking Sikhs wish a separate state of their own from Punjabi-speaking Hindus. Once Pakistan had happened religion could not be ignored as a factor in defining nationhood. Once Bangladesh had happened, religion by itself is shown to be not enough to define nationhood. If Khalistan is not realized, one reason, though by no means the major one, will be that unlike East Pakistan which was distant from West Pakistan, Punjab is contiguous with Indian territory. Territoriality will remain the residual reason for defining nationhood at the Indian level. Thus again it is the fragmented nation state that in its turn has the need to construct a nationhood to suit its territory.

Conclusion

Despite its length, this paper must be considered preliminary and somewhat short on details. In one sense the parallel between Germany and India seems slight. The German national question was solved by sovereign German princes without any formal pressure from outside. The formal proceedings of Frankfurt were the shadow and the cabinet manoueverings were the substance. It was a swift war in 1866 that settled the issue in favour of *Kleindeutsch* and against *Grossdeutsch*. In the Indian case, the context was colonial but the negotiations were the real theatre. The issue was discussed again and again in a legalistic atmosphere as much due to the nature of British Parliament as due to the circumstance that most of the leading negotiators (Jinnah, Gandhi, Nehru, Patel) were lawyers. It was not a swift war but a rising climate of communal violence from August 1946 onwards that forced the pace as did the determination of the Labour Government to give up India. But here again the issue was settled against the inclusive solution.

The formal similarity is thus the *Gross—Klein* dichotomy and the rejection of the *Gross* alternative. But beyond that, there is the unsustainability of the solution. In Pakistan's case within 25 years there was a break-up. In Germany's case, there were three constitutions within 75 years and then a break-up.

The real structural similarity is about the relationship between nation and nation state. The nationalist movement in both cases had liberal parliamentary connotations. But the nationalist movement also was ambivalent about whether it wished to realize the cultural nation or was willing to settle for what would prove effective and powerful. The German Liberals suffered the same dilemma as the Indian National Congress. Ultimately they preferred a strong state to the nation they championed. But the strong state in turn compelled them to redefine the nation.

There is a further similarity in the rapidity with which the situation changed. In Germany's case the 1860s was the crucial decade; for India the 1940s. There is perhaps a further parallel to explore between Bismarck and Jinnah, in their combative style. Each started with virtually no popular base but read the changing circumstances shrewdly − let the opponents make the running and all the mistakes − and made rapid gains which no one gave them credit for. But that needs to be argued elsewhere.

10

The Varieties of the Nation State in Modern History: Liberal, Imperialist, Fascist and Contemporary Notions of Nation and Nationality

Wolfgang J. Mommsen

The nineteenth century was in many ways the century of the nation state. It was a period which witnessed the gradual decline, if not collapse, of older types of states, built upon traditional forms of legitimacy and not upon the principle of national self-determination which since the French Revolution had come to be considered the only viable base for legitimate government. The nation state as a new form of political unit emerged in Europe in a long series of revolutions, wars, and internal conflicts of various sorts. It is with hindsight surprising that the European system of powers survived the period of nation state formation largely intact up to the First World War, as a system of balance of power within which five major powers by and large managed to maintain political control. Since decolonization we have observed a similar process of nation building in the extra-European world, and on the whole it must be considered a far more painful and bloody process than the one which Europe experienced during the nineteenth and early twentieth centuries.

It is, of course, true that some of the West European states, such as France, Spain and – to some degree at least – Great Britain, had been established along national, or rather ethnic and cultural lines since the sixteenth century. Long before the French Revolution the idea was born that at least ideally state and nation ought to be identical with one another. But it may be doubted whether these states could be considered nation states in the modern sense of the word at all before the end of the *ancien régime*. The rise of constitutional government through which the people, or rather the educated bourgeois elites, were given at least some say in the running of political affairs, is an essential precondition of the nation-state in its modern meaning. Since Helmut

Plessner coined his famous phrase '*verspätete Nation*' in 1932, it has become a standard argument that nation states which were established only comparatively recently, that is to say in the second half of the nineteenth century, had been at a distinctive disadvantage; many of the shortcomings in their internal systems are supposed to be explainable on these grounds. However, this is in many ways an interpretation which is influenced by a sort of self-pity. Moreover, it tends to unduly isolate the German experience from that of many other European nations. Besides it does not live up to the fact that the process of nation-formation is not just a matter of establishing national independence *vis-à-vis* other rival nations; it was also an internal process which created a high degree of internal cohesions within a particular political fabric. Neither were the Germans the only ones who went through great difficulties on their developmental path toward nationhood. In many respects the West European nations also experienced substantial internal crises during the process by which they were formed into nation states in the modern meaning of this term.

During the first half of the nineteenth century there was almost universal agreement among the educated middle classes in Europe that the nation state was the only viable political organization worthy of an age of liberalism and enlightened politics. Giuseppe Mazzini heralded what was in fact a general assumption of the time, that the reconstruction of Europe according to the principle of national self-determination would not only result in greater freedom and prosperity, but also bring about a more peaceful world. For it was assumed that the variegated and colorful multitude of traditional monarchies, principalities and in particular the older empires, like the Habsburg or the Ottoman empires, were a source of constant strife and conflict, whereas in modern nation states governed in accordance with constitutional principles and public opinion the peaceful pursuit of the welfare of all would be dominant. This was a powerful idea created by the intelligentsia; it soon became an essential element of the liberal ideology of the rising middle classes, but it also was taken up by parts of the older aristocracy which at times managed to put themselves at the helm of this new movement. Indeed more recent research tends to argue that liberalism as a political movement was successful only where and when the aristocratic elites took up the ideas of liberalism at least in part, as in Great Britain, in Italy and in Hungary.

The liberal idea of the nation state is in many ways still with us today. On the other hand we know from hindsight that things did not quite work out according to the assumptions of classic liberalism. Rather the nations themselves often tended to be more bellicose and aggressive than their former aristocratic masters. It is, of course, possible to argue that the beneficial effects of a reorganization of Europe according to the principle of national self-determination were largely lost because the aristocratic elites and their fellow-travellers did everything to hang on to their traditional privileges and their power positions; indeed Arno Mayer went so far as to argue that the *ancien régime* lasted until 1914, if not even longer. However, it is perhaps more correct to say that the ideal of the nation state changed its substantive meaning during the course of events in the later nineteenth and early twentieth centuries. To put it in another way, it gradually lost its emancipatory dimensions and instead took on more and more antiliberal features. Indeed, the nation state became increasingly aggressive and militarist in its relations with other states, and authoritarian and at times even repressive in the domestic arena. This, however, has much to do with the rise of imperialism, as a major element of international politics. Perhaps it would be correct to speak of a deformation of national politics during the age of high imperialism (roughly to be dated from 1880 to 1918).

I should like to take a well-known saying by Jacob Burckhardt as my point of departure for an analysis of the deformation to which the idea of the nation state was subjected during the age of high imperialism. In 1870, commenting upon the creation of the German nation state thanks to Bismarck's skilful policies and the momentous victories of the Prusso-German armies over France, Jakob Burckhardt wrote: '. . . in the first place the nation wants power more than anything else . . . one wishes to belong to something great and thereby reveals that power is the first and culture at best a secondary objective'.[1] In other words, Burckhardt predicted that the idea of the nation state was not so much concerned with creating the necessary external preconditions for the free and unhindered development of one's own national culture, but rather it founded upon the desire to be part of a strong, powerful political unit which would be able to impose its will, if needs be, upon neighbouring peoples. Rather than acting as the guardian of a high culture, while respecting the existence of other high cultures from the start the nation state developed an aggressive dynamic. It was concerned in the first place about the exertion of political power, while the free unfolding of one's own national culture came to be considered as secondary.

This argument certainly would require further differentiation in view of the fact that within Europe a variety of developmental paths toward the formation of the modern nation state based upon a particular high culture and enjoying a comparatively high degree of internal cohesion can be observed. It is not intended to develop here a comprehensive model of different types of nationalist development. But certainly a variety of developmental paths must be distinguished in the European arena; not all of them abandoned altogether the heritage of liberalism, even though they all were imbued with the notion of power.

Great Britain and France are the most important cases of a fairly continuous development toward the modern nation state which could build upon long-established historical foundations. In these cases the middle and lower classes were gradually given a higher degree of say in political affairs, which seems to be one of the necessary ingredients of modern nationalism, without major internal conflicts or upheavals. This process was, furthermore, only occasionally

---

1 *Gesammelte Werke*, vol. 4, p. 70.

impeded by outside factors, that is to say rival nations or power politics. Accordingly in these cases the national idea retained a good deal of the liberal features which were associated with it from the start. This can be gathered from the non-doctrinaire manner in which nationality was defined in Western Europe, emphasizing the subjective aspect of the idea of national identity. Nationality was defined here in terms of the subjective political option by the individuals concerned rather than by 'objective' factors like language, ethnicity and/or religion.

Compared with the West European model in Central Europe the national development was from the start far more dominated by comparatively small bourgeois elites closely associated with traditional territorial states; some of them recognized that positioning themselves at the head of the national movement offered great opportunities to extend their power—status and their territory by exploiting the national idea. The political elites were prepared, if needs be, to bring about the nation state through war and military might, and, if necessary, to use traditional state power in order to force their fellow countrymen to eventually accept the new order of things, if not by administrative means, then by force. Here, from the start, the idea of the nation state was closely associated with the traditional militarist power state of the late eighteenth century.

In Italy the national idea was in the first place a weapon to establish and justify the hegemony of a still fairly small bourgeois elite over the broad masses who cared little for politics. For a long time the Italian catholics, the huge majority of the population, were told by the Catholic Church not to engage directly in the affairs of the 'secular' nation state which therefore remained the domain of the upper middle classes throughout the nineteenth century. Hence the nation state was for a long time to come a very partisan affair which did not enjoy the support of the people at large.

In Germany nationalism was considered by the intelligentsia and in particular the rising bourgeois classes as a means to break the fetters of an outdated system of petty principalities dominated by two rival major 'German' powers, namely Austria and Prussia, and to create the preconditions for economic growth and social reform. German liberalism always assumed that it could win the struggle against the established powers only if it put itself at the helm of the popular movement for creating a greater degree of national unity, and the establishment of a powerful nation state. But, as is well known, the German nation state eventually came about through a 'revolution from above', skillfully engineered by Bismarck, and the rising middle classes were largely onlookers. Accordingly it was not a liberalized Prussia which would be gradually dissolved in the new German nation state, but the traditional power state which set the tune. Accordingly Prussia's hegemony over the rest of Germany imbued the German nation state from the start with a distinctively authoritarian character.

Even more authoritarian in nature were the smaller national movements which gradually developed in East Central Europe and in particular on the Balkans. These regions had for centuries been subjected to the domination by empires of a pre-modern type, notably the Ottoman Empire, which had ruled in an absolutely authoritarian manner over many extremely variegated territories, but which, as a rule, had tolerated a great deal of ethnic, religious, cultural and national differentiation provided that the essential demands of the authorities were met. Here existed little of a political tradition on which the new national movements could build; moreover, there existed a great diversity of ethnic, cultural and economic conditions. In East Central Europe the nationalist movements were from the start involved in bitter struggles not only against their former hegemonial powers, notably Russia, Austria-Hungary, the Ottoman Empire and, at least initially, also Prussia, but also against rival claims of neighbouring peoples. This explains the particularly violent character of the nationalist movements in these regions, as well as the inclination to stick to 'objective' criteria of nationality, rather than let people decide for themselves to which nationality they wished to belong. Ethnicity, religious affiliation, economic interests and the resistance to traditional rulers together provided the dynamite of national conflicts which eventually led to violent convulsions and major wars. Here as elsewhere it usually was small intellectual elites which exploited the national feelings of the masses in order to entrench themselves in positions of power. In East Central Europe the idea of the nation state was little more than a concept manipulated by dominant ethnic or cultural groups, often of a very small size, in order to strengthen their hegemonial positions within the polity; for that matter nationalism tended to be in these cases all the more belligerent and repressive towards counter-claims by other national groups.

Yet we nowadays tend to forget that even in relatively advanced and civilized nations like Great Britain or Imperial Germany the national ideal had become a new secular religion of the educated elite, often massively associated with a religious doctrine of Christian origin; here also nationalism asserted itself, above all, in contrast to rival nationalist movements. This new nationalist creed which was preaching the extension of control by the nation state as far as possible, was in many ways closely associated with a belief in a particular *Sendungsbewußtsein*, that is to say, the *manifest destiny* of one's own nation, supposedly ordained by God to play a dominant role in the history of mankind. Cecil Rhodes' famous 'Last Will and Testament' springs to mind; here he argued that God had made the English race his instrument to bring the ideals of justice, freedom and peace to the whole world, if only by painting red as much as possible of the map of the world. Friedrich Fabri, head of the Rhenisch Missionary Society and one of the foremost propagandists of colonial expansion in Imperial Germany, argued in a similar fashion. The German people had been 'designated by God' to rise to 'a mighty position in the world'.[2] Religious zeal and nationalist thought in fact became closely correlated. Protestantism was, on the whole, more prone to embrace the new nationalist

---

2 Klaus J. Bade, *Friedrich Fabri und der Imperialismus in der Bismarckzeit*, Freiburg 1975, p. 96.

idea than catholicism, but in the end, the catholics were not far behind. The symbiosis between religious and nationalist attitudes, supported by a cluster of material interests of diverse sorts, became an important factor which worked against the liberal origins of the national idea and was a breeding ground for intolerance and even repression against those groups who stood outside the mainstream of national politics.

The creation of the Italian and German nation states in the centre of Europe set a pattern for what was to come. Both embraced above all the idea of state power, to be exercised against recalcitrant citizens. The idea of the nation state progressively lost those elements which in the first half of the nineteenth century had made it an emancipatory ideology, directed against the arbitrary rule of princes and small aristocratic elites, and an intellectual weapon in the campaign for constitutional government. Instead it came to be associated with the power–status of the established national culture, and the imposition of its values on ethnic or cultural minorities both within and beyond the body politic was now considered essential.

The nation state found it difficult to tolerate national or cultural minorities within its boundaries. National homogeneity was seen as the new ideal, and increasingly the nation state was willing to bring this about by force. National cultures were, as Ernest Gellner has argued only recently, always hegemonial cultures, formed by establishing themselves as high cultures and gradually drawing rival local cultures into their orbits, largely thanks to the cultural, economic, and political advantages to be gained by joining a superior culture.[3] This may be seen to a large degree also as a class phenomenon inasmuch as the economically or politically superior class usually also enjoyed a hegemonial status in cultural or even national terms.

But what happened during the latter part of the nineteenth century was in many ways different. For now the hegemony of the dominant national group was strengthened by the power of the nation state, and frequently it was ruthlessly used to expand the sphere of influence of the dominant culture by administrative measures, or, if needs be, by force. Now national homogeneity was seen to be an essential requirement of the nation state. Accordingly the dominant groups showed little patience with ethnic, cultural or minority groups within the boundaries of the nation state. Assimilation of minority groups into the dominant national culture now became the battle cry, partly for cultural reasons, but primarily for reasons of state, as the ethnic and cultural homogeneity of the nation was increasingly considered an essential precondition of the external strength of the nation state in its perennial struggle against rival states. Minority groups with relatively autonomous status were suspected of being open to inimical influences from outside forces.

In a way this was the reverse side of the process of the gradual democratization of the modern nation state. The more the people at large, and not just small

---

3 Ernest Gellner, *Nations and Nationalism*, Cornell University Press, Ithaca & London 1983, esp. pp. 55–7.

traditional elites, plus, to a degree, the intelligentsia, began to actively participate in the political process, or the more the 'political nation' came to be identified with the population at large, the more urgent appeared the need to impose a sense of national unity upon all citizens alike. The traditional aristocratic elites in pre-modern Europe had found no particular difficulties in governing diverse ethnic or national groups; with the entry into the political arena of ever larger sections of the middle classes this seemed to be no longer possible. It is interesting to see that now even in multi-national states like Tsarist Russia or the Habsburg Monarchy, and eventually, with the rise of the Young Turks to power, also in the Ottoman Empire, the old principle of respecting the cultural autonomy of various ethnic or cultural groups increasingly gave way to a policy of assimilation *vis-à-vis* ethnic or religious minorities. Poland provides a particularly interesting case. When it was divided among Tsarist Russia, Prussia, and the Habsburg monarchy in 1797 and again at the Congress of Vienna, the statesmen of Europe did not find it difficult to concede to the Polish people that their cultural autonomy and even their common national usages should be respected across the borders which divided this ancient nation state into three segments; by the 1860s little or nothing of such trans-national arrangements survived. By the 1880s the policy of assimilation directed against the Polish population was in full swing both in Tsarist Russia and in Prussia; only relative weakness prevented the Austrian authorities from doing the same. How much suppression and assimilation by a combination of political pressure and economic incentive was possible, was perhaps best demonstrated by the Magyars in the Transleithanian part of the Habsburg Monarchy. They practised a ruthless policy of Magyarization of the various Slav peoples within their sway, even though Austria-Hungary was itself a multi-national empire which could never hope to live up to the principles of national self-determination and the nation-state.

The tendency to impose one's own national culture upon others by a variety of administrative and economic measures, backed up by the power of the state, did not only apply to national minorities which could be considered genuine rivals in the process of nation-building. Increasingly the ideas of the dominant national culture were imposed upon all minorities alike, ethnic, religious, social and otherwise. Loyalty to the nation state was not considered enough; instead a greater degree of homogeneity in cultural, linguistic and political terms was enforced by growing collective pressure against all those groups which seemed to stand outside the main stream of the national tradition. In 1878 Heinrich von Treitschke published a famous pamphlet *Auch ein Wort über das Judentum*. In it, he demanded that the Jewish minority in Imperial Germany fully assimilate into the German national culture, even though German Jewry had come to share the political views and cultural values of the German bourgeois middle classes to a surprising degree. At this time, Treitschke did not argue his case on racialist grounds: he merely demanded that German Jews should give up their traditional faith and let themselves be baptized, as quite a few German Jews indeed had done. This led to a fervent debate in Germany, in which Treitschke was rebuked from many quarters for his statements which, though not directly anti-semitic, nonetheless lent support to anti-semitism which was then beginning to gain ground in Germany. Yet, in fact, he merely had given expression to what was part of a view held generally, namely that the nation state ought to be in every respect homogeneous and that minority groups would have to adjust to the values, cultural traditions and political principles of the nation.

This is to say, however, that the national idea took on distinctive authoritarian features; in almost all spheres of national life strong collective pressures were at work in enforcing loyalty to the national state; these were directed against all groups whose religious, cultural or political views deviated from the main stream of national politics. Those groups which were not prepared to concur with these demands were threatened with marginalization. The socialists, and particularly the social democratic movements, were the prime targets of these policies. But those religious minorities which allegedly did not accept the primacy of the national idea were subjected to similar pressures. In the predominantly protestant countries it was usually the catholics who were considered unreliable in terms of national loyalty, as can be gathered from the grossly exaggerated fears of what was at the time called 'Ultramontanism'. Later the Jewish communities were looked at with increasing suspicion.

This new, *integralist* variety of the idea of the nation state was considerably strengthened by the policies of high imperialism. The arrival in the 1880s of the imperialist ideology as a new mass phenomenon provided powerful support for the idea that nations should be homogeneous. The imperialist ideology also gave an additional impetus to the idea of the racial superiority of one's own nation, even though this type of racialism was still fairly innocent, compared with the racialist policies which were practised in the 1930s and 1940s. High imperialism was, in general terms, only the last stage, or very nearly so, of a long process of European expansion overseas; but by the 1880s nationalism and imperialism became intertwined in a way which had never been the case before. In 1882 John Seeley somewhat naively described the long process of empire-building as the expansion of the English nation, or rather, as he put it, the English race, over large parts of the globe, almost totally losing sight of the many millions of coloured peoples subjected to British colonial rule. Half a generation later most people in Europe were in agreement that the nation state could no longer do without colonial empire, if it was to hold its own against its rivals in a future likely to be dominated by a few great empires. In 1897 Joseph Chamberlain put this view in cogent language in a speech at the Royal Colonial Society: 'It seems to me that the tendency of the time is to throw all power into the hands of the greater empires, and the minor kingdoms – those which are non-progressive – seem to be destined to fall into a secondary and subordinate place.'[4] Much the same

4   George Bennett, ed., *The Concept of Empire*, London 1953, p. 320.

argument was put forward by Jules Ferry who lectured his fellow Frenchmen who in 1885 did not particularly care for French colonial policies overseas about the necessity of empire. If a great nation like France were to abstain from taking part in the race for colonial empire this would be tantamount to its abdication from the first rank among the great powers and its decline to the status of a third-rate power.[5] Heinrich von Treitschke argued in much the same vein. By the 1890s Treitschke, notwithstanding his great admiration for Bismarck who had always considered Imperial Germany a 'saturated power', had come round to the opinion that the German nation state had to acquire a colonial empire in order to maintain its status among the great powers in a future world which was likely to be dominated by only a few world powers, with everybody else reduced to a secondary status. 'Up to now Germany always came last in the partition of the non-European world, but the question of whether we will become an overseas power also is about our future status as a great state. Otherwise we will have to face the potentiality that England and Russia will divide the world among themselves, and I don't know what would be more immoral and frightful − [the rule of] the Russian stick or the English purse.'[6] But such a course of events would be contrary to the very nature of the nation state, namely to establish itself as a powerful entity *vis-à-vis* rival states, for − as he put it − 'the state' − and this applied in particular to the nation state − '*is* power; only a powerful state corresponds to its idea'.

A few years later Max Weber argued in his famous Inaugural Lecture at Freiburg university: 'We must grasp that the unification of Germany would have been a youthful spree, indulged in by the nation in its old age, and it would have been better if it never would have taken place, since it would have been a costly extravagance, if it was the conclusion rather than the starting-point for German power politics on a global scale.'[7] Colonial empire was described here as a necessary corollary of the formation of the nation state, or its logical consequence. The creation of an overseas empire seemed to be the only way of preserving the status of one's own national culture in the coming age of world-power politics.

Initially colonial expansion had been justified by many of the propagandists of the imperialist idea as a means − indeed as the only means − of revitalizing the national culture. Through imperialist expansion national cultural life would receive a new impulse; its growth would in itself strengthen the vitality of national culture; literature, the arts and the sciences would all benefit from an extension of the territory controlled by one's own nation state, and by extending their beneficial effects to the peoples of the non-European world. This was argued, for instance, by the great French economist and colonial propagandist

5 *Discours et opinions de Jules Ferry*, ed. Paul Robiquet, vol. 5, Paris 1897, p. 218.
6 *Politik. Vorlesungen gehalten an der Universität Berlin*, ed. M. Cornicelius, Leipzig 1922, pp. 42–3.
7 *Max Weber: Selections in Translation*, ed. W. G. Runciman, Cambridge 1978, p. 266 (transl. adapted by W. J. M.).

Leroy-Beaulieu in his book *La colonisation chez les peuples modernes*. 'The expansive force of a nation, its capability to reproduce itself, its expansion and multiplication beyond territorial boundaries, all this is involved in colonization. Colonization is the subjection of all or parts of the universe to its language, its morals, ideals and laws. A colonizing people lays the foundations for its future greatness and its supremacy. All vital forces of the colonizing nation are intensified by this expansion.'[8] Imperialist policies were looked at from this vantage point as a source of strength to the nation, not only in terms of power and economic resources, but also in moral terms. For this was a new great task, the fulfillment of which would require the best skills and the best minds of the white nations. This also would have beneficial effects upon the body politic, quite apart from the territorial and economic gains to be made by colonial policies. Max Weber, for one, argued that a new powerful *Weltpolitik* would help the German nation to overcome the prevailing mood of resignation and stagnation in which it found itself a generation after the *Reich* had been founded; an energetic imperialist policy would provide liberalism with a new, popular set of political objectives and would give a strong impulse to constitutional and social reform. In Great Britain the Liberal Imperialists talked likewise; the strengthening of empire would also help to raise the standard of living of the working classes in the motherland; a nation 'proud of the British Empire' would have to be 'satisfied with the living conditions of all citizens alike – conditions of life which make it possible to fulfill this great mission of empire'.[9] Similarly it was argued that imperial policies would lead to greater 'efficiency' in public and private affairs alike, with most beneficial effects for the whole body politic.

However, the most effective argument in favour of imperialist policies was certainly that put by the establishment; that through the expansion of empire the political and cultural traditions of one's own nation would be extended to other regions and peoples overseas, thereby widening the sphere of political, economic and cultural influence of the nation state considerably. In most European countries the imperialists believed that this was a mission which they had to fulfil in order to live up to the great and sacred traditions of their ancestors. In 1893, Lord Rosebery put this in the most persuasive terms: 'We have to look forward beyond [...] the passions of party to the future of the race of which we are at present the trustees, and we should in my opinion grossly fail in this task that has been laid upon us did we shrink from responsibilities and decline to take our share in a partition of the world which we have not forced on, but which has been forced upon us.'[10] The most consequential of British imperialists were prepared to take this message seriously enough to argue that the British would have to go even a step further

8   pp. 748–9.
9   *Liberal League Publications*, no. 10. London School of Economics, Library.
10   Speech at the Royal Colonial Institute, 1 March 1893, Bennett, p. 311.

by transforming the British Empire into one great world state which would bear the imprint of British cultural traditions, British constitutional wisdom, British industrial and commercial skills, united under the British crown, although not necessarily governed any more by a parliament located in Westminster. Elsewhere the expectations went by no means quite so far, but the basic features of this colonizing zeal, which saw itself as an extension of the national will, can be easily traced here as well. Gabriel Hanotaux put it as follows: 'What is this [i.e. colonialism] all about? By no means just about spectacular annexations, neither about increasing our public or private fortunes, it is about extending to uncivilized countries overseas the principles of a civilization, of which one of the oldest nations on the earth justly can be proud. We must create as many Frances as possible near by and in distant regions of the world. The issue at stake is to preserve our language, our customs, our ideals, the reputation of France and of the Romanesque peoples in the midst of a bitter competition with other races which entered upon the same path.[11]

Politics, economics and culture all played a part in the imperialist ideology which reached its highest peak in the last two decades before the First World War. But the most effective justification of empire was the appeal to national feeling. Certainly this was to some degree an ideology created by intellectuals for the consumption of intellectuals, and it reflected, as Max Weber already recognized, the ideal and material interests which the intelligentsia associated with a policy of imperialist expansion. But its impact on the bourgeois classes and beyond, and not least the *classes dirigentes* was lasting and far-reaching. Under the impact of this new ideology not only the great European powers and, since the 1890s, also the United States turned imperialist, but also – and this is most significant – powers of a secondary or even tertiary rank, like Italy and the Balkan states even though some of them had in fact not yet completed the process of national emancipation in full.

It is usually argued that imperialist expansion was motivated above all by economic considerations, real or ficticious. This may or may not be so. But it is most revealing that since the 1880s the pursuit of empire, either directly or indirectly, came to be considered an essential element of national politics quite independently of considerations of economic or material advantage of any kind. There may have been some sensible motivation for the Italians to seek a foothold of their own in North Africa, since in 1881 the French had established a protectorate over Tunisia even though there had existed in Tunis a thriving Italian 'colony' of merchants and middlemen of sorts. But it can only be explained in terms of national prestige that Italy developed an ambitious scheme of territorial *aggrandissement* in the coastal regions of the Adriatic and the Balkans. The *Dreibund* treaties were all about guaranteeing Italy a substantial say in the future arrangements in the Balkans, eventually to be turned into territorial gains on the Adriatic coast. And later Italian diplomacy

11   Gabriel Hanotaux, *L'Affaire de Madagascar*, Paris 1896, p. 272.

struggled hard to ensure its own share of the Ottoman Empire, if the great powers went ahead with partition. It is hard to see any economic or strategic reasons for these imperialist schemes. On the whole it was national pride, and the assumption that thereby the range within which Italian culture was dominant might be extended substantially. Why Austria-Hungary also joined the imperialist race is even more difficult to understand. In a way her statesmen were infected by the general assumption that imperialist expansion was the order of the day. Though it had some economic interests in the Balkans, certainly it had not the economic resources to seriously consider getting engaged in imperialist ventures of any grander scale, let alone the Ottoman Empire itself; nonetheless Austrian diplomacy envisaged that in the case of a partition of the Ottoman Empire it ought to get a proper share of the spoils, if only for reasons of prestige.

The bitter internecine warfare of the Balkan states in the 1880s and again in 1912–13 is a particularly striking example of this new trend. In fact the idea of the nation state had become merged with the notion that one must extend the sway of one's own national culture as far as possible, regardless of the costs and the consequences; the existence of however small an ethnic minority within a particular region, provided it enjoyed a socially dominant position, was considered sufficient justification for violent irredentist policies; the principle of national self-determination had dropped largely out of sight, surviving only as a skilful ideological argument to justify expansionist territorial claims.

From these observations may be concluded that during the period of high imperialism the notion of the nation state was subjected to a process of gradual, if substantial, change. Increasingly it lost its original emancipatory character, and became very closely associated with the exercise of power against rival political units, justified in terms of the extension of the sphere of dominance of the respective national culture at any cost. Under given conditions there was a lot of truth in Treitschke's saying that the nation state was, in the first place, an institution designed to exercise power and not merely the embodiment of a national culture. Its foremost task had become, in fact, to get the dominant culture accepted throughout the body politic, and to expand its sphere of control as far as possible, while criteria like ethnicity and cultural identity became secondary. Ethnic minorities were forced, directly or indirectly, to submit to the dominant national culture, even though this might mean sacrificing their own cultural identity, their own language and/or their religious affiliations. Loyalty to the nation state was increasingly seen to require full identification with the dominant culture, not just obedience to the authorities within the confines of the law. Last but not least, racialist attitudes gradually became more influential, not least under the influence of the colonialist propaganda which emphasized the allegedly racial origins of the cultural backwardness of the indigenous populations.

These illiberal distortions of the nation state closely correlated with the politics of high imperialism. The scramble for territories overseas which began in the early 1880s and which climaxed in the early years of the twentieth century led to an enormous intensification of great power rivalries which not only changed the nature of imperial rule on the 'periphery', but also of the European political system. The pressures of the state upon individuals increased, and governments often succumbed to the temptation to shelve internal reform because of alleged threats from abroad. A new variety of an aggressive militarism emerged, not so much supported by the traditional military establishment, but by important sections of the bourgeois classes who demanded a stronger army and particularly a stronger navy in order to see imperialist policies backed up by force, if needs be.[12] The rearmament race between the great powers, notably Imperial Germany on the one hand, Russia and France on the other, and the even more spectacular naval rivalry of Imperial Germany and Great Britain since 1898 had an important impact upon domestic politics as well. It was not in the first place the governments, but the public which was increasingly inclined toward an aggressive nationalism. To put things in a nutshell, the military build-up in the majority of European powers substantially contributed to what may be described as a partial militarization of the national idea. Increasingly the symbolic representation of the nation state in the public was becoming a military affair, and less so one of royalties, governments or parliaments. The display of military splendour and military power came to be an essential, if not the dominant feature in public ceremonies, and royalties or heads of state tended to surround themselves more than ever before with the insignia of military might.

It should be added that the national ideologies of the day had an important social function in a period of accelerated social change, largely propelled by the rapid advance of the industrial system. While traditional social lineages and loyalties had lost much of their binding force, the national idea proved to be a substitute for them in as much as it provided a new sort of cohesion among the various social and political groupings. At the same time it was an emancipatory ideology of the rising middle and lower middle classes which challenged the privileged position of the traditional ruling elites and demanded a larger share of power for themselves. But nationalism got its aggressive features only because of its interrelationship with the increase of imperialist rivalries, both in the political and the economic arena. The success or failure of imperialist policies was largely believed to decide the economic future of the European nations, and for this reason it was the middle classes and the intelligentsia which were most strongly in favour of 'forward policies' of one kind or another.

The transition from a liberal to an exclusivist notion of the nation state was promoted by imperialism. This was activated by a backlash on the part of the

12 For Germany this was recently demonstrated in Stig Förster's study 'Der doppelte Militarismus. Die deutsche Heeresrüstungspolitik zwischen status-quo-Sicherung und Aggression 1890–1913, Stuttgart, 1985.

periphery against the metropolis. Not only was the maintenance of empire made far more costly by the increasing rivalry between the imperialist powers, as it necessitated not only a steady intensification of control at the periphery, which in turn fostered resistance, but also financial outlays for policing the empire as well as for the maintenance of ever larger armies and navies in order to maintain one's position against the other powers within the European arena. The imperialist rivalries also had a considerable impact upon the internal order within the 'metropolitan' states; not only was the 'new nationalism' which emerged in the wake of imperialist policies essentially anti-liberal and prone to foster racialism, militarism and authoritarian rule, it also in many respects undermined the social position of the traditional ruling elites, while as yet there was no new elite of far-sighted, responsible statesmen and political and military leaders around to replace them.

The coming about of the First World War must be seen in this light. For by 1914 the traditional ruling elites, subjected to considerable pressures by a public which harboured far-reaching imperialist expectations, proved partly unwilling, partly unable to prevent the outbreak of the war. The First World War marked the end of an era of European predominance over the globe and the beginning of the end of empire, even though decolonization began in earnest only after the Second World War. Besides, the racialist attitudes and the militarist mentality which had become widespread among the officers and men of various colonial armies during their services overseas exercised a significant influence upon the public in the 'metropolitan' states in Europe already before 1914; it contributed to the gradually growing readiness to consider war a good thing in as much as it was supposed to have a revitalizing impact upon national culture, allegedly suffering from a bourgeois materialist lifestyle and from economic saturation, at the expense of traditional national values. This message was preached in Imperial Germany by men like Friedrich von Bernhardi and in France by General Lyautey in much the same vein to large attentive audiences; it certainly became part of the 'unspoken assumptions' which in July 1914 made the nations of Europe willing to go to war.

The First World War marked a new peak of nationalist feeling. Right from the beginning of the war the peoples of the aggressor states demonstrated a degree of national cohesion which few of the members of the governing elites had expected. The nationalist enthusiasm which emerged in August 1914 in the majority of the belligerent countries was considered at the time an altogether new phenomenon which could be the basis for most hopeful developments in the future. Political and social divisions were apparently swept away by a sense of loyalty to the nation state; even the Socialist parties joined in the common endeavour to defend the fatherland against what was seen everywhere as unjust aggression by rival nation states. The national idea made it possible to mobilize the physical and moral energies of the masses for the conduct of the war to a much higher degree than ever before. It soon became apparent that this war was unlikely to be ended by a negotiated peace; the question was: victory or defeat? The Western powers proclaimed that they conducted the war in order to ensure that the principle of national self-determination, so grossly violated by the aggression against Belgium, would be respected in the future, whereas the Central powers developed a conservative variety of national thought, the so-called 'Ideas of 1914'. The latter emphasized not the democratic aspects of the principle of nationality, but a combination of the national idea with the idea of a strong bureaucratic organization of the body politic which allegedly was capable of solving the future problems of industrial society far better than Western democracy. On all sides, however, the national idea was invoked to justify large-scale war aims designed to once and for all ensure the dominance of one's own group in Europe. Besides, the Western powers were determined to dismember the Austro-Hungarian Empire, as well as the Ottoman Empire, the former being labelled a '*Völkerkerker*', and to reconstruct East Central Europe according to the principle of national self-determination. The Central Powers planned to give national autonomy to the Poles and the Baltic nations under their hegemonial control.

Woodrow Wilson's 14 Points, which eventually became the basis for the Paris peace settlement in 1919, had proclaimed in Mazzinian terms a thorough reconstruction of Europe on the basis of the principle of national self-determination, in order 'to make the world safe for democracy', though with certain modifications, including giving all the major states access to the sea. By 1919 the moment seemed to have arrived for a genuine revival of the original emancipatory programme associated with the national idea. But this chance, if it was one, was lost almost from the start. The idea of the democratic nation state which had been envisaged by Woodrow Wilson to be implanted throughout Europe, and in particular in East Central Europe, from the start was challenged by the older varieties of an aggressive nationalism. There was little preparedness to relinquish the traditional habit of suppressing the national minorities within the boundaries of the new states which came into being after 1918. Many of the new states embarked upon imperialist policies *vis-à-vis* their neighbours, wherever possible, even in the case of the reconstituted Polish nation state, which had for so long been the cherished ideal of the European liberal movement. Even worse, the new nationalism gradually took on racialist features, and in some ways at least paved the way for the rise of the fascist movements. However, it could be argued that National Socialism and Italian Fascism represented in some ways a negation of the classic idea of the nation state, as their notion of a 'master race' which would subject inferior races to its rule was no longer in line with traditional national thought which, at least in principle, extended the ideal of national self-determination to all peoples alike.

One would have thought that the eventual collapse of the fascist movements after the Second World War should have led to disenchantment with the idea of the nation as the prime organizational principle of modern politics. In pragmatic terms this was not the case. Under the aegis of the two rival super-powers, the United States and the USSR, Europe was reconstituted according to the principle of nationality, though initial plans to preserve the unity of

Germany under the joint control of the victors came to nought. But the idea of the nation state as the prime principle of political organization nonetheless suffered a moral setback. The 1950s witnessed a decline of the idea of the nation state in favour of transnational models of political organization, at any rate in Western Europe. In 1951 Karl Jaspers preached to his fellow men that the last national mission which the Germans had in their long history was to teach the rest of the world that the principle of the nation state had outlived its usefulness, and that transnational forms of political organization were now on the cards, if a new, more peaceful world was to emerge after the disastrous catastrophe of the Second World War. 'The history of the German nation-state has come to an end. As a great nation we can do but one thing for us and the world: to make people realize that today the idea of the nation-state spells disaster for Europe and all the other continents. The idea of the nation-state is presently a destructive force in the world of mighty proportions. We may begin to lay bare its roots and effect its negation.'[13] Indeed, in these years the idea of a United Europe was born, and likewise it was demanded that the nation states should transfer a good deal of their powers to transnational organizations, in order to pave the way for a new era of international under-standing and peace. The idea of the partial abdication of some of their sovereign powers now no longer ran into insurmountable difficulties, as had been the case for so many years.

However, the hope that a metamorphosis of the nation state was around the corner proved to be premature. Certainly in Europe, notably in Western Europe, the nation state has given way in part to transnational forms of political organization. But the fervent expectations of many 'good Europeans' that the nation state would be supplanted by a European state were soon disavowed. De Gaulle's famous plea for a 'Europe of fatherlands' made clear that the European idea was to stop short of disbanding the nation states of Western Europe.

In fact in the last decades there has occurred a universal revival of the nation state principle not only in Europe, but world-wide. Perhaps most spectacular is the fact that the new nations overseas, however much they disowned the colonial heritage otherwise, wholeheartedly took up the traditional Western idea of the nation state, even though in very many cases it was little suited to the local conditions in Africa or Asia, determined by a great variety of ethnic and cultural traditions within largely artificial boundaries. The Western notion of the nation state was considered by the leading Westernized elites who took over from their former colonial masters as a suitable concept in order to turn the newly independent countries into new political entities under their leadership. Often the national idea, together with the idea of anti-imperialism, was little more than an ideology to justify the rule of small elites over a totally diversified body politic, although it actually bore little, if any, resemblance to what nation and nation state had meant during the time when

13   Karl Jaspers, *Freiheit und Wiedervereinigung*, Munich 1969, p. 53.

they were first developed as basic principles of a modern political order. Besides, in many cases the ruling elites in the non-European peoples have adopted the worst aspects of the notion of the nation state, as it developed during the age of high imperialism. They believe that it is all important to have strong military forces, to display military grandeur, and they have had frequent recourse to violence in order to enforce political loyalty and cultural homogeneity. It might be arguable that these varieties of the idea of the nation state are bare of all substance, apparently mere instrumental devices used to keep particular elites in power. They have in fact little in common with the genuine idea of the nation state which used to be closely associated with the principles of constitutional government. Rather they resemble the early twentieth-century derivatives.

However this may be, it should be realized that right now we are witnessing a return to the principle of nationality throughout the world on a far more fundamental plane. After the end of the cold war and the period during which world politics were dominated by a sharp antagonism between the two rival world systems of Western capitalist democracy and Marxism−Leninism, almost everywhere national emancipatory movements have re-emerged. Sometimes they express themselves in violent forms, and at times even in terrorist activities, as in Ireland, in the Basque region, or in Brittany; in other cases nationalist movements demanding political autonomy for their own ethnic group have been pacified by democratic means, as in Belgium or in Canada. In the non-European world, ethnic conflicts of a similar sort are endemic, a fact which in view of the great diversity of ethnic, cultural and political traditions within these largely artifical 'nation states' is hardly surprising. Recently, ethnic conflicts have surfaced also in the USSR which for many years was thought to be the most unlikely place for such things to happen.

This allows the conclusion that the age of the nation state is far from over; rather we observe a revival of the nation state, notwithstanding the increasing interdependence of the world which would suggest that transnational forms of political and economic organization are increasing in importance. This revival may be in part a reaction against the increasing planification of political, economic, social and cultural affairs on a world-wide scale which threatens to undermine all traditional identities, cultural, ethnic, political or otherwise. Even so, the traditional idea of a world of sovereign, self-reliant nation states claiming the right to assert themselves and pursue their essential national interests by taking recourse to force, against their own nationals or against other nations, appears to be on the way out. The nation state is still with us as an essential principle of political organization, but it is to be hoped that it will not resemble too closely its forerunners of the late nineteenth and early twentieth centuries.

Contributors

DAVID P. CALLEO   is Professor (and Director) of European Studies at the Johns Hopkins University.

MEGHNAD DESAI   is Professor of Economics at The London School of Economics.

ANDREW GAMBLE   is Professor of Politics at the University of Sheffield.

MICHAEL MANN   is Professor of Sociology at the University of California, Los Angeles.

JOHN A. HALL   is Associate Professor of Sociology and Social Studies at Harvard University.

WOLFGANG J. MOMMSEN   is Professor of History at the University of Dusseldorf.

PATRICK K. O'BRIEN   is Reader in Economic History (and Professorial Fellow) of St. Anthony's College, Oxford.

MANCUR OLSON   is Professor of Economics at the University of Maryland.

SIDNEY POLLARD   is Professor of Economic History at the University of Bielefeld.

GILBERT ROZMAN is Professor of Sociology at the University of Princeton.

Index